# Lewis Carroll

*Revised Edition*

## Twayne's English Authors Series

Herbert Sussman, Editor

*Northeastern University*

TEAS 212

LEWIS CARROLL.
*Portrait by O. G. Rejlander.*

# Lewis Carroll

*Revised Edition*

## by Richard Kelly

*University of Tennessee, Knoxville*

TWAYNE PUBLISHERS
An Imprint of Simon & Schuster Macmillan
New York

Prentice Hall International
London • Mexico City • New Delhi • Singapore • Sydney • Toronto

*Lewis Carroll, Revised Edition*
Richard Kelly

Copyright 1990 by G. K. Hall & Co.
All rights reserved.
Published by Twayne Publishers
TWAYNE PUBLISHERS
An Imprint of Simon & Schuster Macmillan
1633 Broadway, New York, NY 10019-6785

First Edition © 1977 by G. K. Hall & Co.

Copyediting supervised by Barbara Sutton
Book production by Gabrielle B. McDonald
Book design by Barbara Anderson

Typeset in 11 pt. Garamond
by Compset, Inc. of Beverly, Massachusetts

Printed on permanent/durable acid-free paper
and bound in the United States of America

First published 1990.
10   9   8   7   6   5   4   3

**Library of Congress Cataloging-in-Publication Data**

Kelly Richard Michael, 1937-
     Lewis Carroll / by Richard Kelly. — Rev. ed.
          p. cm. — (Twayne's English authors series ; TEAS 212)
     Includes bibliographical references.
     Includes index.
     ISBN 0-8057-6988-9 (alk. paper)
     1. Carroll, Lewis, 1832-1898—Criticism and interpretation.
     I. Title.   II. Series.
     PR4612.K38     1990
     828'.809—dc20                                              89-36943
                                                                       CIP

# Contents

# *About the Author*

Richard Kelly received his doctorate from Duke University in 1965. He joined the English Department of the University of Tennessee, Knoxville, in September 1965, where he is currently Lindsay Young Professor of English. He is the author of *The Best of Mr. Punch: The Humorous Writings of Douglas Jerrold* (1970), *Douglas Jerrold* (1972), *The Andy Griffith Show* (1981/1985), *George du Maurier* (1983), *Graham Greene* (1984), *Daphne du Maurier* (1987), and *V. S. Naipaul* (1989). He is currently working on a critical study of the short fiction of Graham Greene. His articles on nineteenth- and twentieth-century British literature have appeared in such journals as *College Literature, University of Toronto Quarterly, Studies in English Literature, Studies in Browning, Studies in Short Fiction, Victorian Poetry,* and *Victorian Newsletter.*

# Preface

The number of books and articles that have been written about Lewis Carroll has continued to grow over the years. Derek Hudson's revision of his *Lewis Carroll* (1977); the publication by the Lewis Carroll Society of North America of *The Wasp in a Wig* (1977); Morton N. Cohen's three scholarly and informative works, *The Letters of Lewis Carroll* (1979), *Lewis Carroll and the House of Macmillan* (1987), and *Lewis Carroll, Photographer of Children: Four Nude Studies*; Anne Clark's biography, *Lewis Carroll* (1979); Edward Guiliano's two collections of critical essays, *Soaring with the Dodo* (1982) and *Lewis Carroll: A Celebration* (1982); and Michael Hancher's *The Tenniel Illustrations to the "Alice Books"* are among the notable books that have appeared since my study was first published in 1977.

Despite the excellence of all of these recent works, there still is no single book that offers a broad critical study of Carroll's life and writings. It is my hope that this volume will fill that gap while also indicating the many specialists to whom one might go for more detailed consideration of specific aspects of Carroll's life and writings.

The principal aim of this book is to demonstrate Carroll's mastery of the art of nonsense, a genre that his works practically define. Underlying all of Carroll's writings is his fear of disorder and the void that threatens the sweet reasonableness of his logical and Christian perspective. I view Carroll's nonsense as an elaborate defense against his anxiety about the possible meaninglessness of life and the unthinkable prospect of annihilation after death. For my exploration of this fascinating subtext I am indebted to Donald Rackin for his perceptive and groundbreaking critical essays on this subject.

I have attempted to incorporate all of the recent criticism and scholarship into this revision and have added a new chapter about the illustrations of the *Alice* books. The chapter on Carroll's life, for example, has been expanded to reflect new insights provided by the publication of his letters. Furthermore, many of my critical evaluations of Carroll's writings have been significantly modified. Having enjoyed over a decade since the publication of my book to reflect upon Carroll's work and critical discussions of it, I hope that my judgments about his strengths and weaknesses may now be more mature.

For helping me in this study, I want to thank Professor Morton N. Cohen, who generously made many valuable suggestions for the revision, and Professor Herbert Sussman, whose careful scrutiny of the revision sharpened and stimulated my thinking about this unique and enigmatic author. I am also thankful to the members of the Lewis Carroll Society of North America for helping to enliven Carroll scholarship through its meetings and excellent publications. Finally, I regret that this revision will appear before the publication of Professor Cohen's definitive life of Lewis Carroll, a work all Carrollians eagerly look toward for new inspiration.

Richard Kelly

*University of Tennessee, Knoxville*

# Chronology

1832    Charles Lutwidge Dodgson born 27 January 1832 at Daresbury, Cheshire; son of Frances Jane Lutwidge and the Reverend Charles Dodgson.

1843    Reverend Dodgson becomes rector of Croft, Yorkshire, where the family moves.

1844–1845    Attends Richmond Grammar School, Yorkshire.

1845    Produces the family magazine *Useful and Instructive Poetry*.

1846–1849    Attends Rugby School.

1850    Studies at home preparing for Oxford; contributes prose, verse, and drawings to the family magazine the *Rectory Umbrella*; matriculates at Christ Church, Oxford, on 23 May.

1851    Comes into residence as a commoner at Christ Church on 24 January; mother dies 26 January.

1852    Student at Christ Church.

1854    Begins to establish himself as a freelance humorist; spends summer with a mathematical reading party at Whitby; contributes poems and stories to the *Oxonian Advertiser* and the *Whitby Gazette*; obtains first class honors in the Final Mathematical School; earns B. A. 18 December.

1855    Becomes sublibrarian at Christ Church (holds post until 1857); composes the first stanza of "Jabberwocky," preserved in his scrapbook *Mischmasch*; begins teaching duties at Christ Church as mathematical lecturer (until 1881); contributes parodies to the *Comic Times*.

1856    Nom de plume "Lewis Carroll" first appears in the *Train,* a comic paper in which several of his parodies, including "Upon the Lonely Moor," appear; purchases his first camera 18 March; meets Alice Pleasance Liddell 25 April.

1857   Meets Holman Hunt, John Ruskin, William Makepeace
       Thackeray, Alfred Tennyson; photographs the Tennyson
       family; receives his M. A.

1860   *A Syllabus of Plane Algebraical Geometry* and *Rules for
       Court Circular.*

1861   Ordained deacon 22 December.

1862   On 4 July makes a boating excursion up the Isis to God-
       stow in the company of Robinson Duckworth and the
       three Liddell sisters, to whom he tells the story of Alice;
       begins writing and revising *Alice's Adventures under
       Ground.*

1863   Completes *Alice's Adventures under Ground* in February.

1864   In April John Tenniel agrees to illustrate *Alice*; on 10
       June Carroll settles upon the title *Alice's Adventures in
       Wonderland*; on 26 November sends manuscript of *Alice's
       Adventures under Ground* to Alice Liddell.

1865   Sends presentation copy of *Alice's Adventures in Wonder-
       land* to Alice Liddell on 4 July; *Alice's Adventures in Won-
       derland* first published in July, withdrawn in August,
       and remaining copies sent to America; the book's true
       second edition published in England in November by
       Richard Clay (erroneously dated 1866).

1866   Appleton of New York publishes the second (American)
       issue of the first edition of *Alice's Adventures in
       Wonderland.*

1867   Writes "Bruno's Revenge" for *Aunt Judy's Magazine*;
       tours the Continent and visits Russia with Dr. H. P.
       Liddon.

1868   Father dies on 21 June; moves his family to Guildford
       in September; in October moves into rooms in Tom
       Quad, Oxford, where he lives for the rest of his life.

1869   *Phantasmagoria* (verse) published in January.

1871   Completes *Through the Looking-Glass and What Alice
       Found There* in January; the volume is published in De-
       cember (though dated 1872).

1875   "Some Popular Fallacies about Vivisection" published in
       the *Fortnightly Review.*

1876 *The Hunting of the Snark,* illustrated by Henry Holiday.

1879 *Euclid and His Modern Rivals.*

1881 Resigns mathematical lectureship (but retains his studentship) to devote more time to writing.

1882 Elected curator of the Senior Common Room (holds post until 1892).

1883 *Rhyme? and Reason?,* a collection of verse.

1885 *A Tangled Tale,* a series of mathematical problems in the form of short stories, originally printed in the *Monthly Packet.*

1886 Facsimile edition of his original illustrated manuscript of *Alice's Adventures under Ground.* Theatrical production of *Alice in Wonderland.*

1887 *The Game of Logic.*

1888 *Curiosa Mathematica, Part 1,* a highly technical analysis of Euclid's 12th Axiom.

1889 *Sylvie and Bruno* and *The Nursery Alice.*

1893 *Sylvie and Bruno Concluded* and *Curiosa Mathematica, Part 2.*

1896 *Symbolic Logic, Part 1,* the last book by Carroll to appear in his lifetime.

1898 Dies 14 January at his sisters' home at Guildford and is buried there; *Three Sunsets and Other Poems* published posthumously.

# Chapter One

# Life and Time

## Family and School

Charles Lutwidge Dodgson was born 27 January 1832 in the parsonage of Daresbury, Cheshire. The third child and the eldest son of the eleven children of the Reverend Charles Dodgson and Frances Jane Lutwidge, he was descended from two North Country families with a long tradition of service to church and state. His family tree contains several clergymen and a few military men, and there is even a possible claim to a distant relationship to Queen Victoria. Morton Cohen aptly describes the Dodgsons as "an upper-crust family: conservative, steeped in tradition, self-conscious, reverential, pious, loyal, and devoted to social service."[1] Despite his good family name, all the world has come to know Charles Dodgson as Lewis Carroll, a pseudonym he chose in 1856 for his fictional and poetical works—he reserved his family name for his academic books and essays.

During his sixteen years at Daresbury, the Reverend Charles Dodgson established a Sunday School, arranged lectures, and served the poor of the parish. In addition to his strenuous duties as a clergyman, he published a translation of Tertullian and wrote several books on theological and religious subjects. His austere, puritanical, and authoritarian personality helped to mold the public character of his son who was later to become a quiet, reserved mathematician. There was, however, an equally important side to the Reverend Dodgson's character that helped to inspire his son's creative genius. The following excerpt from a letter he wrote to Carroll at age eight reveals his unique sense of whimsy and nonsense, a sensibility that foreshadows some of the absurdities of Wonderland:

you may depend upon it I will not forget your commission. As soon as I get to Leeds I shall scream out in the middle of the street, *Ironmongers, Ironmongers.* Six hundred men will rush out of their shops in a moment—fly, fly, in all directions—ring the bells, call the constables, set the Town on fire. I WILL have a file and a screw driver, and a ring, and if they are not brought directly, in forty seconds, I will leave nothing but one small cat alive in the whole town of Leeds, and I shall only leave that, because I am afraid I shall not have time to kill it. Then what a bawling and a tearing of hair there will be! Pigs and babies, camels and butterflies, rolling in the gutter together—old women rushing up the chimneys and cows after them—ducks hiding themselves in coffee-cups, and fat geese trying to squeeze themselves into pencil cases. At last the mayor of Leeds will be found in a soup plate covered up with custard, and stuck full of almonds to make him look like a sponge cake that he may escape the dreadful destruction of the Town.[2]

Years later Carroll would refine this violent and destructive theme to help shape his own nonsense. Pigs and babies would be brought even more closely together, a lizard instead of women would rush up a chimney, a dormouse and a teapot would replace the geese and the pencil cases, and the White Queen in her tureen would replace the mayor of Leeds and his soup plate.

Mrs. Dodgson has been described as "one of the sweetest and gentlest women that ever lived, whom to know was to love. The earnestness of her simple faith and love show forth in all she did and said: she seemed to live always in the conscious presence of God."[3] Although this sketch of her is obviously exaggerated, Carroll's love and affection for his mother was exceptional. It has even been suggested that because of his all-embracing love for his mother Carroll was never able to displace her and develop mature feelings for another grown woman and thus was never able, it seems, to gain reasonable confidence in himself as a man.[4]

Carroll's self-confidence may also have been diminished by his habit of stammering, a childhood affliction that persisted throughout his life. It is possible, but unproven, that this disability may have been caused by attempts to correct Carroll's left-handedness, a condition, Florence Becker Lennon observes, that "may have produced a feeling that something about him was not 'right'"[5] Throughout his life Carroll was fascinated by peculiar symmetries and odd reversals, including mirror-writing, looking-glass worlds, and spelling words backwards (Bruno, in *Sylvie and Bruno,* exclaims that "evil" spells "live" backwards). In 1856 he wrote the following lines, which later became part of "Upon the Lonely Moor": "And now if e'er by chance I put / My fingers into glue / Or madly squeeze a right-hand foot / Into a left-hand shoe."[6] The White Knight, who sings this song, is the prototype of the left-handed man in a right-handed world. "If Charles was reversed," Lennon argues, "he took his revenge by doing a little reversing himself."[7] In any event, Carroll was disturbed enough by his stammer to seek professional help. In 1860 and 1861 he went for therapy to James Hunt, one of the foremost speech therapists of his day. Despite Hunt's assistance Carroll's stammer stayed with him for the rest of his life. Less than two weeks before his death he wrote to a Guildford friend to explain why he could not assist as a reader in church: "The hesitation, from which I have suffered all my life, is always worse in *reading* (when I can *see* difficult words before they come) than in speaking. It is now many years since I ventured on reading in public."[8]

Little is known about the years Carroll spent at the parsonage in Daresbury. A poem written in 1860, however, offers evidence that Carroll recalled those early years with great pleasure: "An island farm, mid seas of corn / Swayed by the wandering breath of morn— / The happy spot where I was born."[9] In any event, after having lived in that secluded pastoral town for eleven years, Carroll was removed to the rectory of Croft, just inside the Yorkshire boundary, where his father proudly assumed his new duties as rector, a position awarded him by Sir Robert Peel.

By this time Lewis Carroll was very fond of inventing games for the amusement of his brothers and sisters. He constructed a crude train out of a wheelbarrow, a barrel, and a small truck, and arranged "stations" at intervals along the path in the rectory garden. Some of Carroll's rules for the railway indicate the boy's rich imagination:

Rules I. All passengers when upset are requested to lie still until picked up—as it is requisite that at least 3 trains should go over them, to entitle them to the attention of the doctor and assistants.

II. If a passenger comes up to a station after the train has passed the next (i.e. when it is about 100 m. off) he may not run after it but must wait for the next.

III. When a passenger has no money and still wants to go by the train, he must stop at whatever station he happens to be at, and earn money—by making tea for the station master (who drinks it all hours of the day and night) and grinding sand for the company (what use they make of it they are not bound to explain?).[10]

Carroll's lifelong delight in number and logic and his interest in meticulous and well-ordered detail are already in clear evidence. Later he was to devise for the King in *Alice's Adventures in Wonderland* "Rule Forty-two. *All persons more than a mile high to leave the court.*"

While at Croft Carroll also amused his family by putting on home theatricals. With the help of a village carpenter he made a troupe of marionettes and a theater for them to perform in. Carroll wrote most of the plays himself, the most popular being *The Tragedy of King John and La Guida di Bragia*. A burlesque of *Bradshaw's Railway Guide, La Guida* is a further example of Carroll's interest in rules and orderliness, and Bradshaw's speech at the close of the drama looks toward the nonsense of *The Hunting of the Snark*: "I made a rule my servants were to sing: / That rule they disobeyed, and in revenge / I altered all the train times in my book."[11] Carroll extended the world of play into the various magazines the Dodgson family produced for their own entertainment. The first of these magazines was *Useful and Instructive Poetry,* composed for Carroll's younger brother and sister. It contains several pieces that anticipate his mature nonsense: "A Tale of a Tail," with a drawing of a very long dog's tail, suggestive of "The Mouse's Tail," is a poem about someone who, like Humpty Dumpty, insists upon standing on a wall but who eventually falls off, and there are numerous morals that sound like those of the didactic ugly Duchess of *Alice's Adventures in Wonderland*.

He also edited and wrote for some other family magazines, the most important of which are the *Rectory Umbrella* and *Mischmasch*. It was the plan that all members of the Dodgson family should contribute; but as their enthusiasm waned, Carroll was left with the whole task. He furnished all the material for the *Rectory Umbrella* and all but two poems for *Mischmasch*. One of the more interesting pieces in the *Rectory Umbrella* is "The Vernon Gallery," a series of caricatures of popular English paintings of the eighteenth and nineteenth centuries. Carroll's parody of Sir Joshua Reynolds's "The Age of Innocence" replaces the young girl in the painting with a hippopotamus. His caption reads: "'The Age of Innocence,' by Sir J. Reynolds, representing a young Hippopotamus seated under a shady tree, presents to the contemplative mind a charming union of youth and innocence."[12] Curiously, Reynolds's young girl exhibits an artificiality in her frozen posture of innocence that uncannily anticipates Carroll's own songs of innocence and numerous photographs that sentimentalize young girls.

Most of the sketches and comments in "The Vernon Gallery" caricature the anecdotal paintings of the Victorian period, especially those that depict scenes from everyday life. "The Scanty Meal," for example, attributed to "John Frederick Herring," makes fun of the sentimental pictures showing the hard times experienced by the poor. In this caricature the serving man announces to a middle-class family seated at the table, "Please'm, cook says there's only a billionth of an ounce of bread left, and she must keep that for next week!" In cartoon-balloon fashion, each member of the family responds to the dire news with a concern for the mathematics of the occasion rather than for their hunger. A spectacled old woman exclaims, "I must really get stronger glasses, this is the second nonillionth I've not seen" (13). The other members join in the mathematical discussion prompted by the servant, thereby feeding their minds instead of their stomachs.

The animal world always held a fascination for Carroll. In a series of sketches called "Zoological Papers," printed in the *Rectory Umbrella,* he displays a whimsical bestiary suggestive of the zany animal creatures of Wonderland. The first paper deals with pixies: "the best description we can collect of them is this, that they are a species of fairies about two feet high, of small and graceful figure; they are covered with a dark reddish sort of fur; the general expression of their faces is sweetness and good humour; the former quality is probably the reason why foxes are so fond of eating them" (15). Carroll's typical wit is seen in the equation of a sweet appearance with a sweet taste and in the outrageous idea that these legendary sprites are devoured by foxes. Carroll's later writings are filled with references to creatures eating one another in a Darwinian, matter-of-fact way.

These early works make it clear that Carroll's brilliant genius for nonsense did not spring up full-blown with the *Alice* books. It appeared in his childhood games at Croft and, more developed, in his creations for family magazines. As Florence Milner points out, "it was through editing these little magazines and doing most of the work upon them himself that he made his first semi-formal approach to literature and art."[13]

At age twelve, Carroll began his schooling at the Richmond Grammar School, ten miles from Croft. His classmates at first delighted in playing tricks upon him, some of which are recorded in a letter to his two eldest sisters: "they first proposed to play at 'King of the Cobblers' and asked if I would be king, to which I agreed. Then they made me sit down and sat (on the ground) in a circle round me, and told me to say 'Go to work' which I did, and they immediately began kicking me and knocking me on all sides."[14] Forced to assert himself, he soon adjusted to his new environment and was able to write that "the boys play me no tricks now." Having advanced sufficiently in his Latin and mathematics, he left Richmond at the end of 1845 and entered Rugby at the start of the following year.

Rugby was one of the great English public schools, brought into prominence during the headmastership of Thomas Arnold from 1822 to 1842. Carroll recorded in his diary his impressions of the years spent at Rugby: "During my stay I made I suppose some progress in learning of various kinds, but none of it was done *con amore,* and I spent an incalculable time in writing out impositions—this last I consider one of the chief faults of Rugby School. I made some friends there . . . but I cannot say that I look back upon my life at a Public School with any sensations of pleasure, or that any earthly considerations would induce me to go through my three years again."[15] Nevertheless, Carroll worked hard at his studies and won several prizes in mathematics and classics. His true joy, however, still lay at home in Croft, which must have seemed the land of lost content. After recovering from a severe attack of whopping cough he enjoyed a pleasant interlude entertaining his brothers and sisters once more with the railway games in the rectory garden. His mother recalled the moment in a letter: "At the *Railroad* games, which the darlings *all delight* in, he *tries and proves* his strength in the most persevering way."[16] And, indeed, Carroll's strength was to persevere in the ways of a child for the rest of his life.

## Oxford

Toward the end of 1849, after nearly four years at Rugby, Carroll returned to Croft where he prepared himself for Oxford. He matriculated at Christ Church on 23 May 1850, and went into residence as a commoner (a student who is not dependent upon a foundation for support) on 24 January 1851. Only two days later he received the shocking news of his mother's death and returned home for the funeral. Archdeacon Dodgson was left with his family of eleven children, the youngest of whom was only five years old. His wife's sister, Lucy Lutwidge, came to take charge of the family and remained with them for the rest of her life. Carroll's undergraduate years thus began most unhappily. Derek Hudson wrote that "if there was one lesson above others that he brought away from Croft, it was that he could never in future, so long as he lived, be without the companionship of children. They had already become a necessity of his existence."[17]

Handicapped by a lack of money and an embarrassing stammer, Carroll kept largely to himself. Although he took a mild interest in sports, he delighted more in taking long walks or making expeditions on the river. Two months after the opening of the Great Exhibition in May

1851 Carroll and his aunt visited the splendid Crystal Palace. "It looks like a sort of fairyland," he wrote. "As far as you can look in any direction, you see nothing but pillars hung about with shawls, carpets, etc., with long avenues of statues, fountains, canopies, etc."[18] He continued to work conscientiously at his studies, in 1851 winning a Boulter Scholarship and in 1852 obtaining first class honors in mathematics and second class honors in classical moderations. Dr. Edward Pusey, Oxford professor of Hebrew, acknowledged his success by nominating him to a studentship (a fellowship) of Christ Church. In 1854 he took his "Greats" examination; he was placed in only the third class because philosophy and history were difficult subjects for him.

In preparation for the Final Mathematical School, he spent two months of the summer vacation with a mathematical reading party at Whitby, a seaport and resort town in North Yorkshire. In a letter to his sister he describes the stormy atmosphere: "there is a strong wind blowing off shore, and threatening to carry Whitby and contents into the sea. There is sand and sharp shingle flying in the air, that acts on the face like the smart cut of a whip, and here and there the painful sight of an old lady being whirled round a corner in a paroxysm of dust and despair."[19] A member of that reading party, Thomas Fowler, later recalled that Carroll won great favor with the local children who gathered around him at the seaside to listen to his fascinating stories. In a reminiscence Fowler wrote, "It was there [Whitby] that *Alice* was incubated. Dodgson used to sit on a rock on the beach, telling stories to a circle of eager young listeners of both sexes. These stories were afterwards developed and consolidated into their present form."[20] While scholars are intrigued with Fowler's claim that *Alice's Adventures in Wonderland* had its origin on the sands of Whitby, they are reluctant to take it as gospel. Fowler's account was written forty years after the fact and his version is unconfirmed by any other source. Nevertheless, it would be foolish to discount the testimony of an actual witness. It is not unlikely that Carroll was recalling these pleasant days on the windswept sands of Whitby when he later wrote "The Walrus and the Carpenter" and questioned how long it would take seven maids with seven mops to clear all the sand from the beach. During this period he managed to find time to write the poem "The Lady of the Ladle" and the story "Wilhelm von Schmitz," which he sent to the *Whitby Gazette*. Although these works are not intrinsically interesting, they are significant for being the first published works by Carroll to survive. His dedication to his mathematical studies during this long vacation was

rewarded when, at the end of October 1854, he distinguished himself
by taking first class honors in the Final Mathematical School. On 18
December of that year he received his B.A.

Carroll began keeping a diary in 1855 and meticulously maintained
it at regular intervals to the end of his life. Before returning to Oxford
on 19 January 1855, he enjoyed a period of leisure that he dutifully
records in his diary. He spent several days sketching, dabbling at his
mathematics, and reading such books as *The Life of Benjamin Robert
Hayden,* Richard Monckton Milnes's *The Life of John Keats,* and Samuel
Taylor Coleridge's *Aids to Reflection.* When he returned to Christ
Church from Croft he began tutoring and preparing his mathematical
lectures. In February 1855 he was appointed sublibrarian and in May
was awarded a scholarship. "This very nearly raises my income this
year to independence—Courage!" he wrote in his diary.[21] The last entry
in his diary for 1855 summarizes his fortunes: "I am sitting alone in
my bedroom this last night of the old year, waiting for midnight. It
has been the most eventful year of my life: I began it a poor bachelor
student, with no definite plans or expectations; I end it a master and
tutor in Christ Church, with an income of more than 300 a year, and
the course of mathematical tuition marked out by God's providence for
at least some years to come. Great mercies, great failings, time lost,
talents misapplied—such has been the past year."[22]

Carroll always favored the company of young girls over that of boys.
In fact, he developed a positive distaste for boys that increased as he
grew older, an attitude that may be traced back to his early attempts
at teaching them. He found his pupils noisy and unmanageable; in his
diary for 1856 he records some of his unpleasant experiences in the
classroom: "Feb. 15. School class again noisy and troublesome—I have
not yet acquired the arts of keeping order. Feb: 26. Class again noisy
and inattentive—it is very disheartening, and I almost think I had
better give up teaching there for the present."[23] Finally, three days
later, he decides to discontinue his lectures, noting that "the good done
does not seem worth the time and trouble."[24]

The unexpected and disorder of any kind greatly disturbed Carroll.
His childhood games with their elaborate rules, his lifelong interest in
mathematics, and his elaborate file and index of all his correspondence
all attest to this compulsive orderliness. If he failed to regulate the
behavior of the boys in his class, he was no less disturbed that same
year when he witnessed one of his fellows suffering an epileptic fit. He
wanted to help him but did not know what to do: "I felt at the moment

how helpless ignorance makes one, and I shall make a point of reading some book on the subject of emergencies, a thing that I think everyone should do."[25] Three days later he ordered *Hints for Emergencies* and began a lifelong interest in medicine. Once again, this incident suggests Carroll's methodical approach to life. If he could not control his class at least he could learn how to conduct himself in emergencies. Despite his compulsiveness and his anxieties, however, Carroll enjoyed teaching. Besides his public lectures, he was responsible for as many as fourteen private pupils. Teaching, after all, was the means by which he earned his living; and if he felt that some of his class work was a waste of time, he more than compensated for that feeling by instructing many students and scholars during his life through his serious writings on logic and mathematics. As a man who considered to his dying day that life was a puzzle, Carroll always held the art of teaching to be an essential part of his work.

Throughout the 1850s Carroll continued to read contemporary novels and poetry. His remarks on literature are not of much critical interest, but they do shed some light on his own temperament. Of *Wuthering Heights,* for example, he wrote that "it is of all the novels I ever read the one I should least like to be a character in myself. All the 'dramatis personae' are so unusual and unpleasant. . . . Heathcliff and Catherine are original and most powerful drawn idealities: one cannot believe that such human beings ever existed: they have far more of the fiend in them."[26] When one recalls that Carroll worked out elaborate mathematical puzzles while falling to sleep in order to check his sexual fantasies (or "unholy thoughts," as he called them), it is small wonder that the violent passions of Heathcliff and Catherine seemed fiendish and fantastic to him.

A significant day in Carroll's life was 18 March 1856, when he purchased his first camera. Discouraged by the rejection of his sketches by the *Comic Times,* he abandoned his notion to work as a free-lance humorous artist and turned to the new and exacting medium of photography. Carroll's artistic and scientific talents could thus be nicely balanced, and he greatly enjoyed mastering the complicated and awkward paraphernalia that photography required at that time. During the course of his life he photographed such famous contemporaries as Alfred Lord Tennyson, Michael Faraday, the Rossettis, John Everett Millais, Holman Hunt, and John Ruskin, as well as members of his own family, friends, and innumerable children. Helmut Gernsheim, a historian of photography, has published a collection of Carroll's photographs. In his critical introduction he states that Carroll's "photographic achievements are truly astonishing: he must not only rank as a pioneer of British amateur photography, but I would also unhesitatingly acclaim him as the most outstanding photographer of children in the nineteenth century."[27]

It was through his photography that Carroll developed his relationship with Tennyson. In 1857 Mrs. Charles Weld, Tennyson's sister-in-law, visited the Croft Rectory with her daughter Grace. Carroll took some photographs of Grace, the most famous of which depicts her as Little Red Riding Hood. Carroll was delighted to learn later that Tennyson liked the photograph. Obviously anxious to pursue a meeting with the great poet, Carroll "just happened" to be in the area where the Tennysons were staying during the summer and called on the family. Although Tennyson was away, his wife received Carroll and introduced him to her two children, Hallam and Lionel. A few days later he returned to photograph the Tennyson boys and met the laureate himself. Having admired Tennyson's poetry since he was a boy, Carroll was star-struck. As if to immortalize the moment of their meeting in words as well as in pictures, Carroll recorded in his diary:

After I had waited some little time the door opened, and a strange shaggy-looking man entered: his hair, moustache and beard looked wild and neglected; these very much hid the character of the face. He was dressed in a loosely fitting morning coat, common grey flannel waist-coat and trousers, and a carelessly tied black silk neckerchief. His hair is black: I think the eyes too; they are keen and restless—nose aquiline—forehead high and broad—both face and head are fine and manly. His manner was kind and friendly from the first: there is a dry lurking humour in his style of talking.[28]

It is uncharacteristic of Carroll to lavish such descriptive detail on the people he writes about, including his fictional characters. This was indeed a *"Dies mirabilis,"* as he noted in his diary. Although Tennyson could not have known it at the time, it was also a remarkable day in the history of photography, for it led to some of Carroll's most memorable photographs of the poet, images that to this day help to shape our perception of Tennyson.

Over the years Carroll had a few occasions to visit or correspond with the Tennysons. Whatever friendship may have developed between the two men, however, came to an abrupt halt in 1870. Carroll wrote to Tennyson requesting permission to keep and show to his friends a copy of one of the poet's unpublished poems that had been printed for private circulation. He also requested permission to keep a copy of an unpublished poem that Tennyson had written when he was eighteen. Displeased with both of these works, Tennyson was apparently irritated by Carroll's request. His wife, Emily, replied that "when an author does not give his works to the public he has his reasons for it."[29] Believing that he was being charged with being ungentlemanly, Carroll fired off a response that made clear that he had always acted with scrupulous concern for the Tennysons' wishes. Tennyson's reply to Carroll's defensive but conciliatory letter has not been discovered, but Carroll's response to Tennyson's letter shows that a near irreparable breach in their friendship had taken place. Carroll's letter opens with a dialogue that appears to summarize the Tennysons' accusations and Carroll's response to them:

"Sir, you are no gentleman."

"Sir, you do me grievous wrong by such words. Prove them, or retract them!"

"I retract them. Your conduct has been dishonourable."

"It is not so. I offer a full history of my conduct. I charge you with groundless libel: what say you to the charge?"

"I once believed even worse of you, but begin to think you may be a gentleman after all."

"These new imputations are as unfounded as the former. Once more, what say you to the charge of groundless libel?"

"*I absolve you.* Say no more."

The other side of the letter reads as follows:

Thus it is, as it seems to me, that you first do a man an injury, and then forgive him—that you first tread on his toes, and then beg him not to cry out!

Nevertheless I accept what you say, as being in substance, what it certainly is not in form, a retraction (though without a shadow of apology or expression of regret) of all dishonourable charges against me, and an admission that you had made them on unsufficient grounds.[30]

Carroll was perhaps guilty for having been too insistent and forthright in his requests. But Tennyson, who was frequently hounded by the public, also apparently overreacted to Carroll's letter. Both of the poems in question were later published anyway. The two men lived on two different planes: Tennyson, the most famous poet of his age, did not seem very interested in Carroll, except for his photography; Carroll, however, hero-worshiped the laureate. Hudson's analysis of Carroll's character, as revealed through his relationship with Tennyson, is noteworthy:

Endowed with a most exacting conscience, he set himself the highest standards of personal conduct and was incessantly engaged in a struggle for perfection. Thus from one aspect he might appear fussy, difficult, touchy; from another—the side that was turned most often to women and children—he would be all generosity and kindness. Of his essential goodness there is no doubt; but an artist had been mixed up with a puritan—and Dodgson's goodness was not of the sort that makes for inner tranquility.[31]

Among the most important children in Carroll's life were the Liddell sisters: Lorina, Alice, and Edith. Soon after Henry George Liddell became dean of Christ Church in 1855 Carroll befriended his children. He first met Alice on 25 April 1856, when she was approaching her fourth birthday. He and a friend had gone to the deanery to photograph the cathedral, and his diary for that day reads, "The three girls were in the garden most of the time, and we became excellent friends: we tried to group them in the foreground of the picture, but they were not patient sitters." Apparently Carroll was very impressed with the children, for the entry concludes, "I mark this day with a white stone,"[32] a comment that he reserved for extraordinary occasions. The attention he gave the Liddell children was soon interpreted by some people as an attempt on his part to win the good graces of their governess, Miss Prickett, and this rumor led him to write that he would "avoid taking any public notice of the children in future, unless any occasion should arise when such an interpretation is impossible."[33]

Although Carroll's family expected him to emulate his father by marrying and establishing himself as a parish priest in one of the Christ Church livings, he grew apprehensive about such a life as the date of his ordination grew nearer. He decided to take deacon's orders, and was ordained on 22 December 1861; but despite the urging of Dean Liddell, Carroll chose not to go on to take priest's orders. Meanwhile, his work in mathematics was progressing; and in 1860 he published his first book, *A Syllabus of Plane Algebraical Geometry*. In the same year he published a small pamphlet entitled *Rules for Court Circular,* which set forth the rules for a new card game he had invented.

A surprise visit by Queen Victoria, Albert, the prince consort, and some of their children to Christ Church in December gave Carroll his first close-up look at the queen. "I had never seen her so near before," he wrote, "nor on her feet, and was shocked to find how short, not to say dumpy, and (with all loyalty be it spoken), how *plain* she is."[34] Like most of the English, Carroll was fascinated by the queen, but unlike them, he enjoyed a playful irreverence, as evidenced in his well-known depictions of queens in the *Alice* books. In his correspondence he occasionally feigned an acquaintance with the queen, as when he wrote a child friend that he refused to give a photograph of himself to Her Majesty. He explains that he wrote to the queen that "'Mr. Dodgson presents his compliments to Her Majesty, and regrets to say that his rule is never to give his photograph except to *young* ladies.' I am told she was annoyed about it, and said, 'I'm not so old as all that comes to,' and one doesn't like to annoy Queens, but really I couldn't help it, you know."[35]

At the outset of 1861 he began his compulsive "Register of Correspondence," which was to include details of every letter he wrote or received from that year to 1898. The last piece of correspondence is numbered 98,721. The register he kept of the letters he sent and received as curator of the Common Room has not survived. Also, it is not known how many letters he wrote during the first twenty-nine years of his life. The total sum of his correspondence, therefore, must be a staggering number. In 1890 Carroll published an essay entitled "Eight or Nine Wise Words about Letter-Writing" as part of *The Wonderland Postage-Stamp Case.* Both whimsical and practical, the essay has four divisions: On Stamp-Cases, How to Begin a Letter, How to Go On with a Letter, and On Registering Correspondence. Had Carroll not been such a methodical and indefatigable letter-writer (and had not Morton Cohen spent twenty years tracking down most of the letters) we would have been denied several volumes of fascinating insights into Carroll's mind and character. Unlike some authors who, when they become famous, write their letters with an eye to their future publication, Carroll painstakingly designed his letters exclusively for their recipients. Like the original story about Alice, a large number of his letters, sparkling with wit and nonsense, were directed exclusively to children.

## The Birth of *Alice*

Between 1856 and 1862 Carroll continued to visit the Liddell children and amused them with many stories; but the date 4 July 1862 is special, even though Carroll recorded it straightforwardly in his diary: "Robinson Duckworth and I made an expedition *up* the river to Godstow with the three Liddells: we had tea on the bank there, and did not reach Christ Church again till quarter past eight, when we took them on to my rooms to see my collection of microphotographs, and restored them to the Deanery just before nine." On the opposite page Dodgson added in February 1863: "On which occasion I told them the fairy-tale of *Alice's Adventures under Ground,* which I undertook to write out for Alice, and which is now finished (as to the text) though the pictures are not yet nearly done."[36]

Twenty-five years later the diary's matter-of-fact account of that eventful day was superseded by Carroll's idyllic description: "Full many a year has slipped away, since that 'golden afternoon' that gave thee [*Alice's Adventures in Wonderland*] birth, but I can call it up as clearly as if it were yesterday—the cloudless blue above, the watery mirror below, the boat drifting idly on its way, the tinkle of the drops that fell from the oars, as they waved so sleepily to and fro, and (the one bright gleam of life in all the slumberous scene) the three eager faces, hungry for news of fairy-land, and who would not be said 'nay' to: from whose lips 'Tell us a story, please' had all the stern immutability of Fate!"[37] It is little wonder that a man whose imagination thrived on the idealized past turned to photography in order to strike out against the passing years that were to steal his many child friends from him.

In 1863, one year after the famous outing up the Isis, Carroll was no longer to see Alice Liddell with any regularity. In fact, by the time that Alice was thirteen, in 1865, Carroll wrote that she "seems changed a good deal, and hardly for the better—probably going through the usual awkward stage of transition."[38] The idyllic Alice he preserved in fiction, but the real girl, entering puberty, was now lost to Carroll forever. No one knows precisely what caused the rupture of Carroll's relationship with Alice, but in June 1863 the Liddell family withdrew its friendship from him and Mrs. Liddell destroyed all the letters that Carroll had written to her daughter. Morton Cohen speculates that a "disagreement between her and Dodgson may have led to the act, it may reflect her own personality, or it may have been her way of breaking off a relationship between the thirty-three-year-old don and her eleven-year-old daughter that she feared was growing too serious or moving outside the limits of propriety."[39]

During the 1860s Carroll made the acquaintance of several literary and artistic figures, including the poets Dante and Christina Rossetti, the painters John Everett Millais, Holman Hunt, and Arthur Hughes, the dramatist and editor of *Punch* Tom Taylor, and the novelist Charlotte Yonge. Carroll saw to it that many of the presentation copies of *Alice* got into the hands of such prominent and influential people. Christina Rossetti's acknowledgment reads, in part: "My Mother and sister as well as myself have made ourselves quite at home yesterday in Wonderland, and (if I am not shamefully old for such an avowal) I confess it would give me sincere pleasure to fall in with that conversational rabbit, that endearing puppy, that very sparkling dormouse. Of the Hatter's acquaintance I am not ambitious, and the March Hare may fairly remain an open question."[40] Her brother, Dante Gabriel Rossetti, thought that "Father William" and Alice's snatches of poetry were the funniest things he had seen in a long time.[41]

In 1863 Carroll spent several days photographing the drawings of Dante Gabriel Rossetti in the artist's studio. As Jeffrey Stern has pointed out, Carroll had been in Rossetti's studio and photographed his work before he illustrated (though after he wrote) *Alice's Adventures under Ground.*[42] Rossetti's Pre-Raphaelite women, especially his portrait *Helen of Troy,* bear an uncanny resemblance to Carroll's drawing of Alice in the White Rabbit's house. Stern suggests that both Rossetti and Carroll exhibit a desire to be Pygmalion. Rossetti worked with a model named Annie Miller, a poor, uneducated girl whom he idealizes in some of his paintings. Carroll worked with the image of a child model, Alice Liddell, which he romanticizes under Rossetti's powerful influence. Stern writes that "The vital similarity was that they were both seen as an intellectualized visualization of an emotional and psychological need. To men captivated by an image, it may also have been important for Annie and Alice to have been intellectually inferior to their admirers."[43]

Carroll's relationship with the artist Arthur Hughes also had an influence upon his visualization of Alice. A common theme in Hughes's paintings is the celebration of female innocence, a theme that endeared his work to Carroll. The only important original painting that Carroll owned, in fact, was Hughes's *Girl with Lilacs,* a portrait of a rather melancholy looking maiden. Carroll's drawing of Alice holding the "Drink me" bottle seems clearly modeled after Hughes's young girl.

Both figures have their heads tilted at the same dramatic angle and both faces are remarkably similar in execution and expression. As Stern points out, one reason that Carroll was drawn to such artists as Rossetti, Millais, and Hughes is that they were obsessed with a vision of threatened innocence and virginity.[44] If Alice seems less melancholy in Tenniel's drawings than in Carroll's, the fact remains that she, like all innocents, is heading for a fall.

Ever since he was a child writing plays and manipulating the puppets of his marionette theater Carroll was entranced by theatrical performances. During his Oxford days he delighted in visiting London in order to attend the plays at the Princess's Theatre. His especial joy, however, arose from watching child actors. In 1856 he had the good fortune of witnessing the debut of Ellen Terry who, at age nine, played Mamilius in *A Winter's Tale.* Although Carroll had no way of knowing that she would eventually become one of the most popular actresses of her day, he instinctively sensed something extraordinary about her. He later described her as someone he had always most wished to meet. It was not until 1864 that he finally was introduced to her. Although now married and much in demand as an actress, she seemed to enjoy Carroll's attentions and to share his interest in child performers.

It should be pointed out that Carroll took a courageous stand toward the theater at a time when such men as Bishop Wilberforce openly condemned public theaters as places of sin and debauchery. His apologia is expressed in a letter he wrote to Alfred Wright in 1892. Having befriended Wright's nine-year-old daughter, he sent her one of his books and in return received a letter from her father saying that he teaches his children that no true Christian can attend theaters. Carroll's response is worth quoting in its entirety:

Dear Sir,

I thank you for your kind and candid letter, with the *principle* of which I am in hearty sympathy, though, as to the practical *application* of that principle, our views differ.

The main *principle,* in which I hope all Christians agree, is that we ought to abstain from *evil,* and therefore from all things which are *essentially* evil. This is one thing: it is quite a different thing to abstain from anything, merely because it is *capable* of being put to evil uses. Yet there are classes of Christians (whose *motives* I entirely respect), who advocate, on this ground only, total abstinence from:

    (1)   the use of wine;

    (2)   the reading of novels or other works of fiction;

(3)  the attendance at theatres;

(4)  the attendance at social entertainments;

(5)  the mixing with human society in any form.

All these things are *capable* of evil use, and are frequently so used, and, even at their best, contain, as do *all* human things, *some* evil. Yet I cannot feel it to be my duty, on that account, to abstain from any one of them.

I am glad to find that *you* do not advocate total abstinence from No. (2), which would have obligated you to return the book I sent to your little daughter. Yet *that* form of recreation has sunk to far more hideous depths of sin than has ever been possible for No. (3). Novels have been written, whose awful depravity would not be tolerated, on the stage, by any audience in the world. Yet, in spite of that fact, many a Christian parent would say "I do let my daughters read novels; that is, *good* novels; and I carefully keep out of their reach the *bad* ones." And so *I* say as to the theatres, to which I often take my young friends, "I take them to *good* theatres, and *good* plays; and I carefully avoid the *bad* ones." In this, as in all things, I seek to live in the spirit of our dear Saviour's prayers for his disciples: "I pray not that thou shouldst take them out of the world, but that thou shouldst keep them from evil."[45]

In 1866 Carroll attempted to write a play for Ellen Terry and Percy Roselle (who, though eighteen years old, could play roles of younger boys). He sent a synopsis of the play to Tom Taylor, the famous dramatist, asking him to show the outline to Terry. The hero of the play, played by Roselle, is to be kidnapped from his widowed mother, played by Terry, by his father's younger brother. Carroll wrote that "The main idea is that the boy should be of gentle birth, and stolen away, and (of course) restored at the end. This would exhibit him in scenes of low life, with thieves, in which he should show heroism worthy of his birth."[46] Taylor was at first enthusiastic about the idea but after he showed the synopsis to Terry they decided that the play lacked the melodrama necessary to please the popular taste.

Carroll's own taste in this proposed drama leaves much to be desired. The play is highly derivative of Dickens's *Oliver Twist* and is filled with characters and actions that are sorry stereotypes. Like his serious poetry and much of *Sylvie and Bruno,* this work illustrates Carroll's failure as a creative artist when he wanders outside of the nonsense mode. Victorian drama seems to have had a corrupting effect upon some of the era's greatest writers, including Tennyson, Browning, and Arnold, all of whom were tempted to write for the stage and all of whom produced theatrical failures. Perhaps, however, we can thank Carroll's intense interest in theater for the crisp dialogue of the *Alice* books—dialogue that anticipates the work of such modern dramatists as Samuel Beckett and Harold Pinter.

## Russia

Unlike his fellow nonsense writer, Edward Lear, Carroll was not a great world traveler. He did, however, spend several holidays at various seaside resorts in England. He loved the sea, the sand, the open sky, and the children he would meet in these places. The many allusions to the sea in his writings stem from these memorable escapes from his busy but routine life at Oxford. He also made a few short excursions to Wales and the Isle of Wight to enjoy new vistas but on the whole he seemed quite content to stay at home. His only trip abroad came in 1867 when he and Henry Parry Liddon, later canon and chancellor of St. Paul's, visited Russia. He prepared for the tour with the greatest care that he be provided for every contingency. All details of the journey were meticulously planned in advance. He even packed letters requiring answers and the stamped envelopes in which to mail his replies. He also kept a diary during his travels; it reveals, besides the tourist's eye for churches and art works, some very colorful sketches of human interest. When they landed at Calais he noted that the usual swarm of friendly natives greeted them with offers of services and advice: "To *all* such remarks I returned one simple answer 'non!' It was probably not strictly applicable in all cases, but it answered the purpose of getting rid of them; one by one they left me, echoing the 'Non!' in various tones, but all expressive of disgust. After Liddon had settled about the luggage, we took a stroll in the market-place, which was white with the caps of the women, full of their shrill jabbering."[47]

Carroll frequently records the play and appearance of children he came upon. In Germany he encountered a large group of children dancing around in a ring, holding hands, and singing: "Once they found a large dog lying down, and at once arranged their dance around it, and sang their song to it, facing inwards for that purpose: the dog looked thoroughly puzzled at this novel form of entertainment, but soon made up his mind that it was not to be endured, and must be escaped at all costs." (974). Two days later he saw a less pleasant sight: "On our way to the station, we came across the grandest instance of the 'Majesty of Justice' that I have ever witnessed—A little boy was being taken to the magistrate, or to prison (probably for picking a pocket?). The achievement of this fact had been entrusted to two soldiers in full uniform, who were solemnly marching, one in front of the poor little creature, and one behind; with bayonets fixed of course, to be ready to charge in case he should attempt an escape" (975).

When he at last gets to St. Petersburg it appears to him as a sort of spacious and colorful wonderland:

We had only time for a short stroll after dinner, but it was full of wonder and novelty. The enormous width of the streets (the secondary ones seem to be broader than anything in London), the little droshkies that went running about, seemingly quite indifferent as to running over anybody (we soon found it was necessary to keep a very sharp lookout, as they never shouted, however close they were upon us)—the enormous illuminated signboards over the shops, and the gigantic churches, with their domes painted blue and covered with gold stars—the bewildering jabber of the natives—all contributed to the wonders of our first walk in St. Petersburg. (977)

His description of Moscow is equally picturesque, with the ubiquitous droshky drivers adding the touch of unreality:

We gave 5 or 6 hours to a stroll through this wonderful city, a city of white and green roofs, of conical towers that rise one out of another like a foreshortened telescope; of bulging gilded domes, in which you see as in a looking glass, distorted pictures of the city; of churches which look, outside, like bunches of variegated cactus (some branches crowned with green prickly buds, others with blue, and others with red and white), and which, inside, are hung all round with Eikons and lamps, and lined with illuminated pictures up to the very roof; and finally of pavement that goes up and down like a ploughed field, and droshky-drivers who insist on being paid 30 per cent extra today, "because it is the Empress' birthday." (983)

After being abroad for over two months Carroll described his return to England with poetic nostalgia: "I remained on the bow most of the time of our passage, sometimes chatting with the sailor on the lookout, and sometimes watching, through the last hour of my first foreign tour, the lights of Dover, as they slowly broadened on the horizon, as if the old land were opening its arms to receive its homeward bound children" (1005). Carroll never again left England and seldom mentioned his Russian tour in later life. As Hudson points out, the trip "seems not to have touched him vitally, but if anything to have deepened his patriotic insularity."[48] Florence Lennon sees him as a paradoxical traveller who was "most English when travelling, and most foreign at home."[49]

Shortly after his return from Russia in 1867 Carroll sent a short fairy tale called "Bruno's Revenge" to *Aunt Judy's Magazine*. This story, which he later developed into a novel, *Sylvie and Bruno* (1889), greatly pleased the editor, Mrs. Gatty, who wrote, "It is beautiful and fantastic and childlike. . . . Some of the touches are so exquisite, one would have thought nothing short of intercourse with fairies could have put them into your head."[50] The news he received from Croft, however, provided no occasion for joy: his father had suddenly taken ill and died. It was the "greatest blow that has ever fallen on my life," Carroll reflected years later.[51]

As the new head of the family, he spent the next seven weeks at Croft looking after the needs of his brothers and sisters. Since the rectory had to be vacated, Carroll found temporary lodgings for his family until he could locate a permanent home for them. In August 1868 he went to Guildford and discovered a handsome four-story house called "The Chestnuts." He signed the lease in his name, but before he moved his family into their new home he made several trips to Guildford in order to meet with some of the local residents and to establish important social contacts for his family. As Anne Clark observes, "Dodgson's tendency to withdraw from society in the latter years of his life makes it easy to overlook the essential gregariousness of his nature. His eagerness for social links for himself and his family is clearly demonstrated in his early visits to Guildford."[52]

Some months after his father's death Carroll's life began to assume a quiet regularity. In October he moved into a suite of rooms on the first and second floors of Tom Quad. One of the best suites in the college, it consisted of a large sitting-room, a study, two bedrooms, and an entrance lobby. Furthermore, he was granted permission to erect a photographic studio on the upper floor. Surrounded now by his books, paintings, and photographs of his child friends, Carroll would reside at Tom Quad for the remainder of his life.

## *Looking-Glass* and *Snark*

On 24 August 1866 Carroll wrote to his publisher, Macmillan, "It will probably be some time before I again indulge in paper and print. I have, however, a floating idea of writing a sort of sequel to *Alice,* and if it ever comes to anything, I intend to consult you at the very outset, so as to have the thing properly managed from the beginning."[53] In 1868, with the idea progressing, Carroll began writing. After considerable persuading, John Tenniel agreed to illustrate the new book. Carroll incorporated many of his earlier writings into the manuscript, including "Jabberwocky" (the first stanza of which he completed in 1855), and "Upon the Lonely Moor," the parody of William Wordsworth which he published in 1856 in the *Train*.

The first inspiration for *Through the Looking-Glass* came from a conversation Carroll had with his little cousin, Alice Raikes, in August 1868. Alice later recorded the incident:

We followed him into his house which opened, as ours did, upon the garden, into a room full of furniture with a tall mirror standing across one corner.

"Now," he said, giving me an orange, "first tell me which hand you have got that in." "The right," I said. "Now," he said, "go and stand before that glass, and tell me which hand the little girl you see there has got it in." After some perplexed contemplation, I said, "The left hand." "Exactly," he said, "and how do you explain that?" I couldn't explain it, but seeing that some solution was expected, I ventured, "If I was on the other side of the glass, wouldn't the orange still be in my right hand?" I can remember his laugh. "Well done, little Alice," he said. "The best answer I've had yet."[54]

While working on the early chapters of *Through the Looking-Glass* Carroll prepared a small volume of poetry, most of it previously published in magazines, which he published in January 1869 under the title *Phantasmagoria*. The title poem deals with the unhappy experiences of a naive little ghost. The other notable comic poems are "Hiawatha's Photographing" (a parody of Henry Wadsworth Longfellow's "The Song of Hiawatha"), "The Three Voices" (a parody of Tennyson's "The Two Voices"), and "Poeta Fit, Non Nascitur" (a humorous account of the making of a poet).

Meanwhile, after much negotiating over meticulous details insisted upon by Carroll and Tenniel, Macmillan published *Through the Looking-Glass* in time for Christmas, 1871. The sales were encouraging. Macmillan first printed nine thousand copies but the public demand was such that they quickly printed an additional six thousand. The reviews were generally more enthusiastic than they had been for *Alice's Adventures in Wonderland*. The *Athenaeum,* for example, wrote that "it is with no mere book that we have to deal here . . . but with the potentiality of happiness for countless children of all ages."[55]

With the masterful nonsense poem "Jabberwocky" behind him, Carroll proceeded to write the complex and more nearly perfect work of nonsense, *The Hunting of the Snark*. The last line of the poem, "For the Snark *was* Boojum you see," occurred suddenly as Carroll was strolling at Guildford in July 1874, and he composed the final stanza several days later. At odd moments during the next two years he pieced the poem together; Macmillan published the "Agony in Eight Fits," consisting of 141 stanzas, in 1876.

He dedicated the *Snark* to Gertrude Chataway, a young girl he first met in Sandown in 1875. As with Alice Liddell, Alice Raikes, and many other young girls of his acquaintance, Carroll became strongly attached to Gertrude. He later requested permission from her mother to photograph her daughter in the nude, but the request was apparently denied. His dreamlike friendship with her, as with his other child friends, soon faded. In 1878 he wrote to her, "So sorry you are grown-up," and two years later to her mother, "I wonder when I shall, or whether I ever shall, meet my (no longer) little friend again! Our friendship was very intense while it lasted—but it has gone like a dream."[56] His feelings about Alice Liddell when she reached puberty were similar. Nevertheless, Carroll was to revive his friendship with Gertrude, and in 1890, when he heard that she was ill, he wrote her a remarkable letter:

Do you think a visit to the Seaside (Eastbourne) could benefit you? And, if so, will you come and be my guest here for a while?

I put that question *first,* advisedly: I want you just to get over the shock of so outrageous a proposal a bit: and then you can calmly consider what I have to say in defence of asking a young lady of your age to be the guest of a single gentleman. First, then, if I live to next January, I shall be 59 years old. So it's not like a man of 30, or even a man of 40, proposing such a thing. I should hold it quite out of the question in either case. I never thought of such a thing myself, until 5 years ago—then, feeling I really had accumulated a good lot of years, I ventured to invite a little girl of 10, who was lent without the least demur. The next year I had one of 12 staying here for a week. The next year I invited one of 14, quite expecting a refusal, *that* time, on the ground of her being too old. To my surprise and delight, her mother simply wrote "Irene may come to you for a week, or a fortnight. What day would you like to have her?" After taking her back, I boldly invited an elder sister of hers, aged 18. She came quite readily. I've had another 18-year-old since, and feel quite reckless now, as to ages: and, so far as I know, "Mrs. Grundy" has made no remarks at all.

But have I had any one who is *grown-up?* (as I presume *you* are, by this time). Well, no, I've not actually *had* one here, yet: but I wrote the other day to invite Irene's eldest sister (who must be 23 by this time) and she writes that she can't come this year "but I shall love to come another time, if you'll ask me again!"

I would take moderately good care of you: and you should be middling well fed; and have a doctor, if you needed it, and I shouldn't allow you to talk, as that is evidently not good for you. My landlady is a good motherly creature and she and her maid would look after you well.

Another point I may as well touch on, the cost of coming. There has been a difference among my child-guests, in that respect. Some—I fancied, when I began the paragraph, that there had been one, at least, whose railway fare I had *not* paid. But I find there was none. (You see, I travelled from London *with* most of them, so it was natural to pay; though in some cases perhaps they *could* have afforded it themselves: but there were certainly *some* who couldn't have come at all, unless I had said beforehand "I will pay the journey expenses.") Therefore (with no fear that I shall offend you by so doing) I make the same offer to you.

Now, *do,* my dear child, get your parents to say "yes" (I mean supposing sea-air is good for you); and then say "yes" yourself and then tell me whether you would be competent to travel down here alone, or if I had better come to escort you.

At present there is, lying on the sofa by the open window of my tiny sitting-room, a girl-friend from Oxford, aged 17. She came yesterday, and will perhaps stay a week. After she is gone, if *you* could come for a week or longer, I should love to have you here! It would be like having my Sandown days over again![57]

The whole tone of this letter would suggest that Gertrude was still indeed a young child and not a full-grown woman. There is a striking innocence and a sense of terrible loneliness in Carroll's solicitude and persuasion, in his attempt to re-create the past ("It would be like having my Sandown days over again!"). Gertrude did come to stay at Eastbourne but not until 1893. She arrived on 19 September and left on the 23rd, on which day Carroll simply recorded in his diary "Gertrude left. It has been a really delightful visit."[58]

## The Noted Author

In 1881, at the age of forty-nine, Carroll resigned his mathematical lectureship. Financially secure and established as an author, he noted "I shall now have my whole time at my own disposal, and, if God gives me life and continued health and strength, may hope, before my powers fail, to do some worthy work in writing—partly in the cause of Mathematical education, partly in the cause of innocent recreation for children, and partly, I hope (though so utterly unworthy of being allowed to take up such work) in the cause of religious thought."[59] But on 8 December Carroll was elected curator of the Senior Common Room, a demanding job of housekeeping that he accepted "with no light heart."[60] He nevertheless carried out his new duties methodically and brought order to a system of accountancy that previously had been chaotic. His letters to various commercial establishments and associates reveal the painstaking care with which he went about maintaining the creature comforts of the Common Room. Mainly concerned about the quality of the wine cellar, Carroll was also responsible for the servants' wages, for the purchase of coal, newspapers, groceries and, as Hudson observes, "for anything that affected the welfare and comfort of what is virtually a large club."[61]

The following excerpt from a letter Carroll wrote to W. M. Snow, a wine merchant, gives the flavor of Carroll's tough-minded and at times exasperating business dealings:

You thank me for my "order" for 20 dozen Imperial Pints of Moet & Chandon's Brut Imperial 1880. Kindly note that I have *not* yet ordered them: but only said I would take them *if* they contained wine proportionate to their price.

What you say on this latter point is perplexing, because it is in reply to my letter, *in which the figures were wrong.* I had said that an Imperial Pint, to be worth its price, ought to contain 24/25 of a bottle, whereas I ought to have said 9/10. Your reply ("you can *rely* upon the quantity and weight") is (virtually) an assurance that it contains 24/25 of a bottle, which is nearly inconceivable.[62]

The letter goes on at some length to clarify the proportions and prices of the wines in question and surely must have set Messrs. Snow & Co. into a state of mathematical deference and respect, if not downright confusion.

Carroll humorously set forth the problems of his undertaking in *Twelve Months in a Curatorship* (1884), and later, in *Three Years in a Curatorship* (1886), he discussed the ventilation, lighting, and furnishing of the Common Room under the heading "Airs, Glares and Chairs." As time went on, however, Carroll found the responsibilities of the curatorship to be onerous and in 1892 resigned from that office. In his letter of resignation he notes that despite the enormous expenditure of time and energy that the post required, he "thoroughly enjoyed the opportunities afforded me, by the frequent practice of placing a guest next to the Curator, of coming into contact with many interesting strangers, and of doing what I could to make their visits enjoyable to them."[63] Hudson laments the fact that this man of genius should have spent nine years of his life doing a job that any competent administrator could have handled—"housekeeping statistics will not nourish a Wonderland," he observes.[64] But history affords many examples of great writers (from Chaucer to Wallace Stevens) who, for one reason or another, have spent years of their lives devoted to routine business matters. As a child, organizing family entertainments, as the head of household after his father's death, and as curator of the Common Room, Carroll exhibited a fundamental need to put things in order and to keep a rather unruly world under his control. Indeed, this is one of the major themes of his *Alice* books. In a real sense, then, one might argue that housekeeping statistics do, in fact, nourish a Wonderland.

It was during this period that Carroll published a new collection of his verse entitled *Rhyme? and Reason?* (1883). Most of the poems were taken from *Phantasmagoria,* to which he now added *The Hunting of the Snark* and a few poems hitherto unpublished. He had also been publishing a series of mathematical problems in the form of short stories in Charlotte Yonge's magazine for women, the *Monthly Packet.* In 1885 they were published together in a volume called *A Tangled Tale.*

The year 1886 was a busy one for Carroll. He worked with Macmillan on the facsimile edition of *Alice's Adventures under Ground*; gave a series of lectures on logic at Lady Margaret Hall; worked on *Sylvie and Bruno* and *The Game of Logic*; and cooperated with Savile Clarke on the theatrical production of *Alice in Wonderland.* Carroll attended the performance on 30 December at the Prince of Wales' Theatre, and recorded his observations in his diary:

The first act ("Wonderland") goes well, specially the Mad Tea Party. Mr. Sydney Harcourt is a capital "Hatter," and Little Dorothy d'Alcourt (aet. 6½) a delicious Dormouse. Phoebe Carlo is a splendid "Alice." Her song and dance with the Cheshire Cat (Master C. Adeson, who played the Pirate King in *Pirates of Penzance*) was a gem. The second act was flat. The two queens (two of the Rosa Troupe) were *very* bad (as they were also in the First Act as

Queen and Cook): and the "Walrus etc," had no definite finale. But, as a whole, the play seems a success.[65]

Later, in an essay he wrote for the *Theatre,* Carroll commented upon the performance at greater length. In his praise for Phoebe Carlo he reverts to his characteristic idealization of the innocent girl: "But what I admired most, as realizing most nearly my ideal heroine, was her perfect assumption of the high spirits, and readiness to enjoy *everything,* of a child out for a holiday. I doubt if any grown actress, however experienced, could have worn this air so perfectly; *we* look before and after, and sigh for what is not; a child never does *this*; and it is only a child that can utter from her heart the words poor Margaret Fuller Ossoli so longed to make her own, "I am all happy *now.'*"[66]

During 1888 Carroll was hard at work on his *Curiosa Mathematica, Part 1,* a technical analysis of Euclid's Twelfth Axiom. A less abstruse but more interesting project was his *The Nursery Alice,* a shortened version of *Alice's Adventures in Wonderland* for children below the age of five. Published in 1889, the work contained twenty of Tenniel's illustrations, enlarged and colored. Carroll explained in his preface that "my ambition *now* is (is it a vain one?) to be read by Children aged from Nought to Five. To be read? Nay, not so! Say rather to be thumbed, to be cooed over, to be dogs'-eared, to be rumpled, to be kissed, by the illiterate, ungrammatical, dimpled Darlings, that fill your Nursery with merry uproar."[67]

Carroll finally completed his novel *Sylvie and Bruno* and published it in December 1889. Its sequel, *Sylvie and Bruno Concluded,* appeared in December 1893. The novel fell far short of the success of the two *Alice* books, a fact due in part to the work's heavy moralistic tone and in part to the difficult theory that man may go through three stages in relation to the supernatural. Nevertheless, by 1890 Carroll's reputation was secure and a reviewer could not blithely dismiss his latest work. The *Athenaeum* was fairly generous in its review of *Sylvie and Bruno*: "Being written by Mr. Lewis Carroll, it is needless to say that it is full of amusing things, and not without some of 'the graver thoughts of human life'; nevertheless it falls far below *Alice in Wonderland,* and the illustrations by Mr. Harry Furniss are by no means worthy of his reputation." It is remarkable that the reviewer goes on to say that the characters Sylvie and Bruno are "from first to last . . . delightful."[68]

Although Carroll enjoyed the fame that he acquired after the publication of the *Alice* books, in his old age he scrupulously avoided public attention. He denied requests for autographs and to all but children would be recognized only as Charles Dodgson. When Alexander Macmillan invited Carroll to a publisher's party he received this response: "Many thanks for your kind intimation of the days of your 'receptions' in Bedford Street: but (how many 'buts' there are in life!) I fear that in such an assembly it would be almost impossible to preserve an incognito. I cannot of course help there being many people who know the connection between my real name and my 'alias,' but the fewer there are who are able to connect my *face* with the name 'Lewis Carroll' the happier for me. So I hope you will kindly excuse my non-appearance."[69]

Toward the end of his life Carroll acquired a reputation as a preacher in Oxford, Guildford, and Eastbourne. His stammer, of course, continued to make his speaking in public an ordeal. In a letter to a friend he confided his anxiety: "A sermon would be quite formidable enough for me, even if I did *not* suffer from the physical difficulty of hesitation: but, with *that* super-added, the prospect is sometimes almost too much for my nerves."[70] He nevertheless was apparently happy in his ministry. After he preached his first sermon at Eastbourne he wrote, "I am very thankful to have had this opportunity of work."[71] The text of his sermon was "Lead us not into temptation."

Throughout the *Alice* books there are many references to death, from Alice's fear of killing someone if she drops the jar of marmalade to the threat to Alice's life posed by the Red King's awaking. And in *The Hunting of the Snark* there is the theme of annihilation. In his sixty-fourth year Carroll, anticipating his own death less than two years later, wrote to one of his sisters, "It is getting increasingly difficult, now, to remember *which* of one's friends remain alive, and *which* have gone 'Into the land of the great departed, Into the silent land.' Also, such news comes less and less of a shock: and more and more one realises that it is an experience each of *us* has to face, before long. That fact is getting *less* dreamlike to me now: and I sometimes think what a grand thing it will be to be able to say to oneself, 'Death is *over*, now: there is not *that* experience to be faced, again!'"[72]

On 5 January 1898 Carroll, then ill himself, received a telegram informing him of the death of his brother-in-law, the Reverend C. S. Collingwood, and requesting that he attend the funeral. He wrote a letter of sympathy to his sister, Mary, explaining that he has come down with "a feverish cold, of the bronchial type"[73] and that his doctor forbids him to travel. Characteristic of his generosity, he enclosed fifty pounds to help his sister and her two sons to deal with the financial burden. That same day he wrote another letter to his nephew, Stuart Collingwood. It was the last letter Carroll was to write before he himself died nine days later:

When my dear Father died in 1868, we gave almost *carte blanche* to the undertakers, without any stipulations as to *limit* of expense. The consequence was a *gigantic* bill—so large that we had great difficulty in getting the authorities at Doctors' Commons to sanction such extravagance.

If I had the thing to do again, I should say to the undertaker "Now that you know *all* that is required, I wish you to give me a signed promise that your charges *shall not exceed a stipulated sum.*" I should then take the advice of experienced friends as to whether the limit named was a reasonable one; and, if they said "no," I should apply to another undertaker.

You and your mother will have to live with the strictest economy; you have no money to throw away.[74]

Carroll's bronchial congestion developed into pneumonia, and on 14 January, at 2:00 P.M., he died at "The Chestnuts," Guildford. Carroll requested that his funeral be "simple and inexpensive, avoiding all things which are merely done for show, and retaining only what is, in the judgement of those who arrange my Funeral, requisite for its decent and reverent performance."[75] His wishes were honored and his funeral in the Guildford Cemetery was attended by only a few mourners. The gravestone reads simply: "Where I am there shall / Also my servant be. / Rev. Charles Lutwidge Dodgson / (Lewis Carroll) / Fell asleep Jan. 14, 1898 / Aged 65 years."

Lewis Carroll remains a mysterious, complex, and paradoxical individual, perhaps never to be understood despite the numerous psychological probings of his life and writings. Despite his reclusive life-style, Carroll enjoyed hundreds of friendships including those with other writers and their families, artists, editors, theater people, and numerous children and their parents. His love for and generosity toward his family and friends are well documented. Throughout his life he devoted an enormous amount of his creative energy to the children around him, taking them on outings, giving them presents, writing them long and imaginative letters, paying bills for their lessons, and even for their visits to their dentists. He possessed a deep and religious feeling and conviction and lived a priestly life even though he chose not to take holy orders.

Love of God, family, and children may have comprised the greater part of his life but he was nevertheless tormented by powerful fears, anxieties, and insecurities. Mrs. Liddell's intervention in his relationship with her daughter must have left a serious wound in Carroll's feelings and a sense that he was perceived to have done something wrong. He obviously kept a tight rein on his sexual desires: his social, professional, and literary life all reflect his sense of Victorian decorum and propriety. Still, one suspects that his relationships with the numerous young girls he entertained and with such special people as Alice Liddell and Ellen Terry were intensified and complicated by his sexual feelings.

In contrast with the seeming placidity and orderliness of his life at Oxford, Carroll's writings exhibit considerable violence and disorder and a powerful struggle to control and contain those forces underground. This contrast seems to mark a fundamental conflict within Carroll himself, a ruthless battle between emotion and reason, sentiment and satire, chaos and control. Carroll was sometimes an intensely lonely man, one who needed the nonthreatening company of children to buoy his spirits and to distract him from the void. The riddles, games, and stories that he created for his child friends helped to bridge their disparate worlds. His quest for a child audience, however, amounted to a passion and consumed countless of his hours in writing letters and in meeting with child friends throughout his life. He continued this activity even in his latter years, after he withdrew from most social contacts. He became more and more open in inviting girls and even young women to visit him and seemed to enjoy defying Mrs. Grundy. Even though one of his sisters cautioned him about the potential for gossip from his seeing young girls in his rooms, Carroll always insisted upon his innocence. One wonders, however, if he did not satisfy a hidden desire to be defiant and, like Alice, dismiss the judge and jury as a mere pack of cards. In the company of children and young women Carroll could relax, grow expansive, bestow affection, and allow his imagination to play itself out in supple forms. Their presence gave him a profound sense of well-being and inspired him to transform his joys and depressions, his tender feelings and violent desires, and his sense of control and his fear of chaos into literary masterpieces. God may have been Lewis Carroll's Savior but the countless children with whom he spent the greater part of his life were his salvation.

# Chapter Two
# Poetry: Approaching the Void

## Serious Verse

Lewis Carroll's serious poetry is very dull. Most of his comic verse, on the other hand, is generally amusing and sometimes exhibits a genius that remains unrivaled. The gulf between his serious and humorous poetry is as vast as that between Carroll the Oxford don and Carroll the creator of Alice. A fundamental duality in Carroll's thinking is clearly exhibited in these two poetic modes. His serious poetry is largely derivative, romantic, sentimental, lyrical, and moral. His nonsense poetry, on the other hand, is highly original, cerebral, amoral and sometimes sadistic. Nonsense poems such as "Jabberwocky," "The Walrus and the Carpenter," and *The Hunting of the Snark,* and parodies like "You are old, Father William," "Speak roughly to your little boy," and "Twinkle, twinkle, little Bat" are inspired works that have become an integral part of our literary and popular culture. Underlying and unifying both modes of poetic expression is Carroll's profound and obsessive concern with order and meaning in a world that constantly threatened him with anarchy and absurdity.

As Donald Rackin observes,

the biographical evidence indicates that Dodgson was passionately devoted to order in his everyday affairs and that his rage for order sometimes even bordered on the pathological. But he was by no means unique. We recognize the type all around us. People like Dodgson, people who manifest their extraordinary need for order by obsessively regulating their everyday lives, seem also to manifest through this behavior a deep-seated anxiety about the messiness that surrounds us, an anxiety about the morally random nature of existence. On guard against this apparently mindless chaos that threatens their beliefs and their very vanity, they fill their waking lives with artificial structure— with manufactured systems and rules their wills impose on all the disorderly matter and events they inevitably encounter.[1]

Rackin's term "artificial," however, might more accurately be changed to "human." Science, art, literature, philosophy, religion—in short, civilization—are dedicated to creating order and meaning out of the chaos of human experience and history. What makes Carroll's efforts to structure his life and thought interesting is the intensity and compulsiveness with which he goes about this monumental task.

It must be remembered that Carroll was living during a time when geologists, astronomers, biologists, and archaeologists began to investigate the origins and antiquity of the universe, Earth, and the human race, making the story of creation in Genesis no longer believable. Methods of scientific scholarship (called the "higher criticism") were applied to the study of biblical texts. The historical accounts of the life of Christ by such noted authors as David Strauss and Ernest Renan disturbed the English public with their analyses of Jesus as an historical figure instead of a divine being. As Rackin points out, new developments in science during the Victorian period undermined one's sense of a comfortable, purposeful universe: "the broadly operative teleological vision that found or mythologized an orderly metaphysical structure within nature's bewildering multiplicity, fecundity, and waste was swept away in the nineteenth century by modern science hitting its full stride, an inescapable science that now began to demonstrate conclusively the true cold order of nature."[2]

In his serious poetry Carroll allows us to glimpse some of his heartfelt emotions of grief, anxiety, and love but not without maintaining a firm control over those emotions. By writing in conventional poetic forms, by alluding to established poets such as Coleridge, Keats, and Tennyson and by modelling his poems upon theirs, and by adopting an accepted sentimental tone, Carroll carefully modulated, refined, and made socially agreeable to his audience and to himself the raw emotions that threatened his sense of order and psychological integrity. He was especially drawn to such poems as "The Rime of the Ancient Mariner," "La Belle Dame Sans Merci," "In Memoriam," and "Mariana," all of which dwell upon such disturbing themes as guilt, depression, or sexual temptation. In short, he attempted to shape his anxieties within a poetic tradition and to hallow them against the riotous swirl of fear, chaos, and despair. Later on Carroll defended himself against the somber themes of some of these same poets by employing humor and wit in his parodies and burlesques of their work.

Carroll's nonsense verse, on the other hand, is much more complex and paradoxical than his serious poetry. Much as he relaxed and allowed his imagination to blossom in the presence of his young girl friends, Carroll ignored and even challenged some of the conventional literary constraints in writing his comic poetry. These poems are rebellious in

the way that children are. They are visceral, instinctive, and free, in
their confrontation of authority and convention. While they assume
the poetic forms and meters of traditional English poetry, they undermine that tradition by their comic tone, bizarre logic, and unsettling
assumptions. Carroll's nonsense verse embodies his primal feelings
about the possible meaninglessness of life, his repressed violence and
sexuality, and his growing awareness that order and meaning within
the context of a poem do not necessarily reflect a corresponding order
in the terrifying void of cosmic reality. The soothing effects of regular
meter and rhyme may offset the beating of a child who sneezes ("Speak
Roughly to Your Little Boy") and the use of one's brother as fish bait
("The Two Brothers"), but the madness and cruelty of an unhallowed
world nevertheless encompasses Carroll's unblinkered vision.

Most of Carroll's serious verse appeared as part of the first edition of
*Phantasmagoria* (1869) and was reissued in 1898 in *Three Sunsets*. A
recurring theme of these poems is the loss of innocence or love. "Three
Sunsets," for example, deals with a man who has known "the star of
perfect womanhood," a creature who made him bless the world "where
there could be / so beautiful a thing as she." But then the two lovers
bid farewell and time begins to wreak its havoc upon the man:

> So after many years he came
> A wanderer from a distant shore:
> The street, the house, were still the same,
> But those he sought were there no more:
> His burning words, his hopes and fears.
> Unheeded fell on alien ears.
>
> Only the children from their play
> Would pause the mournful tale to hear
> Shrinking in half-alarm away,
> Or, step by step would venture near
> To touch with timid curious hands
> That strange wild man from other lands.[3]

Cast out of his romantic paradise, the lover is now alienated from the
real world, with which he refuses to compromise. Carroll's outcast is a
composite of Coleridge's Ancient Mariner, who both fascinates and
terrifies his audience, and the narrator of Tennyson's *In Memoriam*,
who desperately seeks consolation: "Dark house, by which once more I
stand / Here is the long unlovely street, / Doors, where my heart was

used to beat / So quickly, waiting for a hand" (stanza 7). Carroll creates a comfortable distance between his depressed lover and himself by modelling his poem after these other writers. He thereby protects his own sense of alienation and loneliness by casting his hero in the role of a literary figure, one whose grief is modulated and restrained by the regular rise and fall of metrical accents, expected rhymes, and recognizable allusions.

As Carroll's poem continues it incorporates the theme of Tennyson's "Mariana" and "The Palace of Art," that emotional self-indulgence is spiritually and psychologically destructive. Sounding very much like Mariana, the lover sighs, "She will not come to-day"; and he invents "new luxuries of agony." Carroll's didacticism gradually emerges: "So all his manhood's strength and pride / One sickly dream had swept aside." Finally, his lover does indeed return to him but he was "Too rapt in selfish grief to hear / even when happiness was near," and thus he dies despising the present and powerless to recapture the past. One suspects that Mariana's grief was equally self-indulgent and that her lover's return would spoil the luxury of her gloom. Carroll simply could not resist the impulse to set the moral record straight. But even Tennyson, in "The Palace of Art," heavy-handedly condemns the immorality of selfish aestheticism. What is interesting about both poets, however, is that they are fascinated and drawn to those very emotions that their rational selves distrust. Carroll, for example, freely indulged himself in wistful memories of the "island farm" of his childhood without any recrimination. "Three Sunsets" simply demonstrates that the past, when it consumes the present, is dangerous and potentially destructive.

"The Valley of the Shadow of Death," on the other hand, affirms the healing power of the past. An old man on his death bed tells his son the story of how he was rescued from despair by happy, innocent cottage children who were reading from the Bible "Come unto Me, come unto Me— / All ye that labour, come unto Me— / Ye heavy-laden, come to Me— / And I will give you rest" (415). This event not only redeemed his dark day but continues to strengthen his prospects for the future, as he can now interpret his passing years as "home-ward-speeding" towards his departed wife; "So with a glad and patient heart / I move toward mine end." The poem never makes clear what caused the old man to despair in the first place. There were simply "evil spells that held me thrall" (the language suggests "La Belle Dame Sans Merci" and may imply sexual anxiety). The movement from suicidal thoughts ("What need to lag and linger on / Till life be cold and gray?") to affirmation of life ("Blest day!") is similar to that in Tennyson's "The Two Voices," where the sight of a happy family going to church enables the poet to repress the barren voice for one that proclaims "Rejoice! Rejoice!" "The Valley of the Shadow of Death" serves as a companion poem to "Three Sunsets" in that one shows the past to be redemptive and the other to be destructive, the former associated with childlike innocence, the latter with romantic eroticism.

In his poem "Solitude" Carroll makes a wistful attempt to recapture the lost innocence of his childhood. In a pensive mood the poet retreats to a silent woods: "Here from the world I win release, / Nor scorn of men, nor footstep rude, / Break in to mar the holy peace / Of this great solitude" (417). He glories in the memories of "Life's young spring, / Of innocence, of love and truth!" and concludes: "I'd give all wealth that years have piled, / The slow result of Life's decay, / To be once more a little child / For one Bright summer-day." Carroll was only twenty-one when he wrote these lines, a fairly typical age for a poet to write his "old age" poem. Keenly aware of the passage of time and mortality, Carroll relentlessly sought refuge from decay in memories of golden fairy lands, in photography, and in constant association with children.

"Beatrice" sets forth the comforting theme that youthful innocence can control and structure the violence and disorder of experience. Beatrice, the "sainted, ethereal maid," can tame a wild beast:

> For I think, if a grim wild beast
> Were to come from his charnel-cave,
> From his jungle-home in the East—
> Stealthily creeping with bated breath,
> Stealthily creeping with eyes of death—
> He would all forget his dream of the feast,
> And crouch at her feet a slave.
>
> (420)

These lines, richly romantic in sentiment, suggest that innocence is a stay not only against a violent eroticism but against mortality—and perhaps those two forces are related in Carroll's mind. Beatrice has the same powers as Robert Browning's Pippa ("Pippa Passes"), whose song enabled Sebald to repent his crimes of murder and lust:

And be sure, if a savage heart,
In a mask of human guise,
Were to come on her here apart—
Bound for a dark and a deadly deed,
Hurrying past with pitiless speed—
He would suddenly falter and guiltily start
At the glance of her pure blue eyes.

(420)

The entire poem is, of course, sentimental—most of the innocents in Carroll's serious verse are emblems of abstract forces that perform almost magical feats in his fantasy world, such as thwarting murderous erotic crimes or preserving the hope of despairing old men. In this and other of his poems Carroll is strongly influenced by the Romantic poets, especially Wordsworth, who glorified the child in many of his poems. Carroll's innocents, however, seem more faceless and undefined. They are literary stereotypes rather than vital presences, hollow forms into which Carroll pours his fantasy of uncomplicated, unthinking innocence and joy.

Another sentimental poem, "Stolen Waters," resembles Keats's "La Belle Dame Sans Merci" with the addition of a happy ending. Christina Rossetti's "Goblin Market" appeared the year Carroll wrote his poem and also may have influenced it. A lithe, tall, and fair maiden, possessing sinister powers, offers the narrator (a knight) the juice of "rarest fruitage": "I drank the juice; and straightway felt / A fire within my brain: / My soul within me seemed to melt / In sweet delirious pain" (423). "Youth is the season to rejoice," the maiden counsels, and lures the knight into her dark dream of sexual pleasure: "The very heart from out my breast / I plucked, I gave it willingly: / Her very heart she gave to me— / Then died the glory from the west." Upon his commitment to her, the horrific effects of time and mortality blight his dream: "In the gray light I saw her face, / And it was withered, old, and gray; / The flowers were fading in their place, / Were fading with the fading day." He flees from the fatal lady, senses that his heart has turned to stone, and longs to die in order to be released from his misery. But, as in "The Valley of the Shadow of Death," the narrator hears a voice that renews his hope: "'Be as a child— / So shalt thou sing for very joy of breath— / So shalt thou wait thy dying, / In holy transport lying.'" Unlike Keats, who leaves his seduced hero a ruined, despairing man,

Carroll echoes Rossetti's theme in his conclusion by asserting the redemptive power of Christian love.

As in some of the previous poems, eroticism triggers in the mind of
the narrator the horrors of passing time, decay, and death. John Skinner notes that Carroll "offers a solution to the insoluble dilemma of
adulthood by substituting a state of childish existence, aimed not at
the realization of a mature adult life, but fixed at a level of innocence
in life until the adult-child passes into the larger innocence of death."[4]
The fascination with erotic love and the impulse to repress it coexist
in Carroll's verse and in his life as well:

He was a man who carried his childhood with him; the love that he understood
and longed for was a protective love. He had a deep instinctive admiration for
women, yearning for their sympathy and often finding it. But it is possible
that he could not reconcile in himself love and desire, and likely that he
avoided problems of adult love and intimacy in his own life because he knew
that he was pulled in two different ways (ambivalence is the modern term),
and that in any close relationship something compelled him to seek distance
and detachment.[5]

In "Faces in the Fire" the poet anticipates his lonely future and idealizes a lost but haunting love. Curiously, this love from his past does
not sweep away "all his manhood's strength and pride" as it did in
"Three Sunsets." The romantic melancholy of the poem is real but it
is not portrayed as destructive. In fact, there is a kind of pleasurable
brooding over the lost innocent: "Oh, Time was young, and Life was
warm, / When first I saw that fairy-form, / Her dark hair tossing in
the storm" (437). She has since aged, he recognizes, "And she is
strange and far away / That might have been mine own to-day." A. L.
Taylor believes that the idealized woman of the poem is Alice Liddell.[6]
Alice was four years old when Carroll first met her and seven and a half
in 1860, when he wrote the poem. If Taylor is correct and Alice is
indeed the "little childish form," then she is merely imagined to have
"locks of jet . . . turned to gray." Taylor's assumption would help to
explain why the love relationship in this poem is not threatening or
destructive but simply wistful and melancholy. The "aged Alice" is as
safe and beautiful as Keats's unravished bride of silence. She is a haunting face in the fire, a memory stirred from Carroll's recollection of the
distant paradise of his own childhood: "An island farm—broad seas of

corn / Stirred by the wandering breath of morn— / The happy spot where I was born." And if his lover's face vanishes among the "dust and ashes white," leaving him alone in the darkness, at least it is a love he can indulge and understand, one that has been purged of eroticism.

Carroll's *Three Sunsets* volume clearly reflects his recurrent interest in the themes of lost innocence, the fatal attraction of sexuality, and the melancholy nature of memory. It has been argued that "the shadow of some disappointment lay over Lewis Carroll's life"[7] and that it is this unspecified unhappiness that produced the melancholy tone of the book. Some critics and biographers infer that Carroll's frustrated love for Ellen Terry was the shadow of disappointment that lay over his life, but recent scholarship has dismissed this conjecture.[8] The melancholy tone of this volume of poems is more likely traceable to Carroll's growing sense of the instability of all things and the resultant failure of even language and pictures to insure the comfortable company of young girls, their brilliant innocence, and the sense of family, belonging, and love that their presence gave to his grand illusion. Carroll's sadness was bred from his own perceptions of mutability and nurtured and shaped by the romantic melancholy of Keats and Tennyson.

It may be clearer now why Carroll's serious verse is so unsatisfactory. It is the product of an analytical and logical mind that shuns the richness of ambiguity and symbolism. At his serious best, Carroll writes lines that resemble in diction and prosody second-rate Romantic poetry. His emotional impulses are carefully organized, controlled, and submerged through the use of regular meters, strict rhymes, and conventional, often hackneyed, phrases, so that finally no real feeling, no mystery, emerges from the work. But exactly those qualities of mind—meticulousness, logicality, and orderliness—that hamper Carroll as a serious poet enable him to be the genius of nonsense. When he "relaxes" into his nonsense mode he implicitly acknowledges the terrifying absurdity and chaos of reality and proceeds to deal with it as if it were capable of control. Tweedledee and Tweedledum fighting over a rattle, the Snark hunters, the Walrus and the Carpenter—all go about their business with a cool, logical, and careful determination. Their actions, however, ultimately make no sense because they are all emblems of the unknowable void that underlies Carroll's nonsense. They are comic characters because they act *as if* they are operating in a comprehensible, ordered world. Thus the importance of puzzles, numbers, formulae, rules, and regulations in his comic poetry and nonsense. His most elaborate fantasies are as carefully controlled as a mathematical process, comically suggesting order and reason in a bizarre world.

## Humorous Verse: The Theory of Nonsense

Elizabeth Sewell, in her book *The Field of Nonsense,*[9] has provided the most perceptive and comprehensive analysis of nonsense to date. The world of nonsense, she contends, is a universe not of things but of words and ways of using them. The straightforward, unambiguous nature of nonsense is usually reinforced by the use of pictorial illustration. Nonsense is by nature logical and antipoetic, an attempt to render language as a closed and consistent system on its own. It reorganizes language, not according to the rules of prose or poetry, but according to those of play; and the objects of that play are words. Since what is highly variable cannot be played with, ambiguity must be stripped as far as possible from the language. Nonsense works with discrete units, or words, and organizes them within a strict self-referential framework (a Boojum *is* a Boojum). Nonsense disorders references that words have to the familiar sequence of events in everyday life.

The defining characteristic of the game of nonsense, then, is the order-disorder dialectic in the mind. Just when a line or passage of nonsense begins to make sense (that is, when it refers to the everyday world), that sense is cancelled by a subsequent passage that demands one not go outside of the work, outside of the language, for an explanation. The natural tendency of a reader is to ask, What does this line mean? The answer, in nonsense, is that it means what it says and nothing more.

Sewell's analysis is a useful corrective to the many rigid interpretations of the allegorical and symbolic meanings of Carroll's poetry, especially *The Hunting of the Snark,* a work that steadfastly begrudges and denies any consistent "reading." When it comes to the prose works, however, she acknowledges that she is on more dangerous grounds: "it may be that Nonsense goes better in verse than in prose."[10] There are obviously many aspects of the Alice books that do relate to the everyday life of both Victorian England and our own day.

Thus nonsense selects and organizes words in such a way as to frustrate the mind's tendency to multiply relationships. The nonsense universe must be the sum of its parts and nothing more, the emphasis always being upon the parts and not the whole; for there must be no fusion or synthesis. Illustrations aid in inhibiting the imagination because "they sterilize the mind's powers to invention and combination of images while seeming to nourish it, and by precision and detail they contribute towards detachment and definition of the elements of the Nonsense universe."[11] In summary, "all the finer points of the Nonsense game . . . contribute to the main aim: to create a universe which will be logical and orderly, with separate units held together by a strict economy of relations, not subject to dream and disorder with its multiplication of relationships and associations."[12]

Sewell's analysis of the nature of nonsense is brilliant, the best there is, but it does not and cannot explain the total experience of one's reading of Carroll's works. It does not explain, for example, why general readers and sophisticated literary critics alike are fascinated by a poem like "Jabberwocky" and ignore one like "The Two Brothers," or why everyone loves the *Alice* books but hardly a soul cares about *Sylvie and Bruno.* The implications of her argument that the language of nonsense, in its purest form, is self-contained, may be taken a step further. Recent studies in linguistics and literary criticism propose the notion that language itself is purely self-referential and that the meanings of words are infinitely deferred. We define words with other words and it is impossible ever to get to the "thing" itself. Language is something like the Dodo's Caucus race, taking us around in endless circles. Carroll was keenly aware of the disparity between the real world and the world designated by words, evidenced by the episode in *Through the Looking-Glass* where he has Alice enter the forest of no names, a place that enables her to become close to an otherwise frightened deer. But more will be said about this later.

The self-referential world of Carroll's nonsense might best be approached as a circle within the larger circle of language itself. Given the many connotations that we bring to words, we often find the two circles intersecting, and it is at these points that we "make sense" of what we are reading. Thus in "Jabberwocky," for instance, we know that a young man killed a monster and that this act pleased his father even though we have no idea what a "borogove" or a "mome rath" are. If a work of nonsense shuts out too many of our ordinary experiences and understandings, it will fall flat. We shall see later that Humpty Dumpty's poem does exactly that. We must be able to get a handle on a work, a sense, however misguided, that we understand it, before we can have an intelligent interaction with it. Successful nonsense seems to play on that delicate border between reason and unreason, order and disorder, genius and gibberish.

## Humorous Verse: Juvenilia

Very little attention has been given to Carroll's early humorous verse. Much of it is obviously inferior to his later work, but an examination of his youthful attempts at humor will reveal his development into a poet of nonsense. As W. H. Auden pointed out, Carroll was greatly aided in his development as a writer by having an audience with which he was intimate and in which he had no literary rival.[13] Carroll therefore was assured of an immediate and personal response to his works, usually from family and friends of the rectory; for most of his early writings and drawings appeared in family magazines such as the *Rectory Umbrella, Mischmasch,* and *Useful and Instructive Poetry.* Although many of the pieces that appeared in these family productions were slight, the approval and applause of his family and friends greatly strengthened and reinforced Carroll's determination to continue to amuse those surrounding him, particularly the children.

The first of the family magazines was *Useful and Instructive Poetry,* written about the year 1845, when Carroll was only thirteen years old. Some of the humorous verses show that he was remarkably precocious. "Rules and Regulations" pokes fun at copybook maxims:

> Learn well your grammar,
> and never stammer,
> Write well and neatly,
> And sing most sweetly.
>
> . . . . . . . . . . . .
> Drink tea, not coffee;
> Never eat toffy.
> Eat bread with butter.
> Once more, don't stutter.
>
> . . . . . . . . . . . .
> Starve your canaries.
> Believe in fairies.
> If you are able,
> Don't have a stable
> With any mangers.
> Be rude to strangers.
>       *Moral*: Behave[14]

Still a far cry from the sophisticated nonsense of *The Hunting of the Snark,* this early piece nevertheless anticipates the later nonsense in several particulars. One of the characteristics of nonsense noted by Sewell is what she calls a "thing series": "Anything can go into the thing series provided that the list when drawn up will defeat the dream tendency of the mind to run things together."[15] "Rules and Regulations" sets forth an incongruous list of social commandments that the moral, "Behave," simply cannot synthesize, except as a joke. Many of the rules are dictated solely by the requirements of rhyme, not reason: "never eat toffy" is an auditory corollary of "Drink tea, not coffee." In a sense, rules are arbitrary whether formulated by a disciplinarian or by the necessity of rhyme. The emphasis in the poem is clearly upon the parts and not upon the whole. Furthermore, there is no ambiguity in any of the lines. It may make no ordinary sense to be told to starve one's canaries, but there certainly is no question about the single meaning of the command. The poem creates a logical and orderly program of behavior (helped by the couplets and regular meter), with distinct units (incongruously welded together by the couplets), not subject to the disorder occasioned by the multiplication of relationships and associations.

Some of the lines, however, refer clearly to one's everyday world and make conventional sense, such as the first four lines quoted above. The reference to stammering, in fact, derives from Carroll's own speech difficulty. The entire poem makes an implicit reference to the social world of maxims and moral precepts, although, as with a parody, the poem may still have a life of its own, perhaps a limited one, even when not read in the context of the work it pokes fun at. There is a certain comfort in being surrounded and controlled by rules and regulations. They shape our perceptions and behavior, regulate our hours, and protect us from psychological and social disorder. When we mature and discover that these rules are arbitrary, that they do not inhere in the nature of things, that the world is really unruly and dreadful, then we can begin to relax into our freefall into the absurd and become rule-makers ourselves: starve your canaries and be rude to strangers. All maxims make sense and none of them do.

Another poem from *Useful and Instructive Poetry* that illustrates some of the principles of nonsense achieved at this early date is "Brother and Sister."[16] A brother peremptorily orders his sister to go to bed, to which she replies, "Do you want a battered hide, / Or scratches to your face applied?" The brother then resorts to a greater threat: "I'd make

you into mutton broth / As easily as kill a moth!" She dares him to do
so, and he runs to the cook for a frying pan. The cook asks him what
he needs one for, and he answers, "I wish to make an Irish stew." When
she discovers that the boy's sister will be the meat, she refuses to lend
him her pan, and the poem ends with the moral, "Never stew your
sister." The poem resists any "interpretation" and could be passed off
as simply silly. As with many of Carroll's famous angry and ill-tem-
pered characters, such as the Duchess and the Red Queen, the aggressive behavior of the brother seems gratuitous. Furthermore, his
attempt to implement his verbal threat of stewing his sister into mutton broth suggests a literal-mindedness that comes as a surprise, horrific and comic at once. There is a great deal of hostility and
aggressiveness throughout Carroll's writings, and it is particularly refreshing to find those qualities in poems and stories about children; for
it leads away from the conventional pietistic treatment of childhood
that grew out of the Romantic period and flourished in the Victorian
era. The poem's moral, never stew your sister, follows as night follows
day. The cook's refusal to lend the boy a frying pan terminates the
boy's cannibalistic plan and forces the moral.

Psychoanalytical critics, such as Phyllis Greenacre, have observed
that the theme of oral aggressiveness is found in most of Carroll's writings and derives from his jealousy of his sisters who displaced him from
his mother's physical and emotional affections: "The wish to eat up and
the fear of being eaten up are written over and over again in his fantasies, and appear on nearly every page of *Wonderland*."[17] Greenacre
does not mention "Brother and Sister," but it is a classic illustration of
sibling rivalry.

Between 1855 and 1862 while at Oxford Carroll compiled a scrapbook called *Mischmasch*. One of the more interesting nonsense poems
that appeared in that volume is "The Two Brothers" (1953),[18] a work
that not only embodies the themes of sibling rivalry and oral aggressiveness, but cleverly plays with language. The poem, crudely illustrated by Carroll, is about two brothers who, upon leaving Twyford
school, decide to go fishing. When they get to the bridge, the older
brother joins his fishing rod together and "then a great hook he took
from his book, / And ran it right into his brother." The unexpectedness
of this violence, coupled with the singsong effect produced by the meter and internal rhyme, creates a scene of comic grotesquerie unequaled
since Richard Barham's *Ingoldsby Legends*. After he hurls his brother

into the water the fish come to devour him, "for the lad that he flung was so tender and young, / It gave them an appetite." The younger brother asks, "What have I done that you think it such fun / To indulge in the pleasure of slaughter." The response is a series of joking puns:

> I am sure that our state's very nearly alike
> (Not considering the question of slaughter),
> For I have my perch on the top of the bridge,
> And you have your perch in the water.
> I stick to my perch and your perch sticks to you,
> We are really extremely alike;
> I've a turn-pike up here, and I very much fear
> You may soon have a turn with a pike.

Suddenly language and the delight in punning displace any human concern for the distress of the baited brother. Such concern, however, exists only in the mind of the reader, whose expectations are defeated and frustrated by the strategy of the poem. The older brother, despite his hostility, is a wit, a comic character, and not a sadistic homicidal maniac. Similar to many of the creatures Alice meets in Wonderland, the older brother chooses to play with language at a moment that in the actual world of ethical behavior would demand anything but detachment and wit for its own sake. Were he a real person he would, of course, be deemed mad. In the universe of nonsense, however, as the Cheshire Cat observes, "we're all mad." "The Two Brothers" ends, as does much nonsense poetry, arbitrarily; for there is no point or thesis or resolution possible. The boys' sister appears, discovers that she has brothers on either end of the fishing pole, and the older brother jauntily exclaims, "I's mighty wicked, that I is!" and says that he is going off to sea and never coming back. The younger brother, not surprisingly, is almost totally forgotten, except for the final detached observation by the sister: "One of the two will be wet through and through, / And t'other'll be late for his tea!"

Despite the playfulness of "The Two Brothers," it exhibits the sadistic, antiromantic instincts that Carroll harbored throughout his life. Carroll's repressed violence surfaces later in such portraits as those of the Dormouse, the sneezing boy baby, and the Red Queen. He is able to distance himself from and control these strong feelings through the techniques of comedy. Violence, like sex, he saw as a form of extreme disorder that he felt must be brought under control. The strategic use of puns, wit, rhyme, and meter all work to this end. There is nevertheless a quiet desperation behind much of Carroll's nonsense that suggests a need for constant discipline of his irrational desires, on the one hand, and a need to escape conventional restraints, on the other. Thus the poem ends with one brother going off to sea, never to come back, and the other returning home merely late for tea.

*Mischmasch* contains a number of poems that are significant in Carroll's development as a writer of nonsense, including "She's All My Fancy Painted Him," which formed the basis of the White Rabbit's "evidence" at the trial of the Knave of Hearts, and the first stanza (written in 1855) of what was to become "Jabberwocky." "She's All My Fancy Painted Him" copies the first line of "Alice Gray," a sentimental song by William Mee popular at the time. The rest of the poem bears no resemblance to the song except in the alternating iambic tetrameter and trimeter lines. The song may have appealed to Carroll because it tells of the unrequited love of a man for a girl named Alice.[19]

The original song opens, "She's all my fancy painted her, / She's lovely, she's divine, / But her heart it is another's / She never can be mine."[20] Carroll's poem also begins with a sense of loss, but the confusing use of pronouns quickly blocks out any meaning: "She's all my fancy painted him / (I make no idle boast); / If he or you had lost a limb, / Which would have suffered most?"[21] By the end of the poem, the relationship between the "I," "he," "you," "she," "we," and "they" is totally obfuscated—and the secret, as Robert Frost says, sits in the middle and knows: "Don't let him know she liked them best, / For this must ever be / A secret, kept for all the rest, / Between yourself and me." Although Carroll made major revisions in his poem before using it in *Wonderland,* the essential sense unnecessary for a Wonderland trial was already pruned from the 1855 version.

"The Palace of Humbug" (1855),[22] which also appeared in *Mischmasch,* opens with a parody of Alfred Bunn's "I dreamt I dwelt in marble halls, / With vassals and serfs at my side" (from *Bohemian Girl*): "I dreamt I dwelt in marble halls, / And each damp thing that creeps and crawls / Went wobble-wobble on the walls." As in Tennyson's "The Palace of Art," there are decorative tapestries hung on the walls, only here the pictures are dreary and socially decadent: "the humbugs of the social sphere." While wandering through the palace the narrator suddenly has a vision of "two worn decrepit men, / The fictions of a lawyer's pen, / who never more might breathe again." The narrator urges the servants of the two fictitious men (Richard Roe and John Doe) to rouse themselves from woe by tales of evidence, suit, demurrer, and defense. The servant of John Doe bends over him and shouts "Law!" at which he smiled and faintly muttered "Sue!"—for "Her name was legal too." Dawn appears, a hurricane sweeps away the narrator's vision, and the speaker says that to this day his spirit crawls when he remembers "that horrid dream of marble halls!"

The opening tercet of this poem is striking, but the remainder of the verse is disappointing. Here is a good example of a nonsense poem that does not engage the reader's interest beyond a few lines. It is too didactic, too many of the tercets make uninteresting sense, and the legal jokes are not very funny. The delicate balance between the social world (in this case, the law) and the world of nonsense, where words refer to other words, is lost—and the poem becomes merely silly. Perhaps Carroll was wise not to go beyond the first four lines of "Jabberwocky" in 1855.

Carroll's parody "The Three Voices"[23] adopts the meter and stanza form of Tennyson's "The Two Voices" and pokes fun at the grave, complex philosophical questioning of that sententious poem. The loudest of the three voices belongs to an old hag who relentlessly harasses the narrator with her umbrella and endless chatter: "She urged, 'No knife is like a fork,' / And ceaseless flowed her dreary talk." She is filled with pointless truisms: "The More exceeds the Less," "Each gives to more than each," and "Notion hath its source in Thought." The narrator is overwhelmed by her: "When he, with racked and whirling brain, / Feckly implored her to explain, / She simply said it all again." The narrator, like the poem, gets nowhere. Words and senseless rhetoric become ends in themselves, and the serious philosophic questions about the purpose of existence that Tennyson was seeking answers to are left far behind. Carroll's illustration of the hag with her umbrella sticking into the narrator's ribs makes abundantly clear that her silence will be dearly bought.

The verbal oppression and nonsense of this poem, however, go beyond a mere parody of Tennyson. Like the Duchess in *Alice's Adventures in Wonderland*, the foolish philosophical hag is full of sententious maxims and observations. She seems to represent the futility of philosophic speculation. She proclaims,

And he, that yearns the truth to know
Still further inwardly may go,
And find Idea from Notion flow:
And thus the chain, that sages sought,
Is to a glorious circle wrought,
For Notion hath its source in "Thought."

Beneath the comedy lies the serious implication that it is impossible to get at the truth of the world. Carroll seems to view the attempt to arrive at a transcendent reality through logic and language to resemble a Caucus race.

In his comic verse Carroll treats not only children with irreverence but also the aged. "Upon the Lonely Moor,"[24] an early version of the White Knight's Ballad, which appeared in the *Train* in 1856, is a parody of Wordsworth's poem about an aged leech-gatherer, "Resolution and Independence." The hostility and violence of "The Two Brothers" has its counterpart here, in a refreshingly antiromantic and sadistic poem. Carroll chose not to use the rhyme royal stanza of Wordsworth's poem but instead focused upon the tone and subject matter of that work for his parody. The alternating tetrameter and trimeter provide a mocking quality in their relentless regularity: "I met an aged, aged man / Upon the lonely moor: / I knew I was a gentleman, / And he was but a boor." Where Wordsworth reveres the simple honesty and stoical independence of the ancient leech-gatherer, Carroll torments his slightly mad old gentleman, who earns his living in such ways as by baking soap-bubbles into mutton pies which he sells in the street: "I did not hear a word he said, / But kicked that old man calm, / And said, 'Come, tell me how you live!' / And pinched him in the arm." The violence continues: "I gave his ear a sudden box, / And questioned him again, / And tweaked his grey and reverend locks, / And put him into pain." In an attempt to regularize the rhyme within each stanza Carroll changed several lines of this poem for the White Knight's song; and the hostility, though still present, is better controlled. Here are the revisions of the eight lines quoted above:

So, having no reply to give
To what the old man said,
I cried, "Come, tell me how you live!"
And thumped him on the head.
. . . . . . . . . . . . . . . . . .

> I shook him well from side to side
> Until his face was blue:
> "Come, tell me how you live," I cried,
> "And what it is you do!"[25]

The revisions are clearly superior in their economy and surprise—"And thumped him on the head" is a delightful non sequitur enhanced by the funny word *thumped*. The original lines are more violent, and consequently "put him into pain" is anticlimactic and unfunny padding to fill out the stanza.

Wordsworth ends "Resolution and Independence" with the narrator finding strength within himself sustained by his memory of the leech-gatherer. The speaker in Carroll's poem concludes on a note of philosophic madness induced by his encounter with the absurd and eccentric old man:

> And now if e'er by chance I put
> My fingers into glue,
> Or madly squeeze a right-hand foot
> Into a left-hand shoe;
> Or if a statement I aver
> Of which I am not sure,
> I think of that strange wanderer
> Upon the lonely moor.

Carroll reverses the idea that the contemplation of the natural world can bring mental stability. His narrator embodies the disillusionment of the Victorian who has lost the Wordsworthian faith in the natural order and for whom such contemplation now leads to madness.

This poem makes no more sense than many of Carroll's earlier verses and yet it is more memorable. The fact that is parodies a well-known poem partially explains its effectiveness, for there is that pleasant tension between the sentimental original and the irreverent imitation. Furthermore, even taken by itself, the poem is comic. The unexplained hostility of the narrator toward the old man, when safely set forth in a jaunty rhythm and comic rhymes, becomes very funny. The fact that the speaker is less than sane himself (for he plans to keep the Menai bridge from rusting by boiling it in wine) enables him to behave toward the old man in the unconventional manner that he does. These early poems, with their emphasis upon the disjunction of language and the external world, demonstrate a distinct move toward Wonderland, where all are mad, save Alice.

## Humorous Verse: *Phantasmagoria*

Carroll's abiding interest in the occult manifests itself in his depiction of the ghosts in his long poem *Phantasmagoria*,[26] and later in his creation of the fairy world in *Sylvie and Bruno*. He regulates and regiments the behavior of these immortal spirits, however, with the same vigor he applied to his own workaday life. Once he explains and codifies the rules under which his ghosts operate, they no longer frighten us. The supernatural creatures in *Phantasmagoria* are as harassed and constrained as any mortal. The Phantom describes the five rules that govern the behavior of all spirits. They address such topics as how to shake a bed curtain or to scratch at a door, how to initiate a conversation, and the importance of treating the victim with respect and of not trespassing upon another spirit's area.

*Phantasmagoria* was not especially popular in Carroll's own day nor has it received much critical attention in ours. It is, nevertheless, a work on which Carroll took great pains and one that merits some comment. The word *phantasmagoria* means a rapidly changing series of things seen or imagined. The narrator of Carroll's poem, however, soon realizes that his nocturnal visitor is no illusion but an actual little ghost, who proceeds to elaborate upon the difficulties involved in his haunting profession.

When the poem was to be reissued with illustrations by the American artist Arthur Burdett Frost, Carroll wrote his collaborator detailed letters in 1880 and 1881 instructing him in the art of rendering ghosts and their human adversary. He wanted the verse and the illustrations to entertain and delight children but cautioned Frost on occasion when the drawings became too frightening or grotesque. Carroll was quite pleased with Frost's ghosts, but found problems with his depiction of the human character: "I candidly admit that I do *not* like the man. . . . He is, to my mind, too *real* in his anger to be funny. . . . also, I think a pillow or bolster would be more hopelessly useless for exterminating ghosts, and therefore more comic than a warming-pan, which would really be a very deadly weapon."[27] In the final illustration the ghost kneels before the man holding a pillow. As we have seen earlier, Carroll's comedy establishes a delicate balance between violence and laughter, and here we see him self-consciously softening the blow of violence to make it comically acceptable.

The English have been in love with their ghosts for centuries. Like their literature, their ancient houses and castles are filled with startling tales of the supernatural. The intimacy that develops between the narrator of "Phantasmagoria" and his spirit visitor, however, is uniquely Carrollian. In contrast with the horror and terror of Gothic novels, this poem humanizes the ghost and makes him a comic and sympathetic character.

When the narrator, a forty-two-year-old Victorian gentleman, arrives home one winter night, he sees "Something white and wavy" that suddenly begins to shiver and to sneeze. His little ghostly visitor explains that he has caught cold while standing out on the landing. Without further ado, the narrator and his unexpected guest strike up a long and civil conversation. The ghost takes especial delight in explaining the various categories of spirits and the rules and regulations that govern their behavior. There are specters, phantoms, goblins, elves, sprites, and ghouls. Concluding that the narrator's "place was low" and that he kept bad wine, the specters chose not to haunt his house and the task thus fell to the phantom, who was next in the hierarchy, to make the cold and dreary visit.

The poem also contains a few comic allusions to contemporary people and events. The phantom, for example, complains about the design of the victim's room: "'Your room's an inconvenient size: / It's neither snug nor spacious. / That narrow window, I expect / Serves but to let the dusk in—' / 'But please,' I said, 'to recollect / 'Twas fashioned by an architect / Who pinned his faith on Ruskin!'" (132). Carroll, who knew John Ruskin and had made several photographs of him, is poking gentle fun at his enormous influence upon the art and architecture of his time. Ruskin was especially instrumental in resurrecting Gothic architecture.

The Phantom wins the narrator's sympathy with an account of his life. His father was a brownie and his mother was a fairy. His brothers and sisters were each raised as different spirits, including pixies, fays, banshees, ghouls, poltergeists, trolls, goblins, leprechauns, and, of course, phantoms. England's social stratification is clearly reflected in the spirit realm, for the Phantom explains that he always wished he were born a Spectre: "*They* are the ghost-nobility, / And look on *us* with scorn" (136). His entire life's history is filled with examples of how difficult it is to carry out one's duties as a phantom. After a considerable period of time, however, the phantom suddenly discovers that he is haunting the wrong house. He was assigned to haunt a Mr. Tibbs and the narrator's name turns out to be Tibbets. Angry at this situation, the phantom informs Mr. Tibbets that some inferior sprite will come to spoil his soundest naps. "Good-night, old Turnip-top, goodnight!" he cries, and disappears.

The last canto focuses upon the sadness of Mr. Tibbets as he attempts to understand what has transpired. Had he been sleeping or dreaming? Whatever the case, he laments the passing of his "beloved Ghost" with a coronach, a wailing song for the dead, which concludes: "*The hues of life are dull and gray, / The sweets of life insipid, / When thou, my charmer, art away— / Old Brick, or rather, let me say, / Old Parallelepiped*" (156). *Parallelepiped* is a term from mathematics for a solid with six faces, each of which is a parallelogram. Carroll apparently found the polysyllabic term amusing, for several years earlier, in 1848, he had written to his sister Elizabeth that she name one of her new rabbits "Parallelopipedon" [*sic*]: "It is a nice easy one to remember, and the rabbit will soon learn it."[28]

*Phantasmagoria* thus blends affection, laughter, spirit, and flesh as it tames the horror and mystery of the gothic tradition through a highly civilized, if bizarre, explanation of the rules and social customs of the invisible world. The phantoms, sprites, goblins, specters, and other spiritual creatures that occasionally haunt us live in a world that oddly mirrors ours. Despite Carroll's strong interest in ghosts and the supernatural, he seemed inclined to believe that there were natural explanations for spiritualist phenomena. In 1882 he wrote to James Langton Clark: "trickery will *not* do as a complete explanation of all the phenomena of table-rapping, thought-reading, etc., I am more and more convinced. At the same time, I see no need as yet for believing that *dis*embodied spirits have anything to do with it. . . . All seems to point to the existence of a natural force, allied to electricity and nerveforce, by which brain can act on brain."[29]

The best of Carroll's nonsense verse can be found in the two Alice books and in *The Hunting of the Snark*. Since space precludes a discussion of the many other pieces he wrote, such as "Hiawatha's Photographing" (the difficulties of a photographer set forth in the meter of "The Song of Hiawatha") and numerous topical verses ("The Elections to the Hebdomadal Council," "The New Belfry of Christ Church, Oxford," etc.), the rest of this chapter will focus upon the poems in *Alice's*

*Adventures in Wonderland, Through the Looking-Glass,* and *The Hunting of the Snark.*

## Humorous Verse: Wonderland

The response of a Victorian reader to the poems from *Alice's Adventures in Wonderland* would, of course, be very different from that of a twentieth-century reader. The poems that are parodied and burlesqued were familiar, if not known by heart, to Carroll's contemporaries. The recognizable meter, imagery, and morals of these works had an *immediate* effect upon them. Carroll's poetry, furthermore, asserted a daring challenge to conventional, didactic children's poetry and satirized Victorian morality. The Victorians took seriously the familiar moralistic poetry of Watts, Southey, Langford, Taylor, Howitt, and Sayles. These respectable poets appeared in all the popular readers and, until Carroll, no one had questioned their sanctity. Working out of the traditional poetic forms of these authors and alluding to them, Carroll's verse, in the context of Wonderland, embodies a startling irrationality in conventional forms.

A modern reader, on the other hand, is likely to be ignorant of the original poems. Nevertheless, Carroll's parodies survive and continue to delight for they have generated a self-contained absurdity familiar to an audience raised on such authors as Kafka and Albee. His use of familiar meters and rhymes makes us feel comfortable with the verse, but its surrealistic imagery and disjunctions create an irreconcilable anxiety that can only be accommodated by laughter.

Most of Carroll's comic verse is grotesque in its distortions of conventional wisdom, relationships, and morality. The first poem to appear in *Alice's Adventures in Wonderland* is "How doth the little crocodile," a parody of Isaac Watts's moralistic little poem "Against Idleness and Mischief."[30] Watts uses the bee as an example of wholesome industriousness: "How skillfully she builds her cell! / And labours hard to store it well / With the sweet food she makes" (39). Carroll's crocodile, on the other hand, does its work by remaining passive and merely opening its jaws: "How cheerfully he seems to grin, / How neatly spreads his claws, / And welcomes little fishes in, / With gently smiling jaws" (38). Again, we find the theme of oral aggressiveness noted by Phyllis Greenacre. Watts's sentimental vision of the animal world is replaced by Carroll's Darwinian view of survival of the stronger. There is considerable pleasure to be derived from having such a cold picture of animal behavior presented in the rhyme, meter, and near language of Watts's storybook view. Only the smile of the Cheshire Cat can exceed the sinister gentleness of the crocodile's smiling jaws. The very human—and non-Darwinian—attributes that Carroll gives to his predator suggest all too graphically the reality of social Darwinism. As John Ciardi notes, this poem can be read as a criticism of the hypocrisy in Watts's poem: "Is it too much to argue that the crocodile is a happy hypocrite piously gobbling up the trusting fishes (including the poor fishes among the readers who are willing to take Watts's prettily shallow morality as a true rule of life)?"[31]

Although shaped verse can be traced back to ancient Greece, Carroll's mouse's tale is one of the best-known examples of the form. An earlier version, which appeared in *Alice's Adventures under Ground,* tells the story of some mice who were crushed beneath a mat by a dog and a cat that were pursuing a rat. The revision deals with a dog named Fury who suggests to a mouse that they both go to court, for "we must have a trial" (51). The mouse protests that a trial without judge or jury would be meaningless, to which Fury responds: "I'll be judge, I'll be jury," and "I'll try the whole cause and condemn you to death." Unlike the original tale, the revision is absurd and violent. Fury wants a trial simply because "this morning I've nothing to do," and his view of justice is exceeded only by that of the Snark (which serves as judge, jury, and counsel for the defense). If this poem is a satire on the legal profession that aspect of it is incidental. It is primarily a piece of nonsense, a playing with language—seen in the shape of the poem and the punning introduction: "'mine is a long and sad tale!' said the Mouse. 'It *is* a long tail, certainly,' said Alice, looking down with wonder at the Mouse's tail" (50). The puns, the tail shape of the verse (like an illustration), Fury's lack of motivation (a dog not being the natural enemy of the mouse—whereas, in the early version, a mouse offers a good reason for disliking both cat and dog), and the non sequiturs are the essential aspects of the poem's nonsense. Its "statement," therefore, must be read in the context of Wonderland, where violence is usually verbal and is incapable of harming the real world, represented by Alice.

In Wonderland Alice has difficulty in saying things as she remembers them. When she attempts to recite Watts's poem she speaks the parody. Now, at the request of the Caterpillar, when she tries to repeat Robert Southey's "The Old Man's Comforts and How He Gained

Them," she utters still another parody. As the Caterpillar later comments, her recital "is wrong from beginning to end." This poem is reminiscent of "Upon the Lonely Moor" in its unconventional treatment of old age. Southey's old man is incredibly smug about the comforts that his righteous behavior bestowed upon his age: "In the days of my youth I remember'd my God. / And He hath not forgotten my age" (69). Carroll's old man is also proud of the youthful prowess he still retains, but is wonderfully short-tempered: "'I have answered three questions, and that is enough,' / Said his father. 'Don't give yourself airs! / Do you think I can listen all day to such stuff? / Be off, or I'll kick you down stairs!'" (71). Part of the humor of this conclusion comes from the old man's confusion of a literary convention with a personality—one does not expect him to attack the faceless speaker of the refrain "You are old, father William," who, after all, is simply the conventional questioner that appears in numerous ballads.

When one thinks of the image of childhood presented by nineteenth-century authors, Carroll's parody of G. W. Langford's "Speak Gently" seems all the more refreshing and innovative. Langford's poem counsels that it is better to rule by love and gentleness than by fear: "Speak gently to the little child! / Its love be sure to gain; / Teach it in accents soft and mild; / It may not long remain" (85). This saccharine advice is translated into that of comic violence and absurdity by the Duchess, who sings her lullaby to the pig-baby: "Speak roughly to your little boy, / And beat him when he sneezes: / He only does it to annoy, / Because he knows it teases" (85). In some of the poems previously examined there was no explanation for why the characters behaved the way they did. Here the Duchess's advice is predicated upon the motive of a child teasing its parents, as if he could control his sneezing in a room full of pepper. When one expects motivation in Wonderland, it is not given; and when one does not expect it, it is made explicit.

This poem also embodies Carroll's hostility towards boys. It is inconceivable that he could have written "Speak roughly to your little girl / And beat her when she sneezes." Furthermore, Carroll seemed to accept the dual standard for the treatment of boys and girls during the Victorian period. While middle- and upper-class girls were protected and isolated from the harshness of the world, their brothers were removed from their parents at an early age and sent off to public schools where physical punishment was a normal part of their discipline.

Carroll's skill at undermining romantic and lofty expressions of sentiments through his use of grotesque imagery and bizarre relationships is well demonstrated in his parody of Jane Taylor's well-known poem "The Star." The Hatter sings: "Twinkle, twinkle, little bat! / How I wonder what you're at! / Up above the world you fly, / Like a tea-tray in the sky. / Twinkle, twinkle—" (98–99). Carroll subverts the original four lines ("Twinkle, twinkle, little star, / How I wonder what you are! / Up above the world so high, / Like a diamond in the sky!") into nonsense simply by changing a few key words. Here is one explanation as to why bats and tea-trays are more suitable to nonsense than are stars and diamonds:

A star is something exceedingly remote and beyond control; it has no apparent parts and can be assigned by the ordinary observer no definite qualities other than those of size and degree of brightness; it is beautiful . . . ; it is one of an unnumbered multitude. A bat is something near at hand, reasonably familiar, small; it is a creature whose appearance and habits are familiar; it is grotesque and we feel no attraction toward it; it usually appears alone. The other substitution, that of a tea-tray for a diamond, works on much the same principles, abandoning beauty, rarity, preciousness and attraction for ordinariness. It adds one further distinction, for a tea-tray is the work of man. In other words, the artificial is here preferred to the work of nature. Smallness, ordinariness, artificiality, distinctness of units, and a tendency to concentrate on the part rather than the whole are all helpful in the playing of Nonsense.[32]

Carroll's poem surprises us with its bizarre substitutions of key words in Taylor's poem. Our familiarity with the original work makes the appearance of a bat startling. Even without a knowledge of the original, however, the bat would still be surprising because the two "twinkles" are totally inappropriate verbs to describe the actions of a bat. Furthermore, the reader is unable to fuse together the image of the bat with the tea-tray, thereby keeping the two images discrete. Our imagination can, on the other hand, relate stars and diamonds without any difficulty.

The unnerving instability and inconsistency of Wonderland allow Carroll to shift his critical perspective from poem to poem. Thus he can substitute violence for love in one poem, and playful celebration for death in another. The Mock Turtle's song, a parody of Mary Howitt's poem "The Spider and the Fly," removes the venom of the original. The opening stanza of Howitt's version reads:

"Will you walk into my parlour?" said
the spider to the fly.
"'Tis the prettiest little parlour that
ever you did spy.
The way into my parlour is up a
winding stair,
And I've got many curious things to
show when you are there."

"Oh, no, no," said the little fly, "to
ask me is in vain,
For who goes up your winding stair can
ne'er come down again."

(133)

The Mock Turtle sings very slowly and sadly in the meter of the
original:

"Will you walk a little faster?" said a
whiting to a snail,
"There's a porpoise close behind us,
and he's treading on my tail.
See how eagerly the lobsters and the
turtles all advance!
They are waiting on the shingle—will
you come and join the dance?
Will you, won't you, will you, won't you,
will you join the dance?
Will you, won't you, will you, won't you,
won't you join the dance?"

(134)

The Mock Turtle, living up to its name, appears to be mocking here
the moral of Howitt's poem. There is clearly no lesson to be learned
from the song. Rather, it is an invitation to play, to dance. The rol-
licking rhythm of Howitt's poem is retained for its energetic playfulness, but the intrusive moral lesson has been left out of Wonderland.
The whiting, the lobsters, and the snail, unlike the fly of Howitt's
verse, having nothing to fear—for although they will be thrown out
to sea, the experience will be "delightful" and, furthermore, as the
whiting explains, if they are then far from England, they will be closer

to France. It would be wrong to take this as anti-Gallic sentiment. It is a statement of simple optimism—all that is and will be is right. The whiting concludes by exhorting the "beloved snail" to enter in the excitement of the dance, that is, into the amoral world of play. Donald Rackin has this further point: "Note how the Mock Turtle's song that accompanies the Lobster Quadrille twists the sadistic original . . . into an innocuous nursery rhyme. This parody demonstrates that Wonderland refuses to be consistent to itself: if the above-ground rhymes tend to hide or deny Darwinian theory, Wonderland's poems will be vengefully Darwinian; but if above-ground rhymes admit the cruelty of nature, then Wonderland produces harmless nonsense verses."[33]

When Alice attempts to recite another moralistic poem by Watts, "The Sluggard," it comes out as an amoral, cruel, Darwinian commentary on nature. While Watts's poem preaches the gospel of hard work, Carroll's parody tells of a panther who "shares" a meat pie with an owl. The panther gets the meat pie and allows the owl to have the dish and the spoon. Then "the Panther received knife and fork with a growl. / And concluded the banquet by—" (140). The grim final words, "eating the owl," appear in the 1886 printed edition of Savile Clarke's operetta. This poem not only makes fun of the self-righteousness of Watts's verse but comically subverts the sentimental picture of animal (and human?) behavior that characterized so much of children's literature in the Victorian era. An angry vicar in Essex actually wrote a letter to the *St. James' Gazette* accusing Carroll of irreverence because of the biblical allusion in the first line of his parody.[34] Such an attack is surprising, since Carroll's line " 'Tis the voice of the Lobster," is practically the same as Watts's " 'Tis the voice of the sluggard."

The Mock Turtle's mawkish song about beautiful soup is, of course, an appropriate commentary upon his own destiny and, like the poem Alice just finished reciting, depends upon oral aggressiveness for some of its humor. "Turtle Soup" is a parody of the popular song "Star of the Evening," by James Sayles, which opens,

> Beautiful star in heav'n so bright,
> Softly falls thy silv'ry light,
> As thou movest from earth afar,
> Star of the evening, beautiful star.

Chorus:

Beautiful star,
Beautiful star,
Star of the evening, beautiful star.

(141)

The Mock Turtle, in "a voice choked with sobs," begins: "Beautiful soup, so rich and green, / Waiting in a hot tureen! / who for such dainties would not stoop? Soup of the evening, beautiful Soup!" (141). The substitution of "soup" for "star" is a brilliant deflation of a lofty poetic image. A romantic apostrophe to a star, suggestive of beauty, aloofness, and purity is fairly conventional. But soup is not usually thought of as beautiful, and so an exclamatory song of praise for such a common food is not only hilarious but unnerving in its misdirected romanticism.

## Humorous Verse: Looking-Glass Land

The first poem to appear in *Through the Looking-Glass* is "Jabberwocky," perhaps the best known and most frequently discussed of all of Carroll's poetry. It has been interestingly compared to an abstract painting:

The realistic artist is forced to copy nature, imposing on the copy as much as he can in the way of pleasing forms and colors; but the abstract artist is free to romp with the paint as much as he pleases. In similar fashion the nonsense poet does not have to search for ingenious ways of combining pattern and sense—he takes care of the sounds and allows the sense to take care of itself. The words he uses may suggest vague meanings, like an eye here and a foot there in a Picasso abstraction, or they may have no meaning at all—just a play of pleasant sounds like the play of non-objective colors on a canvas.[35]

Characteristically, most of the nonsense words are nouns or adjectives. Carroll apparently wanted his sentences to look genuine (nouns, verbs, and predicates are usually easy to detect) so that he could avoid mere gibberish. The majority of the verbs, however, are not nonsense words: "In logic, a verb expresses a relation, and this suggests two reasons for the few invented verbs in Nonsense. The first is the impossibility of inventing new relations in logic. The second is that a verb is an expressed relation, and relations in logic have to be simple and exact."[36] The reliability of Humpty Dumpty's explanation of the words in "Jabberwocky" as portmanteaus has been questioned: "*frumious,* for instance, is not a word, and does not have two meanings packed up in it; it is a group of letters without any meaning at all . . . it looks like other words, and almost certainly more than two."[37] The mind will play with a nonsense word and perhaps associate with it several genuine words, but as Carroll says, "if you have that rarest of gifts, a perfectly balanced mind, you will say 'frumious.'" "The mind is encouraged by means of these Nonsense words to notice likenesses; but the likenesses are to other *words.* It is the purely verbal memory and associative faculty which is called into play."[38] The likenesses between images, however, are not perceived in nonsense; and the mind cannot fuse the verbal similarities together into a poetic unity.

There is, nevertheless, formal unity in "Jabberwocky," inasmuch as it is a mock-heroic ballad about an encounter between a young man and an adversary and appears to have a beginning, a middle, and an end (although the last stanza repeats the first). The young man, after being warned by his father of the Jabberwock, the Jubjub bird, and the Bandersnatch, goes off to do battle, slays the Jabberwock, and victoriously returns to his approving father. The conventional ballad stanza, the clear story line, the traditional syntax, and the many common words all provide a sensible framework of reference. The element of nonsense is restricted to the use of certain neologisms strategically placed in each stanza. If pure nonsense is conceived of as a field of closed language that resists an interpretation based upon some other system (e.g., ordinary prose, allegory, symbolism, etc.), then "Jabberwocky" is not pure nonsense. There are not enough "structures of resistance," as Michael Holquist calls them,[39] to close out of the poem ordinary meaning. Carroll maintains a delicate balance between sense and nonsense in this poem. He provides us with a framework of understanding against which we can play with the incongruous details and startling new words.

The central interest in "Jabberwocky" is not in its story line but in its language. Our unfamiliarity with "slithy toves," "borogoves," and "Bandersnatch" makes the poem mysterious fun. The words conjure up associations in our minds that provide a "feeling" for their meanings. The word *galumphing* illustrates the failure of pure nonsense. In the sentence "He left it dead and with its head / He went galumphing back," the syntax makes it clear that *galumphing* describes how he went back. As the only nonsense word in an otherwise perfectly conventional sentence, the tendency of the mind is to break sense out of the word (and not to take it as a collection of letters that only has meaning in the context of the work). Consequently, associated words like *galloping* and *triumphantly* arise to help make sense of the sentence. One may, of course, come to accept *galumphing* as a word on its own, one that suggests a triumphant awkward gallop. If another reader makes similar associations, then we would actually converse with that word and be mutually understood. A. L. Taylor, for example, writes that "the little St. George with his vorpal sword is made very attractive in Tenniel's drawing and could not possibly galumph."[40] Carroll's own interpretation of the nonsense words in the poem, though sometimes whimsical, contributes to the reader's impulse to explain and understand them.

In the final analysis, the poem is a work to have fun with. Martin Gardner in his *The Annotated Alice* has enumerated the various explanations of the nonsense words and notes that eight of them reappear in *The Hunting of the Snark*. Some readers, such as A. L. Taylor, insist upon interpreting the poem.[41] He argues that Carroll is satirizing the religious controversies around him, and sees the Tum-tum tree as "certainly the Thirty-nine Articles which people like Jowett signed, according to Dodgson, for the sake of their bread and butter." The Jubjub bird and the Bandersnatch he explains as the Catholic and Protestant aspects of the English Church. *Vorpal* is a concoction of *verbal* and *Gospel*. And the repetition of the first stanza at the end signifies that nothing has really changed, that one controversy (the Jabberwock) has been slain but the "outgribing" is as strident as ever. The difficulty with making an allegory out of the poem, as Taylor has done, is that such an approach is arbitrary, unconvincing, and limits the interest of the poem if we stop with that reading. The poem has survived and perhaps thrived on countless interpretations of that variety. What the poem finally "means," of course, can never be settled, for it is not a secret language to be eventually decoded but a playful battle between sense and nonsense that can never be completely resolved into simple prose sense. As Alice says, after reading the poem, "Somehow it seems to fill my head with ideas—only I don't exactly know what they are! However, *somebody* killed *something*; that's clear, at any rate.—"[42] Perhaps with Alice's response, the poem should be left at that.

Whereas Carroll renders the violence in "Jabberwocky" in a mock-heroic manner, in "The Walrus and the Carpenter" he portrays a more calculated and cold-blooded form of violence. Spoken by the rather

sinister twin, Tweedledee, "The Walrus and the Carpenter" satirizes
the style of Thomas Hood's *Dream of Eugene Aram*. When Carroll gave
the manuscript of his poem to Tenniel for illustration, he offered the
artist a choice of drawing a carpenter, a butterfly, or a baronet. Tenniel
chose the carpenter. Any of the words would have suited the meter and
rhyme scheme, and Carroll apparently had no strong preference as far
as the nonsense was concerned. Since Carroll acknowledged that some
words in this piece are interchangeable, one would be well advised not
to press such a poem too hard for a meaning. A butterfly or a baronet
would serve equally well as a contrasting member of the pair walking
near at hand along the beach. The nonsense would be less effective,
however, if the walrus were walking with a seal or the carpenter with
an electrician.

The opening stanza sets the tone for the contradictions to follow:

> The sun was shining on the sea,
> Shining with all his might:
> He did his very best to make
> The billows smooth and bright—
> And this was odd, because it was
> The middle of the night.
>
>                    (233)

The nonsense of such "darkness visible" is reinforced by the rhyming
of "bright" and "night" and the matter-of-fact regularity of the meter.
The Walrus and the Carpenter are as disorienting as any of the creatures
in Wonderland or Looking-Glass Land. They say and do things without
the logic of motivation and transition. The Walrus, for example, after
speculating whether seven maids with seven mops could sweep away
all the sand on the beach in a half year, beseeches the oysters: "O
oysters, come and walk with us!" The oysters, who wear shoes even
though they have no feet, resemble a crowd of naive and enthusiastic
little school children lined up for an exciting excursion along the sand.
Placing their trust in their elders, they joyfully follow the odd couple
down the beach away. The Walrus finally speaks his famous stanza:

> "The time has come," the Walrus said,
> "To talk of many things:
> Of shoes—and ships—and sealing wax—
> Of cabbages—and kings—

> And why the sea is boiling hot—
> And whether pigs have wings."
>
> (235)

The alliteration in the third and fourth lines and the rhyming of "things," "kings," and "wings" suggest an affinity between the words that does not, in fact, exist. "Shoes," "ships," "sealing wax," "cabbages," and "kings" make up a list of discrete items that can no more be fused together than can the items in a shopping list for a mad tea party. Nevertheless the whole stanza has come to have a meaning almost independent of the poem—namely, that the time has come to get down to essentials and certainties. (In *The Adventures of Ellery Queen,* for example, the first four lines of the stanza are an important factor in the detective's method of frightening a confession out of a murderer.)[43] This meaning probably derives from the fact that the Walrus's statement is a chronological, though nonlogical, prelude to the eating of the oysters. The reader thus works out the tension between the lack of meaning and the effort to find significance in any set of words.

The theme of oral aggressiveness reappears because the Walrus and the Carpenter eventually devour all of the personified, childlike oysters. The Carpenter is ruthless and the Walrus sentimental, but the fact remains that they both eat the oysters, an action tantamount to cannibalism. Alice likes the Walrus best for he was "a *little* sorry for the poor oysters." But Tweedledum then tells her that he ate as many as he could get, leaving Alice to conclude that "they were *both* very unpleasant characters."[44] This poem resembles Mary Howitt's sadistic verse "The Spider and the Fly" in its delicate, playful, and fatal seduction of innocent, humanized creatures. The poem surpasses Darwinian vengefulness, or "Nature red in tooth and claw," in that Carroll's creatures are humanized, thereby making the cruelty and indifference of the Walrus and the Carpenter monstrous. Still, like Alice, we do not judge them any more harshly than the phrase "very unpleasant" allows. They exist only in the nonsense world of Looking-Glass Land and are, in fact, further removed from Alice (and us) by having their existence in a poem recited by a Looking-Glass character. Cruelty and sadism, no matter how violent in Carroll's writings, are always carefully controlled, tempered, and distanced.

After Humpty Dumpty explains away the mystery (and fun) of "Jabberwocky," he recites for Alice "In winter, when the fields are white" (273), a poem, he tells her, that "was written entirely for your amusement." The problem is that the poem leaves Alice more puzzled than amused. The narrator of the poem sends a message to the fish: "This is what I wish." They reply: "We cannot do it, Sir, because—" (274). At this point Alice remarks that she does not understand, and Humpty Dumpty assures her that it gets easier further on. The narrator urges the fish to obey his previous order and when they refuse he fills a kettle with water. Someone comes and tells him that the fish are in bed. The speaker screams into his ear, "Then you must wake them up again" (275). Getting nowhere with this messenger, the narrator takes a corkscrew and goes to wake them up himself. He finds the door closed, and the last line of the poem reads, "I tried to turn the handle, but—" (275). Alice asks if that is all, to which Humpty Dumpty replies, "That's all," and "Good-bye." Alice's relationship with Humpty Dumpty ends as abruptly as his poem.

This has to be the worst poem in the *Alice* books. The language is flat and prosaic, the frustrated story line is without interest, the couplets are uninspired and fail to surprise or to delight, and such elements of nonsense as the unstated wish of the narrator and the lack of a conclusion to the work are crudely presented. Carroll fails to provide the necessary sense to make the nonsense interesting here. There is no way for either Alice or the reader to gain access to the poem. We are left with mere words and incoherence. But the poem's failure is important for what it reveals about Humpty Dumpty. He is the solemn literary man, the self-appointed critic of language who, though capable of a studious, self-assured explication of hard poems, cannot come up with a successful poem himself.

The last comic poem in *Through the Looking-Glass* is a riddle:

> "First, the fish must be caught."
> That is easy: a baby, I think, could have caught it.
> "Next, the fish must be bought,"
> That is easy: a penny, I think, would have bought it.
> "Now cook me the fish!"
> That is easy, and will not take more than a minute.
> "Let it lie in a dish!"
> That is easy,, because it already is in it.
> "Bring it here! Let me sup!"
> It is easy to set such a dish on the table.
> "Take the dish-cover up!"
> Ah, *that* is so hard that I fear I'm unable!
> For it holds it like glue—
> Holds the lid to the dish, while it lies in the middle:

> Which is easiest to do,
>     Un-dish-cover the fish, or dishcover the riddle?
>
>                                             (333)

Commenting on the riddle, Why is a Raven like a writing desk?, a critic observes that "it is essential for Nonsense that the riddle should have no solution. It is propounded to keep the dream and disorder side of the mind in play, but there must be no answer which could set up some kind of unity between the parts."[45] The point is well-taken and may be applied to the White Queen's fish riddle. A solution would tie the verse together and make sense of it. Perhaps Carroll had no solution in mind but Martin Gardner offers a solution arrived at by a man named Peter Suckling: an oyster.[46] A baby can pick it from an oyster bed, a penny would buy one in Carroll's day, it cooks quickly, it lies in its own dish, it is easily placed on the table, but the "dish-cover" is hard to raise because it is held to the dish by the oyster in the middle. This solution makes perfectly good sense; and one could certainly argue that in Sewell's terms the verse is definitely not nonsense, but simply a conventional riddle.

The solution, however, is not important in Looking-Glass Land, for after the White Queen finishes her recitation the Red Queen says to Alice, "Take a minute to think about it, and then guess"; but she then goes on to drink Alice's health and no opportunity is provided for Alice's response. It is significant that Carroll withholds a solution both to this riddle and to the one about the raven and the writing desk. An unanswered riddle exemplifies Carroll's idea of language games. Unlike mathematical puzzles, which do have solutions and thereby satisfy the mind by finally closing it, Carroll's nonsense riddles are linguistic distractions. They have no answers and leave Alice's (and the reader's) mind open, inquiring, puzzling for a moment, but ultimately unsatisfied, so that she must turn to another distraction. To adopt Carroll's metaphor, riddles, like all of Alice's experiences in Wonderland and Looking-Glass Land, feed her mind but never allow her the time or the framework to digest what she is fed.

## Humorous Verse: *The Hunting of the Snark*

On 18 July 1874 Carroll went out for a walk in Guildford, the town where his sisters lived, and received the inspiration for his odyssey of nonsense, *The Hunting of the Snark:*

I was walking on a hillside, alone, one bright summer day, when suddenly there came into my head one line of verse—one solitary line—"For the Snark *was* a Boojum, you see." I knew not what it meant, then: I know not what it means, now; but I wrote it down; and, sometime afterwards, the rest of the stanza occurred to me, that being its last line; and so by degrees, at odd moments during the next year or two, the rest of the poem pieced itself together, that being its last stanza.[47]

Carroll secured Henry Holiday, a prominent London painter and sculptor, to illustrate the poem, and his drawings successfully lived up to Carroll's desire that they be grotesque. The poem, published in March 1876, received mixed reviews. The following comment on the *Snark* by an anonymous reviewer in the *Athenaeum* for 1876 is typical of the bewilderment that the work generated: "It may be that the author of *Alice's Adventures in Wonderland* is still suffering from the attack of Claimant on the brain, which some time ago numbed or distracted so many intellects. Or it may be that he has merely been inspired by a wild desire to reduce to idiocy as many readers, and more especially, reviewers as possible. At all events, he has published what we may consider the most bewildering of modern poems."[48] Although Carroll intended the book for children, it appealed mainly to adults. Sales at first were slow but began to pick up during the latter part of the century; by 1908 it had been reprinted seventeen times, and the many subsequent issues include several American editions.

Many attempts have been made to read *The Hunting of the Snark* as an allegory. Carroll himself responded to the allegorists: "I have received courteous letters from strangers, begging to know whether 'The Hunting of the Snark' is an allegory, or contains some hidden moral, or is a political satire: and for all such questions I have but one answer. '*I don't know!*'"[49] The allegorists continue into our own century. One such reader argues that the poem satirizes an unsound business venture. Another, a former dean of the Harvard School of Business Administration, says that the Boojum is a symbol of a business slump and the entire poem is a tragedy about the business cycle. Still another reads the poem as an antivivisectionist tract. More recently, the work has been read as an existentialist treatise in which the Boojum is comparable to the atomic bomb.[50] Even W. H. Auden joins the allegorists in his suggestions that the ship can stand for mankind and human society moving through time and struggling with its destiny.[51]

The most interesting commentary on the poem to date is Michael

Holquist's "What is a Boojum? Nonsense and Modernism":

> Lewis Carroll's "agony in eight fits" was not only among the first to exemplify what is perhaps the most distinctive feature of modern literature, it did so more openly, more paradigmatically than almost any other text one knew. That is, it best dramatized the attempt of an author to insure through the structure of his work that the work could be perceived only as what it was, and not some other thing; the attempt to create an immaculate fiction, a fiction that resists the attempts of readers, and especially those readers who write criticism, to turn it into an allegory, a system equitable with already existing systems in the non-fictive world.[52]

Holquist argues that in the *Snark* Carroll achieves pure order, that by employing various "structures of resistance" he keeps the reader consistently off-balance in any attempt he may make to draw "sense" from the poem. He cites six such structures of resistance that ensure the poem's hermetic nature: 1) the acrostic dedicatory poem indicates that Carroll is more concerned with words that will exist in his own idiosyncratic system than in the conventional system of English; 2) the rule of three operates as a system for determining a truth that is absolutely unique to this poem and furthermore indicates that the intrinsic logic of the poem is not that of extrinsic logic which operates in systems outside the construct of the poem; 3) the various names of the crew members all begin with the letter *B,* a parallel that is rigidly observed, which dramatizes itself, but only as a dynamic process of parallelism, and nothing else; 4) the Butcher's proof that two can be added to one sets up an equation that is a process which begins with no content and ends with no content—it is pure process which has no other end than itself, namely the number 3; 5) the portmanteau words create new meanings (unique to the poem) by philologically exploiting the divergence between two old meanings; 6) the rhyme binds together words through their similar sounds, but no associative meaning links them and no resultant new association is possible.[53]

Holquist finally asks, "If *The Hunting of the Snark* is an absolute metaphor, if it means only itself, why read it?" His answer is "that it may help us to understand other, more complex attempts to do the same thing in modern literature."[54] It seems ironic for him to have argued so well that the *Snark* is an autonomous fiction and then to conclude that the reason one ought to read it is to better understand *other* autonomous fictions, like those of Franz Kafka and Vladimir Nabokov.

Although it is impossible to establish a coherent allegorical reading of the poem, it does seem possible to go beyond the limits that Holquist sets down for the poem—namely, the poem itself. Despite the "structures of resistance" Carroll does use words, phrases, and structures that permeate the shabby, disordered world of reality. The circle within which nonsense operates clearly intersects the greater circle of our self-referential language itself. There is, in fact, expressed in this poem anxiety over the threat of annihilation, and the Baker does, indeed, vanish. Furthermore, the section entitled "The Barrister's Dream" not only satirizes the English legal system (a pig is sentenced to transportation for life for leaving its pen but it is discovered that the pig has been dead for several years at the time of the guilty verdict) but also establishes the profound dislocation of form from substance. Ritual, custom, and order reveal a fundamental irrelevance to truth and justice.

I think a more interesting way of looking at *The Hunting of the Snark* is to see it as Carroll's comic rendering of his fear of disorder and chaos, with the comedy serving as a psychological defense against the devastating idea of personal annihilation. *The Hunting of the Snark* is Carroll's most dramatic confrontation with the void. The voyage into the unknown acknowledges the fundamental absurdity of life. The blank map that appears on the cover of the book and that guides the forsaken mariners becomes the visual image of this blind plunge into experience. The threat of annihilation underlies the entire voyage. The Baker's uncle warns:

> "But oh, beamish nephew, beware of the day,
> If your Snark be a Boojum! For then
> You will softly and suddenly vanish away,
> And never be met with again!"[55]

In the climactic Fit the Eighth, the warning of the Baker's uncle is realized. The crew discover the Baker, "their hero,"

> Erect and sublime, for one moment of time.
> In the next, that wild figure they saw
> (As it stung by a spasm) plunge into a chasm,
> While they waited and listened in awe.

"It's a Snark!" was the sound that first came to their ears,
    And seemed almost too good to be true.
Then followed a torrent of laughter and cheers:
    Then the ominous words, "It's a Boo—"

Then silence. Some fancied they heard in the air
    A weary and wandering sigh
That sounded like "—jum!" but the others declare
    It was only a breeze that went by.

(86–87)

The crew searches in vain for any trace of the Baker's body, and the poem closes with the lines, "He had softly and suddenly vanished away— / For the Snark *was* a Boojum, you see" (89). The dominant letter *B* closely associates the otherwise disparate crew. When a Snark is a Boojum, it, too, is brought under the umbrella of the letter *B*. The emphasis upon *was* in the line "For the Snark *was* a Boojum, you see" suggests that it was a Boojum all along, and the recognition of that fact proves to be an alliterative fatality.

Holiday's illustration of the scene shows the Bellman's hand ringing his bell for the passing of the Baker. If one looks carefully into the central darkness of the drawing he will see the huge head of the Baker, terror on his face, and a gigantic beak or claw pulling him by the wrist into total darkness.

In light of the terrifying freedom this world affords and the penalty it promises to extract from the unwary, it is little wonder that the rules and regulations of Carroll's youth are resurrected and revised to meet the challenge. The Bellman's crazy but competent role as director of this mad play, his penetrating Rule of Three, and the linguistic brotherhood of the "B" are among the notable attempts to create a sense of order and meaning out of chaos. There is never any question that the order imposed and the truth enunciated ("What I tell you three times is true) are both arbitrary. The implication of the poem, however, is that all systems of thought are fabricated and lead to truths that can never be tested outside of those systems. We create our own worlds and our own meanings to disguise the chaos that we know will eventually engulf us. The Baker's fate represents the ultimate disorder. In this poem there is no loving God, no transcendent guiding light that leads the pilgrim soul to eternal happiness. The Baker simply and suddenly vanishes into nothingness, into the primal emptiness that makes a mockery of all human enterprises.

Phyllis Greenacre observes that central to Carroll's life and writing is a voyeuristic theme. In the *Snark* the penalty for looking is the disappearance of the spectator. The most constant punitive threat in his writings "is extinction, either by disappearance of the whole body or by decapitation."[56] Another critic observes that "the Boojum is more than death. It is the end of all searching. It is the final, absolute extinction."[57]

Edward Guiliano shares my reading of this poem as an expression of Carroll's unconscious fear of death and notes the progression of Carroll's anxiety through three of his works. In *Alice's Adventures in Wonderland* there is a world in which escape is possible. In *Through the Looking-Glass* Carroll's pessimism grows and manifests itself in his depiction of a world where escape is not possible. Here life is conceived as a chess game, where determinism and fatalism eliminate individual possibilities. *The Hunting of the Snark,* however, is "the saddest of Carroll's writings" because it embodies "a statement of despair over the state of being—Dodgson's despair over the threat of nonexistence and the inescapability of time."[58] I should point out that the theme of determinism and entrapment in *Through the Looking-Glass* is not confined to the metaphor of life as a chess game but as a significant presence in the conclusion of the story. The final chapter, "Which Dreamed It?" has a peculiar affinity with *The Hunting of the Snark.* Is Alice dreaming of the Red King or is he dreaming of her? Is she, as Tweedledum says, only one of the things in the Red King's dream? Or, one might ask, is the Red King—God—only one of the things in Alice's mind? If Tweedledum is correct, then one's life is insubstantial, a kind of dream figment shaped and controlled by an unconscious deity. If Alice is the dreamer, the results are discomforting in another way. Then there is no transcendent being or truth but only her dream or idea of such a reality. The implication of the last chapter is that the ultimate entrapment is to be found within one's own mind and imagination. In *The Hunting of the Snark,* then, Carroll substitutes the Bellman and his Rule of Three for the Red King. The center of authority and truth is no longer aloof, sleeping, godlike, but a member of the crew. He constantly rings his bell (which is depicted in every illustration) reminding everyone of the passage of time and reminding them of their mortality, and he arbitrarily defines truth as anything he repeats three times. Carroll's questors must design their own world, for that is all they have. The mythical Snark in this poem turns out to be a booby trap that destroys all order, all hope, all meaning, and ends the poem. The question, Which dreamed it?, has only one answer here: Carroll himself, and the dream has now taken on the proportions of a nightmare.

Carroll's strong Christian faith, however, would never allow him consciously to think along these lines. There was a God, a clear purpose in life, and an afterlife awaiting the righteous. But as has been pointed out earlier, Carroll frequently expressed a more defiant and complex psychology in his nonsense writings than he did in his serious work. Even as the snark hunters manufactured some form of order as a buffer against madness, Carroll created a comic ballad with the bravado of an English adventurer in order to contain his greatest fear.

## Chapter Three

# Dream Child

*Alice's Adventures in Wonderland*

Although Lewis Carroll wrote *Alice's Adventures in Wonderland* explicitly to entertain children, it has become a treasure to philosophers, literary critics, biographers, clergymen, psychoanalysts, and linguists, not to mention mathematicians, theologians, and logicians. There appears to be something in *Alice* for everyone, and there are almost as many explanations of the work as there are commentators. It is helpful for the reader to know, for example, about Carroll's linguistic playfulness, his mathematical and logic puzzles, his religious opinions, his nostalgia for childhood, and his preoccupation with death. Finally, however, the ideal reader is one who can balance the various critical approaches to the *Alice* books without losing sight of their comedy.

Derek Hudson reminds us that Carroll was primarily a humorist: "The nearest parallel to the humorous method of Lewis Carroll is probably that of the Marx Brothers, whose dialogue not only has many verbal similarities with his but who also, like him, assert one grand false proposition at the outset and so persuade their audiences to accept anything as possible." Hudson goes on to note that it would be as foolish to look for sustained satire in the one as in the other: "Both have been based largely on a play with words, mixed with judicious slapstick, and set within the framework of an idiosyncratic view of the human situation; their purpose is entertainment."[1] Steadied by an awareness of the enduring comic value of these works, the best critics nevertheless rightfully insist upon exploring the serious psychological and philosophical subtexts that make the works profoundly relevant to the modern reader.

The critics fall into several categories: biographical, psychoanalytical, logical-linguistic, aesthetic, Jungian, mythic, existential, sociological, philosophical, theological, and historical. Alexander Taylor's *The White Knight* (1952)[2] attempts to explain *Alice's Adventures in Wonderland* as a commentary upon contemporary ecclesiastical history; William Empson's study, *"Alice in Wonderland*: The Child as Swain"

(1960),[3] views Alice as symbolic of the phallus, and her trip as a reversion to her mother's womb; and Donald Rackin's essay, "Alice's Journey to the End of Night" (1966),[4] argues that the story is an existential commentary on meaning in a meaningless world. Given the diverse interpretations of the *Alice* books, one would do well to be eclectic and to reread the story in the light of the various schools of criticism insofar as they clarify or enrich one's reading—while recognizing that there is no single meaning to the adventures.

**Unorthodox Children's Book.** Carroll completed writing *Alice's Adventures under Ground* before February 1863, but it took him until the autumn of 1864 before he finished illustrating the manuscript. Besides planning this work as his personal gift for Alice Liddell, Carroll had by this time completed a version that expanded the original from 18,000 to 53,000 words to be illustrated by John Tenniel. Carroll rejected the title *Alice's Adventures under Ground* as being "too like a lesson book about mines," and considered *Alice's Golden Hours, Alice Among the Elves, Alice's Hour in Elf-land,* and *Alice's Doings in Elf-land* before finally settling upon *Alice's Adventures in Wonderland.* When Macmillan, the publishers for Oxford University's Clarendon Press, began to issue the first edition of the work, Tenniel was completely unhappy with the printing of his illustrations. Carroll acceded to Tenniel's demand to reprint and in August 1865 took the work out of the hands of the Clarendon Press and turned it over to the printer Richard Clay, who reset the type. The unbound sheets of the first edition, however, were disposed of to Appleton Publishers, New York, who published them as the second issue of the first edition in 1866. The actual second edition was published in November 1865, by Clay.

Sales of *Alice's Adventures in Wonderland* began slowly and then gradually increased, and during Carroll's lifetime over 180,000 copies, in various editions, were sold in Great Britain. Reviewers were both pleased and puzzled with the strange new book. The *Pall Mall Gazette* said that "this delightful little book is a children's feast and a triumph of nonsense." The *Reader* declared it "a glorious artistic treasure." Not all reviews, however, were so complimentary. The *Illustrated Times* thought the story was "too extravagantly absurd,"[5] and the *Athenaeum* was put off with both the tale and its illustrations:

This is a dream-story; but who can, in cold blood, manufacture a dream, with all its loops and ties, and loose threads, and entanglements, and inconsistencies, and passages which lead to nothing at the end of which Sleep's most diligent pilgrim never arrives? Mr. Carroll has laboured hard to heap together strange adventures, and heterogeneous combinations; and we acknowledge the hard labour. Mr. Tenniel, again, is square and grim, and uncouth in his illustrations, howbeit clever, even sometimes to the verge of grandeur, as is the artist's habit. We fancy that any real child might be more puzzled than enchanted by this stiff, overwrought story.[6]

Hard words—but the above review, like most reviews of that day, assumed *Alice* was simply a book for children and, as such, did not satisfy an adult's expectations.

Carroll chose not to follow the established pattern of children's books, which demanded realism and moral didacticism, in favor of characteristics of the fairy tale. The Victorian reader expected a children's book to be realistic, to instruct the child in religion and morals, and consequently, to prepare him for a righteous adulthood. Carroll's book not only lacked a realistic framework but openly poked fun at conventional didacticism. Furthermore, few Victorian authors chose to model their stories upon the fairy tale or to embody elements of the fairy tale in their narratives for children. Hans Christian Andersen's fairy tales were translated into English by 1846, but no English writer had yet followed his practice.

Carroll's tentative title, "Alice among the Elves," suggests that he was aware of his departure from Victorian tradition. Although there are no elves in the books, there are magical transformations and changes in size, talking animals, and magical potions and foods. By choosing a dream structure for his work, Carroll rejects the approach of earlier writers in their appeal to the reason of the readers.

The character of Alice also departs from the conventional girl heroine. The typical Victorian children's book presented "girl angels fated for an early death," or "impossibly virtuous little ladies," or "naughty girls who eventually reform in response to heavy adult pressure."[7] Alice is neither naughty nor excessively nice, but curious and bewildered. She may grow physically, but her experiences apparently do not teach her anything, alter her behavior, or prepare her for adulthood in a conventional way. Compared to the standard literature for children, *Alice* was surprisingly antididactic.

Later critics, however, arrived at a different point of view from that of Carroll's contemporaries. Gilbert Chesterton, for example, declared that "it is not children who ought to read the words of Lewis Carroll, they are far better employed making mud-pies."[8] And Jan B. Gordon argues that the two *Alice* volumes "are decadent adult literature rather than children's literature."[9] Although the *Alice* books were originally intended for children—indeed, very specific ones—they have since been appropriated by adults. Most children today, if they know Alice at all, are familiar with the popular and sentimentalized versions of her presented in films and cartoons. But the twentieth-century adult mind is very much at home in the violent, nightmarish dream world of the original Alice.

**Interpreting the Dream.** In Wonderland all things are possible. It is called Wonderland because, like Alice, the reader is continually astonished, surprised, and puzzled. It is a world made up of contradictions, violence, jokes, anxiety, puns, puzzles, rudeness, rules and anarchy shaped by a dream vision. The chaos that rules in Wonderland is not unfamiliar to us. It is evident in the behavior of children who have not yet been restrained by the rules of decorum. Little Leroy's act of throwing his cereal at W. C. Fields and Chico Marx's behavior when insulting a fat, wealthy lawyer are not unlike the conduct of the Hatter at the tea party. The misconduct of a child is more easily taken for granted—but witness that same behavior in an adult and he will be labelled abnormal or mad. In Wonderland everyone is mad, as the Cheshire Cat points out, and yet everyone is also comic. Alice is faced with a world of adults who behave like children, despite the variety of intellectual sophistication they represent.

*Alice's Adventures* has the fluid structure of a dream vision, a conventional literary form that dates back to the Middle Ages. Alice's dream, however, differs from the traditional form in that it is distinctly episodic, is rendered from the third-person point of view, and resists a coherent symbolic or allegorical interpretation. Alice's character does not appear to develop or significantly change throughout the tale. One chapter does not necessarily evolve out of the preceding one. The book sets forth a series of discrete encounters between Alice and the creatures in Wonderland, and she rarely seems capable of applying what she learned in a past encounter to a new one and consequently moves through her dream world in almost constant amazement. Curiosity above all else impels Alice on to new adventures.

The first two paragraphs of the book provide an important frame for the story in their depiction of Alice falling asleep as her older sister reads a book. Alice peeps into the book and, seeing no pictures or conversations in it, wonders what possible use the book can have. Her remark suggests her rebellion against the boring and didactic Victorian texts used to educate children. This setting thus establishes the motivation for Alice's escape into a dreamworld. Like Alice, Carroll was intent on transforming his small corner of Victorian England into a rigorous and extraordinary adventure, whether playing railroad as a child at Croft Rectory, working puzzles at Oxford, or telling stories to little girls. After three short paragraphs he whisks Alice off the humdrum surface of the earth and has her plummet into Wonderland.

Like the great real-life adventurers of her day, Alice is strongly motivated by curiosity. She resembles a Victorian anthropologist, an explorer encountering strange cultures that she chooses not to understand. At times she almost seems to be a disembodied intellect, so cool is she in the face of danger. While she is falling down the rabbit-hole, for instance, "she had plenty of time as she went down to look about her, and to wonder what was going to happen next."[10] As she continues her fall she rather casually removes from a passing shelf a jar of orange marmalade. To her disappointment it is empty and rather than drop it and risk hitting someone below, she places it in a cupboard as she falls past it. Of course, since she was falling, she could not have dropped the jar even if she chose to.

Her composure is extraordinary (to think of food at a time like that)—and yet she has an intellectual appreciation of her fall, for she says that now "I shall think nothing of tumbling down stairs" (27). The naïveté of her coolness, however, is quietly undermined by a joke the narrator makes about death: "'Why, I wouldn't say anything about it, even if I fell off the top of the house!' (which was very likely true)" (23). There is a connection in Carroll's (and the narrator's) mind between the death of childhood and the child's sexual awareness. The poem that introduces the Looking-Glass ("Come, hearken then, ere voice of dread, / With bitter summons laden, / Shall summon to unwelcome bed / A melancholy maiden") supports the sex-death relationship and elicits a comment by Empson: "After all the marriage-bed was more likely to be the end of the maiden than the grave, and the metaphor firmly implied treats them as identical."[11]

A great deal of the humor found in Alice's encounters with the creatures of Wonderland derives from the solemnity of Alice herself. She is almost totally lacking in a sense of humor; and the reader, along with the narrator, is always a step or two ahead of her. Alice is a kind of "straight man," not only to the inhabitants of Wonderland but to the author as well. More often than not the reader sees things through Alice's eyes, but her vision is limited and flawed by her youthful naïveté. Carroll's choice of third-person narrative, therefore, gives one the perspective necessary for adult comedy.

The double perspective of the narrative reflects Carroll's own fundamental duality, a constant tension in his thinking and sensibility between such forces as emotion and reason, illusion and reality, and sentiment and wit. He could move with ease from the intellectual rigors of math, logic, and wit to the sentimental expression of his feelings in his verse. The dreamy, nostalgic romanticism of the opening poem, for example, stands in marked contrast with the cold and loveless world of verbal assaults of Wonderland itself. The story might be viewed as a battle between the sensibilities of the child and those of an adult. Carroll's dream children—embodiments of his own lost childhood—are filled with hope and wonder. They seek love and understanding, believing that their dreams can be realized. The powerful longings of the child within Carroll, however, are relentlessly undermined, denied, or diffused by his cold reason and wit.

It quickly becomes apparent that Wonderland is not a promised land, a place of sleepy fulfillment. Wonderland stimulates the senses and the mind. It is a *monde fatale,* so to speak, one that seduces Alice (and the reader) to seek new sights, new conversations, new ideas, but it never satisfies her. Conventional meaning, understanding, and the fulfillment that comes with illumination are constantly denied her. That is the secret of Wonderland: its disorienting and compelling attractions make it a Wanderland and Alice herself an addicted wanderer, free of the intellectual and moral burden of ordering her experiences into some meaningful whole. She is never bored because she is never satisfied.

Significantly, she is presented with a stimulating, alluring vision early on in her adventures. Although all the doors around the hall are locked, Alice finds a tiny golden key that opens one that leads into a small passage. She kneels down and looks along the passage into "the loveliest garden you ever saw" (30). Because of her size she is unable to get out of the dark hall to "wander among those beds of bright flowers and those cool fountains" (30). It is not until chapter 8 that Alice reaches the garden, only to discover that the roses in the garden are painted and its inhabitants either mad or cruel. One critic believes that "the story revolves about the golden key to the enchanted garden and Alice's endless frustrations and wanderings in bypaths until she enters at last," and that the garden is a "rich symbol if we call it adult life viewed by a child, or vice versa."[12] Another critic conjectures on the perspective of the adult: "As sublibrarian of Christ Church, Carroll used a small room overlooking the deanery garden when the Liddell children played croquet. How often he must have watched them, longing to escape from the dark halls of Oxford into the bright flowers, and cool fountains of childhood's Eden!"[13]

More basic than either of these two readings, however, is the theme of desire created by Alice's vision of the garden. It becomes a dream vision within a dream. Too large to enter the passage to the garden, she can only imagine being among its delights. In mythic terms, Alice's dream garden corresponds to a longing for lost innocence, the Garden of Eden. Her desire invests the place with imagined significance. Later, of course, when she actually enters the garden it loses its romantic aspect. In fact, it turns out to be a parodic Garden of Life, for the roses are painted, the people are playing cards, and the death-cry "Off with her head!" echoes throughout the croquet grounds.

Alice's dream garden is an excellent example of Carroll's paradoxical duality. Like Alice, he is possessed by a romantic vision of an Edenic childhood more desirable than his own fallen world, but it is a vision that he knows is inevitably corrupted by adult sin and sexuality. Carroll would later combine the innocence of childhood and the sexuality of adulthood in the character of the Mad Gardener in *Sylvie and Bruno*. Here, meanwhile, he allows the romantic dream of the garden to fill Alice with hope and joy for a time but he later tramples that pastoral vision with the hatred and fury of the Queen and the artificiality of the roses and the two-dimensional characters. Carroll's paradoxical attitude here is best summarized by the lines from John Donne's "Twickenham Garden": "that this place may thoroughly be thought / True Paradise, I have the serpent brought."

Alice is constantly at odds with the creatures and situations of Wonderland. It is precisely this tension between her expectations and the actuality of Wonderland that makes the book exciting. Alice is "our" representative, bringing the ideals of reason and morality and a desire for meaning into a world of disorder, contradiction, violence, arbitrariness, cruelty, rudeness, frustration, and amorality. Jan B. Gordon wonders "whether Alice's attempt during her *Adventures* to constitute a social family among the animals is not the burden of the Victorian exile."[14] He sees the character of Alice to be determined by the Victorians' habit of equating the child with the adult, an action that has the unfortunate effect of creating an orphan. Many children do, indeed, develop social and family ties by investing their stuffed animals with human sensibilities. Alice, however, is more than an orphan seeking a surrogate family; she is a victim of a seeming conspiracy of animal, plant, and human characters. These diverse characters comprise a hierarchy of heartless adults who bully and issue orders to Alice. Cruel or indifferent, these creatures exhibit neither compassion nor affection. There can be no families where there are no feelings. Everyone is alone and isolated in Wonderland.

James Kincaid's thesis is that Alice is an invader in Wonderland, that she reenacts the betrayal of innocence: "She carries with her the chief barrier between human beings and comic existence: an implicit belief in a world ruled by death and predation and a relentless insistence upon linear progression and completeness."[15] He contends that Carroll adopts an ironic view that questions the value of human innocence altogether and accepts the sophisticated and melancholy corruption of adults as preferable to the cruel selfishness of children.

This interpretation is a valuable corrective to the sentimental view of Alice held by a few uncritical readers, but it seems to go too far in the other direction. Like patient Griselda in Chaucer's "The Clerk's Tale" and Desdemona in Shakespeare's *Othello,* Alice can be made into an interesting villain because she is so apparently innocent. There is no question that she is an imperfect child—too serious, a bit priggish and prissy, rather conventional, and selfish—and that her innocence is ambiguous, but she is hardly a dark Darwinian invader of paradise. Nina Auerbach describes Alice's role more accurately: "The ultimate effect of Alice's adventures implicates her, female child though she is, in the troubled human condition."[16]

The first thing Alice has to learn in this strange world is to adjust to unexpected changes, as in female puberty. By drinking from a mysterious bottle and eating from a small cake, she experiences great changes in body size until she becomes unsure of her own identity: "Who in the world am I? Ah, that's the great puzzle" (37). Throughout her adventures Alice is confronted with the problem of her shifting identity, a problem aggravated and in large part caused by the inconsistencies of Wonderland. The theme of maturation is also in evidence here: "Children like to think of being so small that they could hide from grown-ups and so big that they could control them, and to do this dramatises the great topic of growing up, which both Alices keep to consistently."[17]

The "nearly universal belief in permanent self-identity is put to the test and eventually demolished in Wonderland."[18] Alice finally overcomes the threat to her selfhood at the conclusion of the story, when, having grown to her full size, she asserts "You're nothing but a pack of cards!" (161). This capability for sudden changes in body size can be seen as an ominous and destructive process that undermines one's sense of natural growth and predictable size. Through the destruction of stability, Wonderland asserts its mad sanity.

Carroll typically grants his heroine incredible powers of distraction, as if to demonstrate that the mind has remarkable defenses against the panic inherent in the human condition. After vainly puzzling over her identity, Alice finds herself swimming in the pool of tears that she wept when she was nine feet tall. Alice not only thinks about marmalade instead of death but now worries about the proper way to address the Mouse she finds swimming in her tears. The prospect of drowning does not enter her mind as she engages the Mouse in conversation. The image of the tears as a sea supplants in dream-like fashion the actual hall in which Alice stands weeping—for the Mouse and Alice, magically joined by birds and other animals, swim "to the shore."

Carroll's need to bring emotion under the reins of reason seems to be the major driving force behind this episode. For centuries poets have seen tears as the essence of human emotion, whether they be tears of sorrow or of joy. John Donne, however, intellectualized this emotional symbol through his metaphysical wit in such poems as "The Canonization" and "A Valediction: of Weeping." Carroll employs a similar wit and comic perspective by threatening to drown his heroine in her own tears. By treating such hyperbole literally (and reinforcing the image through the illustration), Carroll humorously demonstrates the inherent dangers of uncontrolled emotion, of reckless romanticism.

Alice's immersion in her own tears may also suggest an underlying image of sexuality. William Empson, for example, reads this scene in Freudian terms: "The symbolic completeness of Alice's experience is I think important. She runs the whole gamut; she is a father in getting down the hole, a foetus at the bottom, and can only be born by becoming a mother and producing her own amniotic fluid."[19]

Alice's concern for the correct form of address to the Mouse is a reminder that nonsense is a game of words, and chapter 3 reinforces this aspect of the story. The Mouse proposes to dry Alice and the other animals by relating to them a piece of dry history. When the Mouse states that "Stigand, the patriotic archbishop of Canterbury, found it advisable" (47), the Duck interrupts to ask what the antecedent of "it" is: "I know what 'it' means well enough, when *I* find a thing . . . it's generally a frog or a worm" (47). Such analysis and questioning is obviously detrimental to communication; but since the Mouse's purpose in relating this history is to dry off the fellow creatures, such an attack upon grammatical ambiguity is doubly ridiculous.

The Dodo finally settles upon a caucus race to dry everyone off. When Alice asks what kind of a race that is, the Dodo replies that "the best way to explain it is to do it" (48), a remark that suggests the inadequacy of language to explain all things. After the race is run everybody is declared the winner and all are awarded prizes, which seems like a perfectly acceptable democratic arrangement considering that everyone has gotten dry. Like so many anxious children, the animals all crowd around Alice, calling out "Prizes! Prizes!" The Dodo solemnly awards Alice her own thimble, perhaps an emblem of her fated domesticity. The animals all take this ceremony very seriously and cause Alice to look as solemn as she can. The caucus race and the award ceremony seem incomprehensible to Alice because she is an outsider, unfamiliar with the other creatures' games and language system. In Tenniel's illustration of the ceremony there is pictured in the background among the birds the face of an ape. Although never mentioned in the text, the ape is perhaps meant to be a grim reminder of Darwin's recent investigations.

Carroll may have intended the caucus race to satirize the activities of political parties. As one critic suggests, Carroll might have been poking fun at "the fact that committee members generally do a lot of running around in circles, getting nowhere, and with everybody wanting a political plum."[20] This episode also has a biographical interest, for a number of the animals in this race appear to be based upon actual people. The Duck is Canon Robinson Duckworth; the Lory is Lorina Liddell; the Eaglet is Edith; and the Dodo is Carroll. When he stuttered while pronouncing his name it came out "Do-Do-Dodgson."

The caucus race may more significantly be read as a metaphor for the entire story, indeed, for life itself. Many authors, including Saint Paul, have compared life to a race. The circularity and arbitrariness of the caucus race, however, undermines the conventional metaphor. By making drying off the motive for the race, Carroll subverts the usual purpose of such a contest to select the fastest runner. The circle eliminates the finish line and without a goal there can be no losers and no winners. If such is life, then its goals are arbitrary and capricious (though bizarrely practical in the short run). An epistemological equivalent to the caucus race occurs in "The Three Voices" where the sententious old hag observes: "And thus the chain, that sages sought, / Is to a glorious circle wrought, / For Notion hath its source in Thought." Carroll's humor in all of this must not be forgotten, for it provides him with a psychological defense against such a conception of life. His comedy here, as in *The Hunting of the Snark,* diffuses rather than confronts such terribly serious issues as the limits of knowledge and the purpose of life.

The Mouse's tale is still another instance of language as play. "Tale" is confused with "tail," "not" with "knot," and the shape of the verse depicts a tail in Alice's mind. When one thinks back on this chapter he realizes that despite all the dialogue Alice has learned very little from her associates and vice versa. The strategy of Wonderland is to defeat different systems of logic, to keep details from joining to establish some meaningful order. The language, characters, and scenes in Wonderland are all essentially discrete. Attempts to fuse them lead to misunderstanding. Consequently, the reader, not to mention Alice, cannot evaluate past experiences and can only look forward to new and more unusual ones. In the case of the Mouse's tale, however, there is a faint foreshadowing of the trial at the end of the book. The law is an issue in both, and both the tale and the trial exhibit linguistic confusion.

Along with its intellectual emphasis upon language, chapter 4 focuses upon Alice's body and her physical space. After drinking from the magical bottle she grows so large that her body fills the entire house. The illustration reveals a powerful sense of claustrophobia, as if a child had somehow gotten into her doll house and cannot get out. Empson finds in this scene a nightmare theme of the birth-trauma,[21] an idea supported by the fact that in Carroll's drawing of Alice she is much more in the fetal position than she is in the Tenniel illustration. This theme is first introduced when Alice, grown large, longingly looks through the small door that leads into the garden. Alice's response to her entrapment, which would be terrifying to an ordinary child, is unexpected. Her curiosity and simple bewilderment are expressed in a remarkably detached tone: "it's rather curious, you know, this sort of life!" (58). Her reality becomes a kind of fiction: "When I used to read fairy tales, I fancied that kind of thing never happened, and now here I am in the middle of one!" (59). Carroll thus draws a significant parallel between the strangeness of life and that of fiction. Life mirrors fiction; both are fabrications that create the illusion of purpose and meaning. Alice's adventures, however, ultimately reveal no such purpose and meaning, and her experiences in Wonderland are fundamentally different from those of children in fairy tales. She achieves no particular goal in her adventures nor does she learn a morally uplifting lesson. Indeed, the reader discovers in her dream the terrifying vision of the void that underlies the comfortable structures of the rational world.

Carroll's conclusion to this chapter is singularly disappointing. The difficulties Alice experienced as a giant are now balanced by her encounter with an enormous puppy that threatens her life in its exuberant playfulness. Somehow a puppy seems out of place in Wonderland. It barks instead of speaks, it chases a stick, pants, and jumps in the air. It is simply an oversized creature from the familiar world above-ground and its presence disfigures the character of Wonderland that has already been established. There is a little too much of second-rate *Gulliver's Travels* in this chapter to make it memorable; and one is happily relieved when Alice finally comes upon the mysterious large blue caterpillar quietly smoking a long hookah, for here, indeed, is the discomforting dream quality of Wonderland again.

The Caterpillar has a multifaceted significance in the story. It fuses the themes of sexuality, changing body forms, and the mystery of personal identity. The illustration is replete with phallic images: the Caterpillar himself, the mushroom on which he sits and those beneath him, and Alice's mushroom-shaped dress. As a symbol of sexuality, he represents a threat to Alice's childhood innocence. Enclosed in the chrysalislike circle of his pipe, he also represents an image of the mysterious transformation of body form. Alice, who literally has to look up to this hooded creature, has come upon her high priest, who presumably will impart his great wisdom and initiate her into the mysteries of life. Of course, he does nothing of the kind, except by indirection.

Like so many of the creatures Alice meets, the Caterpillar treats her rudely, almost contemptuously. What makes this encounter unsettling is that the author provides absolutely no motivation for the Caterpillar's aggressiveness toward Alice. His insults are gratuitous, funny, and intimidating. Alice, however, expects to be treated in the polite manner customary above-ground. The Caterpillar's first question to her— "Who are *You?*"—is not only contemptuous but especially unnerving considering Alice's previous difficulty in answering that question. It is almost as if the Caterpillar had read her anxieties and set this question to torment her. He does, after all, possess extrasensory perception. As he gets down from the mushroom he tells her that eating one side will make her grow taller and eating the other side will make her grow shorter. "'One side of *what*? The other side of *what*?' thought Alice to herself. 'Of the mushroom,' said the Caterpillar, just as if she had asked it aloud" (73).

The issue of Alice's identity is carried into her next encounter. The Pigeon, believing Alice is a serpent, asks, "Well! *What* are you?" and the best that Alice can come up with is "I—I'm a little girl" (76). But Alice's elongated neck suggests convincingly that she looks more serpentine than girlish to the Pigeon—and, furthermore, since girls as well as serpents eat eggs, it really makes no difference to the Pigeon, for whom girls are a kind of serpent. Defining an entire creature by a single action has a particular logic from the Pigeon's point of view, and the newness of the idea silences Alice. Wonderland thus reveals again its logical subtext, one that poses a constant challenge to Alice's more conventional reasoning. The Caterpillar's and now the Pigeon's aggressive attack seriously threaten Alice's assumption of a permanent identity. Later, when the White Rabbit orders her about like his servant, Alice imagines that her new identity will surface in the world above when her cat Dinah will command her in the same manner. Empson goes behind the question of identity raised in this section to observe, "Alice knows several reasons why she should object to growing up, and does not at all like being an obvious angel, a head out of contact with its body that has to come down from the sky, and gets mistaken for the Paradisal serpent of the knowledge of good and evil, and by the pigeon of the Annunciation, too."[22]

The peculiar behavior of the creatures in Wonderland, possessed of their unique form of logic and reason, is further developed in chapter 6. The Frog-Footman sitting on the step of the Duchess's house takes for granted the chaos around him. When a plate flies out of the door and breaks against one of the trees behind him, he continues talking "exactly as if nothing had happened" (81). The surface image of aristocratic order implied by the livery of the Frog-Footman and the Fish-Footman and by the pillared porch of the Duchess's house is subverted by the raucous noise from within and by the Footman's detachment from the interior mayhem.

This is the home of chaos. Once inside, Alice meets the Duchess, one of the most unwholesome characters in the book. She is incredibly ugly, masculine, sadistic, moralistic, and sexually aggressive. The fact

Alice meets the Duchess.
John Tenniel. *Alice's Adventures in Wonderland.*

that she is first pictured nursing a baby makes her appear even more grotesque, for she is the antithesis of a maternal figure. The Cheshire Cat with its unnerving grin adds still another element of the grotesque to this caricature of domesticity. Pepper fills the air and the Cook is throwing everything within her reach at the Duchess and the baby. When Alice attempts to control the situation the Duchess quickly puts her in her place; "If everybody minded their own business the world would go round a deal faster than it does" (84). And when Alice starts talking about the world spinning on its axis, the Duchess, by way of a pun, escalates the violence: "Talking of axis, chop off her head!" (84). But her violence is aimless and quickly turns upon the baby: "she began nursing her child again, singing a sort of lullaby to it as she did so, and giving it a violent shake at the end of every line" (85). She then tosses the baby violently up and down "and the poor little thing howled so" (85) that Alice could hardly hear the words of the lullaby.

Alice is left to nurse the baby as the Duchess prepares to play croquet with the Queen.

This extended parody of motherhood is finally terminated when the baby turns into a pig. Alice thinks to herself, "If it had grown up it would have made a dreadfully ugly child; but it makes rather a handsome pig, I think" (87). Here again is another reminder that in Wonderland the essence of anything is unstable. If a baby boy can turn into a pig, then perhaps the Pigeon was correct in seeing Alice as a serpent. There are no familiar rules, conventions, or categories—the comedy of seeming chaos reigns supreme. Without stable points of reference, reason is helpless to defend one against disorder. Alice ultimately comes to realize this at the end of the tale where the culmination of her frustrations leads her to deny the meaningless world around her. Meanwhile, her conversation with the Cheshire Cat takes her a step further into the confusion.

In a world devoid of structure and permanent landmarks Alice rather naturally asks directions: "Would you tell me, please, which way I ought to go from here?" The Cat replies, "That depends a good deal on where you want to get to." When Alice hesitates with "I don't much care where—" the Cat quickly interrupts, "Then it doesn't matter which way you go." Alice goes on to complete her remark saying "—so long as I get *somewhere*" (88), but one surmises that Wonderland has already spoken in its usual unsettling tone. Alice seemingly cannot escape the madness of chaos that surrounds her. She protests that she does not want to go among mad people, but the Cat knowingly replies, "we're all mad here. I'm mad. You're mad" (89). The term "mad" seems relative to Carroll: the creatures of Wonderland, with their unique rules and logic, seem mad to Alice, and Alice, with her conventional thinking, appears mad to the Cheshire Cat. Alice, in any case, does not believe that her coming to Wonderland proves her mad. She never comprehends the Cat's revelations about its strange world and persists in her subsequent adventures to expect conventional behavior from the inhabitants of Wonderland.

There is no question that the Cheshire Cat registers its momentary hold upon Alice and the reader. Like the grin of a madman it may have no logical significance whatsoever but the sane observer will of necessity try to interpret it even as a reader of nonsense feels compelled to make some sense of it. Unlike the *Mona Lisa* or the Sphinx, the Cat can speak and poses a threat to Alice with its teeth and sharp claws. Its smile, however, is its most unnerving aspect. The Cat's eyes and smile suggest that it knows something that Alice (and the reader) does not. Curiosity may have killed the legendary cat, but here the tables are turned and the Cat makes Alice curious. Alice's curiosity is quickly beaten down by the domineering Duchess, who boldly asserts that all cats can grin. She proceeds to insult Alice, who quickly changes the subject. Like so many previous issues, the question about the Cat's motivation for grinning is forgotten. In a world without meaning, everything is important and everything is trivial. Wonderland bullies memory, judgment, and reason into submission.

Carroll reinforces the enigmatic nature of the Cheshire Cat by first granting it what appears to be an all-knowing mind and then later undermining its presumed omniscience. After the Cat vanishes it suddenly reappears to ask what became of the baby. Alice replies that it turned into a pig and the Cat remarks, "I thought it would" (90) and vanishes again. It is curious that the Cat should be concerned with the fate of the baby; and its lack of surprise that the boy turned into a pig suggests a disquieting omniscience. The Cat vanishes and again reappears to ask if Alice said "pig" or "fig," a question that suggests, in typical Wonderland fashion, that it really does not matter what happened to the baby after all.

In her own detached and amused aspect, Alice is very much like the Cheshire Cat herself. As the Cat gradually vanishes again its grin remains suspended among the branches of its tree, leading Alice to think: "Well, I've often seen a cat without a grin, but a grin without a cat! It's the most curious thing I ever saw in all my life" (91). The "seemingly indestructible bond between subject and attribute—has been graphically subverted by the appearance of a cat's grin without a cat."[23] Nevertheless, Alice maintains a remarkable coolness in the face of such a bizarre experience. The word "curious," the most frequent adjective used to describe her behavior, suggests a quiet, detached interest in the occurrences surrounding her, an intellectual rather than an emotional response to fantastic sights. Alice is seldom amazed, excited, or dreadfully afraid.

Despite her equanimity, Alice is no match for the Hatter, who demonstrates that life in Wonderland is like a puzzle in which none of the pieces fit together. He challenges her logic with an answerless riddle: "Why is a raven like a writing-desk?" When Alice gives up and asks the Hatter the answer, he replies that he does not have the slightest idea. In Wonderland it is appropriate that the riddle should have no solution,[24] for it keeps the dream and disorder side of the mind in play.

"A Mad Tea-Party."
John Tenniel. *Alice's Adventures in Wonderland.*

Carroll himself admitted that the riddle, as originally invented, had
no answer at all. Like Alice's question to the Duchess as to why her cat
grins, this one also has no answer. As questioner, Alice is bullied by
the Duchess; as the one questioned, she is bullied by the Hatter.

Having presented her with an interesting riddle ("'Come, we shall
have some fun now!' thought Alice"), the Hatter attacks her use of
language and never allows her the opportunity to return to solving the
riddle. The March Hare interrupts to tell Alice to say what she means.
She replies that "at least I mean what I say—that's the same thing, you
know." But the Hatter retaliates with, "Not the same thing a bit! Why
you might just as well say that 'I see what I eat' is the same thing as
'I eat what I see!'" (95). As Roger W. Holmes points out, Carroll the
philosopher-logician is at work here. "We know that if all apples are
red, it does not follow that red things are apples: the logician's technical description of this is the non-convertibility *simpliciter* of universal
propositions."[25]

Alice's sense of time as well as her grammar is undermined in the subsequent dialogue, which is full of puns based upon the nonsensical personification of time. Time itself is defined by and is an extension of the incomprehensible manner of the tea party. The scene Alice has come upon has no beginning and apparently no end. The personified time will not obey the Hatter; consequently it is always six o'clock, always tea time. The disordered conversation, like the ceaseless movement around the table, is endless. Life in Wonderland is indeed a caucus race.

In the midst of the boisterous tea party we find the sleepy Dormouse whose imperturbability appears to anger the March Hare and the Hatter. When the Dormouse drowses off to sleep in the midst of its own story the Hatter pinches it, and as Alice walks away from the interminable confusion she looks back and sees the Hare and the Hatter trying to force the Dormouse into the teapot. There is no explanation offered for any of their actions, and since Wonderland offers no key to understanding its social conventions, this act of gratuitous violence appears as logical as any to conclude the chapter. Rackin believes that at this point in the narrative "the destruction of the foundations of Alice's old order is practically complete."[26] While it is true that most of the conventions that Alice and the reader subscribe to have been challenged and subverted by the inhabitants of Wonderland, it is not Alice but the reader who discovers this fact. In order to maintain the playful tension between the chaos of Wonderland and the conventional assumptions that Alice brings from her world above ground, Carroll has to take care that Alice's understanding of her dream world does not develop, for that would bring an abrupt end to the nonsense. In this respect the nonsense is a form of irony implicit throughout the entire narrative.

The rose garden is a parodic garden of life. The only living creatures besides Alice are the flamingo, the hedgehogs, and the Chesire Cat— all animals. The "people" are cards. Furthermore, the flamingo and hedgehogs, which are living, are employed as surrogates for inanimate things, namely a croquet mallet and croquet balls. Life, as such, is inherently detrimental to the game of croquet where consistency and rigidity are required. Such consistency and rigidity, on the other hand, are to be found in the Queen of Hearts, who constantly calls out "Off with her head," and the King of Hearts, whose paper heart has long been trampled flat by his single-minded wife. As Alice says, "you've no idea how confusing it is all the things being alive" (113).

Against the threat of life to the game of croquet is the constant mock-threat of death to Alice, the soldiers, and the Cheshire Cat. The Queen's cry for beheadings finally materializes in the person of the executioner who has been summoned to cut off the head of the Cat. Wonderland neutralizes its own tension at this point, for the Cheshire Cat's body has vanished, leaving only its grinning head and the metaphysical question, whether one can cut off a head when there is no body from which to cut it off. Although the chapter ends with an academic consideration of execution, the subject of death is turned into an inane intellectual argument, whereby Carroll once again defends himself and the reader against the terrible reality of death.

The Duchess's preoccupation with finding morals in everything parodies the temper of the self-righteous moralists of Victorian England and ironically contrasts with her own sexual aggressiveness. She foolishly applies a moral axiom to everything that Alice says. As Elsie Leach observes, "When Dodgson makes a ridiculous character like the Duchess praise and practice moralizing in this manner, he clearly indicates his attitude toward didacticism directed against children."[27] It is possible that Carroll had in mind the popular children's book by Oliver Goldsmith, *Little Goody Two Shoes.* In that work the wise and mature heroine Margery draws morals from every accident, as when the death of a pet dormouse gives her the opportunity of reading to the children a lecture on the uncertainty of life and the necessity of always being prepared for death.[28]

Carroll's depiction of the Duchess, however, goes far beyond parodying Victorian moralists: she represents a terrifying sexual threat to childhood innocence. Alice is made very uneasy by the Duchess's overtures: "Alice did not much like her keeping so close to her: first, because the Duchess was very ugly: and secondly, because she was exactly the right height to rest her chin on Alice's shoulder, and it was an uncomfortably sharp chin" (120). She tucks "her arm affectionately into Alice's" (119) and shifts the subject to romance: "'Tis so, and the moral of that is—'Oh, 'tis love, 'tis love, that makes the world go round!'" (120). The Duchess digs her chin further into Alice's shoulder and escalates her sexual overtures: "I dare say you're wondering why I don't put my arm round your waist" (121). Since Alice is still carrying her flamingo, the Duchess remarks, "I'm doubtful about the temper of your flamingo. Shall I try the experiment?" "He might bite" (121), Alice cautiously replies, not at all interested in the offer. The word "experiment" to describe putting her arm around Alice's waist seems to be a sinister euphemism for the act of seduction. William Empson, however, suggests that the scene depicts Carroll's fear of being seduced by a middle-aged woman.[29]

At last, it seems, Alice finds someone with whom she can actually communicate and who will show her compassion. Free from the oppressive Duchess, Alice next meets the Mock Turtle and the Gryphon. Whereas most of the Wonderland creatures are lacking in the emotions of love, compassion, or friendship, these two sentimentalists, in their excessive show of feeling, are as sterile and shallow as their mad fellows. They ask her about her previous adventures, and she describes them up to her meeting with the Caterpillar, at which point the Gryphon says, "It's all about as curious as it can be" (138). The Turtle asks her to repeat "'Tis the voice of the sluggard" to see if it will come out different, as "Father William" had in the presence of the Caterpillar. These are hardly reassuring responses to Alice's recounting of her bewildering adventures.

The recurrent theme of the fear of being eaten dominates this episode. Alice's rendition of "'Tis the voice of the sluggard" concludes with a panther feasting upon an owl. The theme continues in the Mock Turtle's song, in which he ironically celebrates the beautiful soup he is destined to become. The idea of death in both cases is distanced by the rhymes and regular meters of the poetry and by Carroll's comic logic that argues that there must be such a creature as a mock turtle to account for the soup made from it.

Many of the creatures who gather at the court for the trial of the Knave of Hearts Alice has met before, suggesting a final assemblage for the approaching conclusion. The time-obsessed White Rabbit appears again, with a trumpet in one hand and a scroll in the other, standing near the King. The conduct of the judge, jurors, and witnesses is, not surprisingly, totally uncivilized (and far too similar to our own legal system). Insignificant details are stressed and important ones overlooked. Justice is as arbitrary as it is whimsical. What is on trial here is the law itself.[30] It is another example of a system that is only a defense against violence and lack of meaning. Wonderland indiscriminately introduces mayhem into everything it touches, from the game of croquet to legal trials. And as in the Queen's croquet grounds, the threat of execution is constantly present in the courtroom.

One of the most preposterous interpretations of the trial is by Shane Leslie, who sees it as an allegorical satire of the Oxford Movement. He argues as follows: the tarts represent the Thirty-Nine Articles of the Anglican faith; a "knavish Ritualist" (John Henry Newman) is accused of "having removed their natural sense"; and the Hatter (High Church) and the March Hare (Low Church) are called as witnesses against him. Leslie concludes: "it is interesting that the King's words to the Knave were exactly those which had been hurled at Newman and at everybody who had tried to equivocate on the Articles. 'You must have meant some mischief or else you would have signed your name like an honest man.'"[31] It is not impossible, of course, that Carroll quietly alludes to Newman in this section, but the real impact of the trial scene lies in its Kafkaesque absurdity. Following the idea of life as a circular race, the trial of the Knave of Hearts subverts normal linear progression for process that demands a verdict from the jury before the evidence is heard.

Alice begins to rebel and her increasing size threatens Wonderland with the ultimate disorder—annihilation. She upsets the jury box, spilling the animals onto the floor. The King objects that the trial cannot proceed until all the jurymen are back in their proper places. Such pointless formality in the midst of gross disorder is commonplace at this point. The Queen calls for the Knave of Hearts to be sentenced before the jury submits its verdict. Alice challenges the Queen with "Stuff and nonsense!," a statement that dangerously threatens to un- ravel the substance of Wonderland. When the Queen shouts "Off with her head!," Alice makes her climactic protest: "Who cares for *you*? You're nothing but a pack of cards!" (161). With this exclamation she annihilates Wonderland as if by word magic, and the suspension of disbelief comes to an end.

From a child's perspective the rules and regulations of adults may seem as arbitrary and capricious as those enunciated in the trial scene. In Alice's act of calling the bluff of the Queen there emerges the theme of a child's rebellion: the "rejection of adult authority, a vindication of the rights of the child, even the right of the child to self-assertion."[32]

Alice's dream becomes her nightmare. A novelty at first, Wonder- land becomes increasingly oppressive to Alice as she is faced with its fundamental disorder. Everything there, including her own body size, is in a state of flux. She is treated rudely, bullied, asked questions with no answers, and denied answers to asked questions. Her recitations of poems turn into parodies, a baby turns into a pig, and a cat turns into a grin. The essence of time and space is called into question and her romantic notion of an idyllic garden of life turns out to be a paper wasteland. Whether Alice, as some critics argue, is an alien who in- vades and contaminates Wonderland or is an innocent contaminated by it, one important fact remains the same: she has a vision that shows the world to be chaotic, meaningless, a terrifying void. In order to escape that oppressive and disorienting vision, she denies it with her outcry that "You're nothing but a pack of cards!" and happily regains the morally intelligible and emotionally comfortable world of her sister.

The systems of the Wonderland creatures may be logical, in the sense of being self-consistent, but Carroll's point is that they bear no relation to the underlying meaninglessness of their world any more than our systems relate to the meaningless of our world. Alice's rejection of Wonderland therefore signals her return to the defenses of Victorian society that, though perhaps no more valid than those of Wonderland, at least afford her familiar conventions of thought and behavior. As one critic astutely observes, "She becomes for many modern readers what she undoubtedly was for Dodgson: a naive champion of the doomed human quest for ultimate meaning and Edenic order."[33]

Contrasting with the uncertainties and anxieties of Wonderland is Alice's sister's idyllic imagination: "Lastly she pictured to herself how this same little sister of hers would, in the aftertime, be herself a grown woman; and how she would keep, through all her riper years, the simple and loving heart of her childhood" (164). The nightmarish tone of the story changes at the conclusion into sentimentality and an idyllic affirmation of innocence. This peaceful, wistful conclusion, with its hope for the preservation of Alice's simple joys and childhood innocence, suppresses the image of Alice's aggressive self. She has met and withstood all the challenges of Wonderland and emerges from the violent dislocation of her dream world totally unaware of the significance of her journey. Equipped with conventional expectations, proper manners, and a moral superiority, Alice possesses powerful defenses against the onslaughts of Wonderland. By denying the nightmare of disorder, by relegating her underground adventures to her subconscious, she is free to enjoy the illusion of order in her waking moments.

Even in the fair gardens of Oxford, however, Alice Liddell would grow up and abandon the pleasant dream of her admirer. Carroll's story is obviously concerned with the anxieties of maturity and the mystery of one's true identity. He poses those anxieties throughout the story, but particularly in the Caterpillar's rough questioning of Alice. Nevertheless, Carroll fails to deal with the subject of sexual maturity in its totality. Once recognizing the pain of growth, he refuses to follow out its implications—for that would be to make Alice's character develop, to replace her innocence with the sexuality of adolescence, and to lose her (as the White Knight does) to other interests. The dream of Alice's sister, then, is the dream of Carroll himself, who, in his anticipation of Alice Liddell's maturity, may well echo the conclusion of the book, that Alice would "find a pleasure in all their [other children's] simple joys, remembering her own child-life, and the happy summer days" (164).

## Through the Looking-Glass

Although he was obviously taking a great risk in writing a sequel to *Alice's Adventures in Wonderland, Through the Looking-Glass* was not only a popular success but it was also well received by reviewers and critics, who had begun to recognize Carroll's comic genius. Unlike twentieth-century critics, however, most continued to see the *Alice* books as children's literature. The novelist Henry Kingsley, on the other hand, wrote that the book "is the finest thing we have had since *Martin Chuzzlewit.*"[34]

Macmillan published *Through the Looking-Glass* in time for Christmas 1871. The initial printing of nine thousand copies proved inadequate and another six thousand were published. Carroll, the perfectionist, was more concerned with the uneven quality of the illustrations than with sales figures and wrote his publisher that no matter what the commercial consequences, he did not want more artistic fiascos. Macmillan, with its usual patience and accommodation, improved the printing of the illustrations and the book went forward with considerable commercial success. By 1893 over sixty thousand copies had been sold.

*Alice's Adventures in Wonderland* stands to *Through the Looking-Glass* as play stands to artifice.[35] The static quality of the latter story is reinforced by the fact that it is set indoors in autumn, whereas its predecessor takes place outdoors in spring. Carroll's self-conscious design in *Looking-Glass* is revealed at the outset when he has Alice say to her kitten, "Let's pretend the glass has got all soft like gauze, so that we can get through" (181–82). Such premeditated transitions do not occur in *Wonderland.* In the first book the emphasis is upon Alice's adventures and what happens to her on the experiential level; in the sequel the reader accepts Alice and with detachment examines nature transformed in Looking-Glass Land's chess-board landscape. The voyage has shifted from the Kingdom of Chaos, with its riotous motion and verbal whirlpool, to the land of stasis, where the landscape is geometrical and the chessmen are carefully manipulated by the rules of a precise game. In Wonderland everybody says and does whatever comes into his head, but in the Looking-Glass world life is completely determined and without choice. Tweedledum and Tweedledee, the Lion and the Unicorn, the Red Knight and the White must fight at regular intervals, whether they want to or not.

There are many philosophical allusions scattered throughout the story that reinforce the intellectual and deterministic character of Looking-Glass Land. After the White Knight has fallen off his horse for the ninth time and is dangling head downward, Alice asks him how he can go on talking so quietly from that position. He replies, "What does it matter where my body happens to be? My mind goes on working all the time" (304). As Roger Holmes points out, his response clearly reflects the Cartesian dualism of mind and body.[36] There is an allusion to the philosophy of Bishop Berkeley in the following dialogue about the Red King:

"He's dreaming now," said Tweedledee, "and what do you think he's dreaming about?"

Alice said, "Nobody can guess that."

"Why, about you!" Tweedledee explained, clapping his hands triumphantly, "And if he left off dreaming about you, where do you suppose you'd be?"

"Where I am now, of course," said Alice.

"Not you!" Tweedledee retorted contemptuously. "You'd be nowhere. Why, you're only a sort of thing in his dream!"

"If that there King was to wake," added Tweedledum, "you'd go out—bang!—just like a candle!" (238)

Holmes notes that the Red King performs the function of God in the philosophy of Berkeley. To be is to be perceived, ultimately in the mind of God—or the Red King. When Alice tells the twins to keep quiet lest they wake the King, Tweedledum answers, "Well, it's no use *your* talking about waking him when you're only one of the things in his dream. You know very well you're not real" (239). Tweedledum raises the central problem of philosophy: whether the mind can ever apprehend anything outside of itself.[37]

There are numerous other allusions to philosophy throughout the book, but the point to observe here is that such references make the texture of Looking-Glass world much more abstract, problematic, and determinstic than that of Wonderland. Whether it be the Red King or the unseen chess master there is a sense of controlled order and determination here. Alice is literally a pawn in a game in a dream. She may believe she is in control of her movements and thoughts, but the reader, with a broader perspective, recognizes that her freedom is an illusion, that she is manipulated by the strict rules of a game and by the dreaming King. Although there are a few vague intimations of such manipulation in Wonderland, such as the mysterious appearance of the "Drink Me" bottle upon the table (Alice noted that it "certainly was not here before"), the essential spontaneity of Alice's adventures and encounters in Wonderland is never seriously impaired by exterior forces. She is totally free to go where she pleases and do what she desires. Having lived with disorder, she now must come to grips with strict rules and unyielding order.

There are several forces of control and order in Looking-Glass Land besides the chess rules, and one of the most important is language itself. Patricia Spacks says that Carroll's world of fantasy, in its semantic aspects at least, is "the sort of world for which such a logician as Charles Dodgson might yearn: a world of truth and order."[38] That it seems disorderly, she argues, is a condemnation of the ordinary sloppy thinking of the reader and the careless traditions of his language. Language relates things in this well-ordered world. For example, Alice is told that when danger comes to the tree in the garden, the tree barks— it says "bough-wough." In the actual world there is obviously no logical relationship between the bark of a tree and the bark of a dog or between "bow-wow" and "bough-wough." In Looking-Glass Land, however, the relationship is established by the identical sounds of the words. Our use of language is more arbitrary and unaccountable than that of Looking-Glass Land. The Frog, for example, cannot understand why anyone should answer the door unless it has been asking something.

Sometimes language has the power of primitive magic to make things happen. Words create distinctions, the sense of self, and the loss of primal unity with one's mother and with nature itself. Alice is able to walk with her arm around the neck of a fawn through the mysterious woods where names are forgotten. When names return to the two on the far side of the wood, the fawn runs away in fear. An interesting modern parallel to this episode occurs in Bernardo Bertolucci's *Last Tango in Paris,* where Paul and Jeanne maintain a sexual relationship in an apartment where names are banned. When the apartment is abandoned and they take on names and personalities their relationship begins to deteriorate and ends with Jeanne shooting Paul.

The power of the word is also displayed in the nursery rhyme. Tweedledee and Tweedledum fight over the rattle not because they want to but because the rhyme says they do, and so they must. Language determines actions with all the force of a deity. Humpty Dumpty knows that if he falls the King will send all his horses and men to pick him up again because the rhyme dictates their assistance. The Lion and The Unicorn will fight for the crown and the action will continue to the drumming out of town—again, because the rhyme says so.

Another force of determinism in Looking-Glass Land is the chessboard itself. The game is not strictly up to chess standards because Carroll was more interested in the implications of the game than he was in working out the actual moves. Alexander Taylor points out that since Alice is a pawn she can only see a small patch of board and, consequently, cannot understand the meaning of her experiences: "This is a pawn's impression of chess, which is like a human being's impressions of life." "Alice never grasps the purpose of the game at all," Taylor continues, "and when she reaches the Eighth Square tries to find out from the two Queens if it is over. None of the pieces has the least idea what it is all about."[39] An understanding of one's role in a game of chess would entail an awareness of the room and the unseen intelligence that is manipulating the pieces. At no time does Alice converse with a piece that is not then on a square alongside her own. Even the eccentric behavior of the engaging White Knight reflects the unique way in which this chess piece moves. The fact that he keeps falling from his horse suggests the Knight's move of two squares in one direction followed by one square to the right or left. The chess game also reinforces the mirror-reflection motif. Not only do many of the pieces come in pairs but the asymmetric arrangement of one player's pieces at the start of the game is an exact mirror reflection of his opponent's pieces.[40] If, then, the chief aim of the game of nonsense is to create a universe that will be logical and orderly, *Through the Looking-Glass* is more purely nonsense than *Alice's Adventures in Wonderland*.

Carroll's mind sometimes worked like a mirror, for it would reverse what it reflected upon. He composed letters to his child friends in mirror-writing that had to be held up to a mirror to be read. He also wrote letters that had to be read by starting from the last word and reading to the first. And he began writing *The Hunting of the Snark* with its last line. The principle of inversion (do cats eat bats or do bats eat cats?), which supplied some of the humor of *Alice's Adventures,* is a dominant force in Looking-Glass Land: Alice must walk backwards in order to approach the Red Queen, the White Queen explains the advantages of living backward in time, and the White Knight thinks best when seeing things upside down.

Related to this technique is the humor of logical contradictions, a humor derived from the fact that math and science seem to contradict common sense. Alice runs as fast as she can to stay in the same place; the Red Queen offers Alice a biscuit to quench her thirst; and the Unicorn is amazed that Alice is alive and not a fabulous monster. The paradoxical progress in Alice's running can be explained as a mathematical trick: "In our world speed is the ratio of distance to time: $s = t/d$. For a high speed, the time is great and the distance small. The higher the speed, the smaller the distance covered."[41]

Another aspect of such logic twisting is Carroll's treatment of nothing as something: Alice wonders where the flame of a candle is when the candle is not burning; the White Knight praises Alice's keen vision in being able to see nobody down the road; and the King of Hearts finds it unusual to write letters to nobody.[42] Here again Carroll exploits the arbitrary rules of language that allow "nobody" to be read as a noun instead of a pronoun. e. e. Cummings cleverly developed this linguistic ambiguity in his poem "anyone lived in a pretty how town."

Like the creatures in Wonderland, the inhabitants of Looking-Glass Land treat Alice rather shabbily and rudely. Alice may be in the tradition of the great Victorian explorers who make adventure an end in itself, but she is also an intruder and can never be at home in the two alien worlds she visits. As explorer, Alice bears the stamp of the English imperialist; her civilized social assumptions allow her to elevate the tone of the foreign world she enters, a task that is simplified by the behavior of the creatures she meets. Like Victorian colonialists, she assumes the natives are rude simply because they are different. Empson observes that Alice is both aristocratic and snobbish and as "the perfect lady" she "can gain all the advantages of contempt without soiling herself by expressing or even feeling it."[43] The rude reception she receives in the Garden of Live Flowers makes it clear from the outset that she is going to be in for hard times. The Victorians, who did so much to sentimentalize flowers in poetry, song, and paintings, now have vengeance wreaked upon them in the person of Alice.

Alice continually approaches but never achieves a sense of unity with nature in her adventures: she can converse with flowers, insects, animals, and inanimate objects such as cards and chessmen. Yet unlike Wordsworth's child of glory, Alice always remains detached, isolated, and self-protective.[44] Perhaps her tentative relationship to her surroundings reflects Carroll's fear of a Darwinian world without God to unify nature and humanity. Despite the humor in her dialogue with the Gnat, there is the subtle undercurrent of the reality of death. She asks what the Bread-and-butter-fly lives on, to which the Gnat replies, "Weak tea and cream in it." "Supposing it couldn't find any?" asks Alice. "Then it would die, of course," answers the Gnat—"it always happens" (223). At the end of their conversation, the Gnat sighs itself away, vanishing completely like the Baker in the *Snark,* and the only response that Alice can make is to get up and walk on.

Carroll raises the philosophically complex question of the relationship of one's name to one's being. An interesting irony is that neither the Gnat nor Alice seems to grasp the intellectual issue here. The Gnat simply takes for granted that Rocking-horse-flies eat sawdust and sap and that Bread-and-butter-flies drink weak tea with cream. Alice, on the other hand, is puzzled because her conventional category of names (which includes rocking-horses and butterflies) does not accommodate these seemingly fantastic combinations. Standing above and beyond his characters, Carroll seems to be asking some profound questions. Do things exist because we name them or do we name them because they exist? What is the relationship between the imagination and reality? Can we ever know the thing in itself or are we irrevocably isolated from reality by the signs and symbols of language?

In the wood in which things have no names Alice becomes a pure child of nature, walking with her arms clasped lovingly around the neck of a fawn. In this prelinguistic fantasy she achieves the mythological unity of Eden. There is no duality here, no "other," no sense of separation from the world. She is in a state similar to Wordsworth's Lucy: "No motion has she now, no force; / She neither hears nor sees; / Rolled round in earth's diurnal course, / With rocks, and stones, and trees."

But the Edenic bliss of this oneness with the world is quickly dispelled as the loving couple emerge from the wood and the fawn recognizes Alice to be a human child: "a sudden look of alarm came into its beautiful brown eyes, and in another moment it had darted away at full speed" (227). Alice watches it run away and is "almost ready to cry with vexation at having lost her dear little fellow-traveller so sud-

"The wood where things have no name."
John Tenniel. *Through the Looking-Glass*.

denly" (227). The tentative unity with nature is breached and Alice is left with only one comfort—she regains her name, the paradoxical power of language that allows her to understand her world by separating her from it.

After it is established that language gives us a mere tentative hold on reality as it fabricates a unity through its symbols and signs, the philosophy of Tweedledum and Tweedledee questions the very nature of reality itself. First of all, these bizarre twins extend the artifice of Looking-Glass Land in that they are mirror-image forms of each other. Tweedledee's favorite word, "contrariwise," and the fact that the brothers extend right and left hands for a handshake reinforce the mirror-image motif. In putting forth the Berkeleyian view that all material objects, including Alice, are only "sorts of things" in the mind of the Red King (God) they reinforce the theme of determinism. Not only does a person relinquish free will, but one's individual essence cannot be distinguished from that of the creator: he or she is a mere fiction shaped by a dreaming mind. Moments earlier Alice had lost her name, and now the reality of her actual being is brought into question.

Confounded at first, Alice begins to cry but then asserts that if she were not real she could not cry. Tweedledum contemptuously replies that her tears are false, and Alice finally dodges the argument by concluding that the brothers are talking nonsense. The ultimate question of what is real and what is dream, however, is never resolved in the book. In fact, the story ends with the perplexing question of who dreamed it all—Alice or the Red King? Presumably, Alice dreamed of the King, who is dreaming of Alice, who is dreaming of the King, and so on. The question of dream versus reality is appropriately set forth in terms of an infinite regression through mirror facing mirror.[45] The apprehension of reality is indefinitely deferred and the only reality may be one's thoughts and their well-ordered expression.

In keeping with the looking-glass principles of logical inversion and contradiction, the White Queen introduces Alice to some of the details of living backwards: here one remembers things that happened the week after next; the King's Messenger is imprisoned, then his trial takes place, and finally he commits the crime. Such a weird chronology strengthens the determinism of Looking-Glass Land where every effect leads to a cause. The Queen's finger, for example, begins bleeding, and she then recollects that she will soon prick it on the brooch that fastens her shawl. For every effect, there must obviously come about a cause.

Even as the Duchess's child had turned into a pig, so now the White Queen becomes a sheep and, as if by dream magic, Alice finds herself in a shop. Shortly thereafter the sheep's knitting needles turn into oars, and Alice is suddenly rowing a boat with the old sheep through the queer shop. After some punning on rowing slang, the boating couple land on some rushes, the sheep moves to the other end of the shop (in chess terms, the White Queen moves to KB8, a position in the last row of the far side of the chess board), and Alice comes into the presence of Humpty Dumpty. Empson suggests that the sheep represents Oxford and the life of learning: "Everyone recognizes the local shop, the sham fights, the rowing, the academic old Sheep, and the way it laughs scornfully when Alice doesn't know the technical slang of rowing."[46] The dreamlike fading of Queen into sheep, knitting needles into oars, and the sudden appearance of the boat not only counterpoint the rigid geometry of Looking-Glass Land, but remind the reader that the entire adventure is encapsulated in a dream.

The episode with Humpty Dumpty is a comic essay on language and comments more extensively on the earlier episode of the wood with no names. Applying the principle of inversion, Humpty makes clear that ordinary words mean whatever he wants them to mean ("glory" for example, means "a nice knock-down argument"), whereas proper names are supposed to have general significance (Humpty explains that his name means the shape he is). In actuality, of course, the reverse is usually true. Humpty assumes the nominalist position that universal terms do not have an objective existence but are mere verbal utterances: "When *I* use a word it means just what I choose it to mean—neither more nor less' (269). When Alice questions whether he can make words mean so many different things, he replies "the question is, which is to be master—that's all' (269).

In *Symbolic Logic* Carroll echoes Humpty Dumpty's thesis by arguing that an author may establish his own definitions: ". . . any writer of a book is fully authorised in attaching any meaning he likes to any word or phrase he intends to use. If I find an author saying, at the beginning of his book, 'Let it be understood that by the word *black* I shall always mean *white,* and that by the word *white* I shall always mean *black,*' I meekly accept this ruling, however injudicious I may think it."[47] Language, like mathematics, must have an internal consistency but it has no intrinsic relationship to reality. The human mind is a great fabricator, but all it can ever know are its own fabrications. Meanings do not refer to external reality but only to a system of communal, social agreements.

Beyond these serious philosophical and linguistic issues raised by Humpty's dissertation on words stands an essential point not to be overlooked: Humpty is authoritarian, pedantic, and a fourth-rate literary critic. As J. B. Priestley has pointed out, "he thinks that every simple question is a riddle, something for him to solve triumphantly."[48] In Humpty Dumpty's discussion of Alice's age he shows himself to be annoyingly pedantic, and his explication of "Jabberwocky" displays a foolish self-assurance: "I can explain all the poems that ever were invented—and a good many that haven't been invented just yet" (270).

Even in the midst of Humpty's discourse on words the idea of death is not far off. His remark to Alice is, indeed, shocking:

"Seven years and six months!" Humpty Dumpty repeated thoughtfully. "An uncomfortable sort of age. Now if you'd asked my advice, I'd have said, 'Leave off at seven'—but it's too late now."

"I never ask advice about growing," Alice said indignantly. "Too proud?" the other inquired.

Alice felt even more indignant at this suggestion. "I mean," she said, "That one can't help growing older."

"*One* can't, perhaps," said Humpty Dumpty; "but *two* can. With proper assistance you might have left off at seven."

"What a beautiful belt you've got on!" Alice suddenly remarked. (265–66)

Humpty's chilling phrase, "with proper assistance," is a grim reminder that Alice dwells in a fallen world and that her innocence is indeed a fragile commodity. Implied in Humpty's remark is A. E. Housman's ironic compliment, "Smart lad, to slip betimes away / From fields where glory does not stay."

With the appearance of the White Knight Alice discovers for the first time someone who seems to be genuinely fond of her and who treats her with courtesy and respect. His character is multidimensional, embodying elements of myth, social satire, and autobiography. He presents a mystical moment for Alice: "Not her own coronation, but that of the true King of the Looking-Glass World. Not a mighty world conqueror, but the gentle man, the pure and innocent hero, the risen Christ radiant with scars—Christ as Clown."[49] He is also a parody

The White Knight.
John Tenniel. *Through the Looking-Glass.*

of the Victorian scientist who "earnestly, patiently, carefully . . . without sensuality, without self-seeking, without claiming any but a fragment of knowledge . . . goes on laboring at his absurd but fruitful conceptions."[50]

Donald Rackin's biographical interpretation of Alice's meeting with the White Knight is more thematically relevant and comprehensive than those previously cited. He views the quest structures of both Alice books as "representations of a failed search for the warm joy and security of love."[51] When the White Knight is about to leave Alice, he senses her sadness and offers to sing her a song to comfort her. Rackin observes that "It is as if the narrator and the narrator's gentle, loving voice have crossed over some boundary between reality and fiction, between Alice's adventures and Carroll's telling of them." Rackin concludes that the song is the "White Knight Carroll's last farewell and last love-gift to his beloved invention Alice. After this he must, like his inventor Dodgson . . . continue his well-practiced falling, alone and unaided to the end."[52]

Besides his argument that Carroll exhibits his own anxieties about love and death in the *Alice* books, Rackin also points out that these fundamental human concerns override the game of nonsense: "Like so much Victorian comedy from Carlyle and Dickens to Eliot and Meredith, Carroll's *Alices* are great and good because they rest finally upon the warm, fusing morality and sentiment the Victorian age cherished as 'humor'—not upon those surface games which have brought Carroll so much critical esteem in recent years, but which his own age would probably have considered mere entertaining 'wit.'"[53]

Carroll probably intended the White Knight to be a playful caricature of himself. Gardner draws some of the similarities: "Like the knight, Carroll had shaggy hair, mild blue eyes, a kind and gentle face. Like the knight, his mind seemed to function best when it saw things in topsy-turvy fashion. Like the knight, he was fond of curious gadgets and was a 'great hand at inventing things.'"[54] He is equipped with strange devices to handle almost any imaginable contingency: a mouse-trap to keep mice from running about his horse, anklets around the horse's feet to ward off shark bites, an upside down little box for his clothes and sandwiches. The White Knight lives by the motto *"semper paratus,"* and his preparedness is a parodic extension of Carroll's own obsessive need to control and order the details of his life. One need only recall Carroll's compulsive record keeping, the mathematical problems he would work out in bed to avoid evil thoughts, his invention of the Nyctograph (a device that allowed him to take notes in the dark), and his elaborate photographic paraphernalia to recognize the model for the White Knight.

His sad farewell to Alice suggests Carroll's own farewell to Alice Liddell when she grew up and left him. Alice's progress toward becoming a queen is indicative of such growth: "'You've only a few yards to go,' he said,—'down the hill and over that little brook, and then you'll be a Queen—But you'll stay and see me off first?' he added as Alice turned with an eager look in the direction to which he pointed. 'I shan't be long. You'll wait and wave your handkerchief when I get to that turn in the road! I think it'll encourage me, you see!'" (313–14). But Alice's youthful eagerness to be crowned queen quickly extinguishes from her mind the affectionate image of the White Knight. After waving her handkerchief to him, she says: "'I hope it encouraged him,' as she turned to run down the hill: 'and now for the last brook, and to be a Queen! How grand it sounds!'" (314).

Such youthful ambition for pastures new is a true valediction forbidding weeping. Alice's eagerness to get on with the coronation belies Rackin's notion that there is a "warm, fusing morality and sentiment" underlying the story but affirms his thesis that the adventures are about a failed search for love, security, and order. Carroll rather dramatically compartmentalizes his reason and emotions. On the one hand, his serious poetry and the *Sylvie and Bruno* books are filled with Victorian sentimentality and unrestrained romantic longings. His nonsense poetry and the *Alice* books, on the other hand, deny any emotional development. Alice's meeting with the White Knight may give the reader a singular and momentary glimpse of sentiment, but the rules of the chess game, of a preordained life, quickly prevail. Human attachments have no place in such an arrangement. Writing to the mother of one of his child friends, Carroll gives us a sense of what his White Knight must have been thinking after his farewell to Alice: "It is very sweet to me, to be loved by her as children love: though the experience of many years have now taught me that there are few things in the world so evanescent as a child's love. Nine-tenths of the children, whose love once seemed as warm as hers, are now merely on the terms of everyday acquaintance."[55]

Although still controlled by the rules of the chessboard, Alice as queen acquires a great new power through freedom of movement. The Red and White Queens, however, set out to give Alice an examination that will rightfully allow her to assume the new title. After badgering her with outrageous questions the two queens fall asleep. Alice then goes through an archway marked "Queen Alice," and enters a large banquet hall filled with animals, birds, flowers, and the two revived queens.

The chapter moves toward a finale that strongly suggests that Alice's coronation is tantamount to a sexual orgasm (she "mates" the King): 'The candles all grew up to the ceiling, looking something like a bed of rushes with fireworks at the top. As to the bottles, they each took a pair of plates, which they hastily fitted on as wings, and so, with forks for legs, went fluttering about in all directions" (335). As she afterwards recalled, "all sorts of things happened in a moment" (335) ("moment" being a much repeated word in the last few paragraphs). The intensity of this moment finally overwhelms Alice and she ends the dream (hers or the Red King's): "I can't stand this any longer" (336), she shouts, and seizes the tablecloth and pulls the plates, guests, and candles down into a crashing heap upon the floor. In chess terms, Alice has captured the Red Queen and checkmates the sleeping Red King. In human terms, she has grown up and entered that fated condition of puberty, at which point Carroll dismisses her once and for all by concluding his story.

Although Carroll surrounds his tales with a golden nostalgic haze, deliberately invoking a sense of the past, the stories themselves suppress any longing for the past. Characters who recall the past—the Mouse, the Mock Turtle, and the White Knight—distort memory by strange anxieties. Their accounts are neither clear nor factual but dreamlike, are usually in verse rather than in prose, and contain a good deal of comic violence. Alice herself lives, for the most part, in the present. As Lionel Morton observes, "the fictional Alice is cut off from her memory because Carroll wants Alice Liddell to be cut off from hers and brought into a world he controls. . . . Little girls must make very frustrating love-objects, after all, and it is unlikely that Carroll can have borne his enslavement to them without some resentment."[56]

Carroll's mind and feelings, Morton believes, were directed toward some past trauma that caused women—his mother and probably his sisters—to have far more importance to him than men. Memory is thus a threat because if Carroll recalled his painful past experience he would destroy the psychological balance on which his relations with Alice Liddell, and so with her fictional counterpart, are based. Here, then, is Morton's assessment of Alice's symbolic role:

Alice functions as a mediating figure between Carroll and the mother hidden in memory, comprising elements of both. To some extent she is Carroll himself, expressing his sense of what it was like to be a child. And she is also a Victorian little mother . . . , always wise and nicer than the characters she meets and ready to take care of them. But for that moment at the end of each story she is the terrible mother withdrawing her love.[57]

This is a fascinating psychoanalytical reading but it seems to raise more questions than its answers. What is the mysterious trauma that Carroll may have had in his past? Is Alice, in fact, always wiser and nicer than the characters she meets? Furthermore, Alice rarely expresses any affection, not to mention love, toward the characters she meets. It is therefore difficult to understand how she can be viewed as a symbol of maternal love. The conclusions of both stories do not exhibit her withdrawal of love, but rather an assertion of her own will against the prevailing chaos that threatens her sanity, an assertion that returns her to the conventional, ordered, and safe world.

## "The Wasp in a Wig"

In 1974 Sotheby Parke Bernet and Company, a London auctioneering firm, listed the following item: "Dodgson (C. L.) 'Lewis Carroll.' Galley proofs for a suppressed portion of *Through the Looking-Glass*." Until 1974 the suppressed episode was believed by Carroll scholars to have been lost. After Carroll's death in 1898 an unknown person purchased the galleys and between that time and the Sotheby auction nothing is known of their history. Norman Armour, Jr., of New York City, now owns the galleys and permitted the Lewis Carroll Society of North America to publish them in August 1977. The publication proved to be a major event for Carroll scholars and critics, and even the popular press heralded the discovery. Carroll's reclusive Wasp found himself on the cover of *Time* magazine.

"The Wasp in a Wig" episode was suppressed because John Tenniel refused to work with it. "Don't think me brutal," he wrote to Carroll, "but I am bound to say that the '*wasp*' chapter doesn't interest me in the least, I can't see my way to a picture."[58] Considering the weird creatures that Tenniel did draw for Carroll's books, it seems odd that he rejected a wasp in a wig as being "beyond the appliances of art." In any event, Carroll suppressed the episode in galley stage but fortunately preserved the galleys.

"The Wasp in a Wig," according to Gardner and Guiliano, is not a separate chapter of *Through the Looking-Glass* but a portion of the chapter on the White Knight.[59] The Wasp represents a bad-tempered, lower-class laborer in his declining years. Alice responds to his cross remarks with incredible patience and kindness. In Gardner's words, "it is an episode in which extreme youth confronts extreme age."[60] Furthermore, it is an episode in which the proper breeding and speech of the middle class confront the rudeness and slang of the lower class. It exhibits the tone, word play, and humorous nonsense characteristic of the rest of the book, but more important, it contrasts—in proper Looking-Glass perspective—Alice's relationship with the White Knight.

The White Knight is an upper-class gentleman who combines youthful vigor with the appearance of old age. It must be remembered that Carroll insisted that Tenniel not draw the White Knight with whiskers and a balding pate. Had Tenniel followed instructions the identification of Carroll with his character would have been enhanced. The Wasp, on the other hand, is a lower-class worker who combines old age with the appearance of youth, thanks to his yellow wig.

Like the White Knight, the Wasp causes Alice a momentary delay on her relentless movement toward becoming queen. Hearing a deep sigh coming from the woods, she senses that there's "somebody *very* unhappy there."[61] Thinking she cannot be of any use to him, she nevertheless stops and returns to the Wasp "rather unwillingly, for she was *very* anxious to be a Queen" (13). Whereas the White Knight recited a poem to comfort Alice, the situation is now reversed as Alice reads a newspaper article to the Wasp to distract him from his bodily pain. The White Knight's ballad celebrates the absurd glories of an old man. The story Alice reads, however, is about an expedition of wasps to a lake of treacle, an adventure that ends with the deaths of two wasps who were "engulphed" by the sweet lake. The old Wasp makes Alice stop her reading at that point. One recalls the story of the Dormouse about the three little girls who lived at the bottom of a well and who lived on treacle. The sweetness that nurtured the children of springtime's Wonderland now has a lethal connotation to the old Wasp in November's Looking-Glass Land. By keeping Alice from continuing with her reading, the Wasp denies his approaching death. Alice, it will be recalled, in her conversation with Humpty Dumpty, similarly denied the idea of death by abruptly changing the subject.

The Wasp explains the cause of his present discomfort in a poem that he recites to Alice. When he was young he shaved off his ringlets and curls because other people (wasps?) told him he would look better in a yellow wig. They then told him that the wig did not fit properly and that it made him look extremely plain. His ringlets would not grow again and now, old and gray, with all of his hair nearly gone, he must endure their jibes. As a solace to his misery, he explains, "I gets cold. And I gets under a tree. And I gets a yellow handkerchief. And I ties up my face" (16). When he tells Alice that the handkerchief is "good for the conceit," she remarks that conceit is not a disease. The Wasp rejoins, "It is though: wait till you have it, and then you'll know. And when you catches it, just try tying a yellow handkerchief round your face. It'll cure you in no time!" (17) One critic notes that the Wasp's "warning against conceit comes at the right moment. Alice is about to become a queen and is in danger of becoming proud."[62]

The short scene that follows the Wasp's history is notable for its grotesque, surrealistic details, and for the theme of oral aggression:

"*Your* wig fits very well," the Wasp murmured, looking at her with an expression of admiration: "it's the shape of your head as does it. Your jaws ain't well shaped, though—I should think you couldn't bite well?"

Alice began with a little scream of laughter, which she turned into a cough as well as she could. At last she managed to say gravely, "I can bite anything I want."

"Not with a mouth as small as that," the Wasp persisted. "If you was a-fighting now—could you get hold of the other one by the back of the neck?"

"I'm afraid not," said Alice.

"Well, that's because your jaws are too short," the Wasp went on: "but the top of your head is nice and round." He took off his own wig as he spoke, and stretched out one claw towards Alice, as if he wished to do the same for her, but she kept out of reach, and would not take the hint. So he went on with his criticisms. (20–21)

Even here there is an interesting contrast between the White Knight and the Wasp. Dressed in armor, the White Knight appears to be dedicated to battle, but he turns out to be a very gentle man. The Wasp, on the other hand, despite its advanced age and obsession with its looks, exhibits a predatory violence in the passage quoted above. By having the Wasp describe Alice as an insect with mandibles that are inadequate to seize and subdue her victim, Carroll conjures up an image as disconcerting as that of Gregor Samsa in Kafka's *Metamorphosis*. This passage also recalls Alice's ominous remark to her nurse in *Through the Looking-Glass*: "Do let's pretend that I'm a hungry hyaena, and you're a bone!" (180). The Wasp's final gesture of removing his wig and reaching out a claw to remove Alice's hair parallels the White

Knight's steadying himself by holding onto Alice's hair as he mounts his horse. The former scene, however, has a terrifying aspect, and Alice understandably keeps out of the Wasp's reach.

Carroll's obsession with the image of hair has an obvious Freudian significance. The cutting off of hair is a familiar symbol of castration. The Wasp, then, could well represent the horror of old age, where concealed impotence is expressed by sexually aggressive language and gestures. A symbol of her own sexuality, Alice's hair is threatened by the Wasp's terrifying claw that attempts to dislodge it.

Growing tired of the Wasp's personal remarks and seeing that he has recovered his spirits, Alice says good-bye. The episode ends with the Wasp thanking Alice, who "tripped down the hill again, quite pleased that she had gone back and given a few minutes to making the poor old creature comfortable" (21). The basis for her self-satisfaction, however, is not at all clear. The story she read the Wasp, with its reminder of death, was not a comforting one, and she pulls away from his frightening attempt to grasp her hair. She has given him an audience and perhaps it is for that reason that he thanks her.

Typical of children, Alice is selfish, energetic, and eager to get on, especially since she was "*very* anxious to be a Queen." Her interludes with the White Knight and the Wasp appear to be based more upon civility than upon love or affection. It is the reader's response to the White Knight, not Alice's, that makes him lovable and memorable. She thinks to herself that it will not take long to see him off. The affecting gesture of waving a handkerchief to encourage him as he heads into the woods is the White Knight's idea. She merely carries out a touching assignment, echoes his hope that it encourages him, and dashes toward the last brook to become a queen. Although he is depicted as a pathetic old man, the Wasp lacks the warm, genial spirits of the White Knight. The fact that he is of the lower class, as well as his advanced age and grotesque appearance, separates him from Alice's sphere. The embodiment of approaching death, a foolish vanity, sexual impotence and aggressiveness, the Wasp affords a grim reminder of a life outside the control of the literary chess master.

## Through Bergson's Looking-Glass

Scholars, critics, psychoanalysts, and logicians have all scrutinized Carroll's writings, but few of them have offered an explanation of why or how his creations are funny. The problem with any serious discussion of humor, of course, is that the analysis inevitably destroys the fun. How much easier it is to elucidate Hamlet's melancholy than to explain Falstaff's jokes! Nevertheless, humor is at the very heart of Carroll's major works, and no discussion of them could be complete without an examination of some of the principles of that humor, especially as they apply to the *Alice* books.

Henri Bergson's essay on *Laughter,* published in 1900, is a classic statement of the principles of humor. Although his analysis focuses upon the comedy of manners, it is applicable to Carroll's humor as well. Like Carroll, Bergson lived through the technological revolution that made the duality of man and machine a vital concern to philosophers, novelists, poets, and humorists. Bergson believed that life is a vital impulse, not to be understood by reason alone, and sees the comical as something encrusted on the living.

Early in his essay Bergson observes that laughter and emotion are incompatible: "It seems as though the comic could not produce its disturbing effect unless it fell, so to say, on the surface of a soul that is thoroughly calm and unruffled. Indifference is its natural environment, for laughter has no greater foe than emotion."[63] In both his comic poetry and prose Carroll maintains a fairly consistent detachment from his characters, and his characters likewise usually remain remarkably detached from their environment. The Cheshire Cat best illustrates Bergson's point. The obvious symbol of intellectual detachment, it wears the fixed grin of an amused observer. It can appear as only a head for it is representative of a disembodied intelligence. Alice maintains a similar detachment from her surroundings. She forms no strong or lasting relationships with any of the creatures or persons of Wonderland and Looking-Glass Land. The temporary emotional bond formed between Alice and the White Knight, therefore, makes a rather serious affair out of her farewell to him. Carroll tempers the somber mood by having Alice observe the White Knight's comic tumbling off his horse as he disappears into the woods.

A sentimentalist might have difficulty in appreciating comedy for, as Bergson notes, "to produce the whole of its effect . . . the comic demands something like a momentary anesthesia of the heart. Its appeal is to intelligence, pure and simple" (63). Carroll's parodies of the didactic and sentimental verses of Isaac Watts, for example, are funny in so far as the reader is aware of the originals and attentive to the intellectual cleverness involved in reshaping them. The emotions that the moral sentiments originally invoked are repressed by the wit of the parodies.

What might pass for cruelty in the treatment Alice receives in Wonderland is, in fact, funny because the emotions are excluded. Alice's conversation with Humpty Dumpty is a case in point: "'I mean,' she said, 'that one can't help growing older.' 'One can't, perhaps,' said Humpty Dumpty; 'but two can. With proper assistance, you might have left off at seven.'" Although Humpty Dumpty is suggesting that Alice might have been killed off at age seven (not a very funny idea), the passage is humorous because Carroll's focus is clearly upon Humpty Dumpty's linguistic playfulness—his intelligence and wit—and not upon Alice's death. One could apply Bergson's observation to countless examples in Carroll's works, from "The Two Brothers" to *The Hunting of the Snark,* and his principle holds up. We are not sickened at witnessing a boy using his brother as bait ("The Two Brothers") any more than we grieve over the annihilation of the Baker (*The Hunting of the Snark*). Carroll rarely allows us to know well and sympathize with his characters and thereby spares us an emotional reaction when they are assailed.

Bergson refines his observation that laughter appeals to intelligence pure and simple by adding, "this intelligence, however, must always remain in touch with other intelligences." He continues: "The comic will come into being, it appears, whenever a group of men concentrate their attention on one of their number, imposing silence on their emotions and calling into play nothing but their intelligence" (65). Alice provides exactly that focus of concentration for the reader. She is the instrument of humor as Carroll the narrator engages the mind of the reader to share with him the absurdity that arises in her various encounters with the creatures of Wonderland. Carroll invites the reader to conspire with him to laugh at their mutual representative battling with foreign intelligences.

Basic to Bergson's conception of the comic is the tension that exists between rigidity and suppleness: "rigidity is the comic, and laughter is its corrective" (74). He sees a laughable expression of the face as "one that promises nothing more than it gives. It is a unique and permanent grimace. One would say that the person's whole moral life has crystallized into this particular cast of features" (76). He concludes that "automatism, *inelasticity,* habit that has been contracted and maintained are clearly the causes why a face makes us laugh" (76). Tenniel's illustrations are significant in this respect, for they help to fix the expressions of such characters as the Cheshire Cat with its sinister grin and the Queen of Hearts with her perpetual scowl. The Queen's favorite expressions, "Off with his head!" or "Off with her head!," likewise are as fixed and predictable as her expression. The sentiment is obviously not funny, but its repetition is.

In more general terms both *Alice* books deal with the battle between rigidity and suppleness. Alice embodies secure conventions and self-assured regulations, and Wonderland is dedicated to undermining those conventions and regulations. In Looking-Glass Land the rigid rules of chess are set against the relatively undisciplined behavior of humans, thereby reversing the situation in Wonderland. In this connection another statement by Bergson is revealing: *"The attitudes, gestures and movements of the human body are laughable in exact proportion as that body reminds us of a mere machine"* (79). In *Through the Looking-Glass* Alice and the other characters are treated as chess pieces to be manipulated in a very rational game. In short, they have become things and, as Bergson notes, *"we laugh every time a person gives us the impression of being a thing"* (97). Similarly, the battles between Tweedledee and Tweedledum and between the Lion and the Unicorn are comic because they are repetitive and predictable.

Discussing the humor of disguise, Bergson argues that "any image . . . suggestive of the notion of a society disguising itself, or of a social masquerade, so to speak, will be laughable" (89). Both the Caucus-race and the trial of the Knave of Hearts illustrate Bergson's thesis. In the former, all the contestants are awarded prizes, thereby ignoring the substance of the race, namely, finding a winner. In the trial scene, the procedures are of paramount importance, the guilt or innocence of the defendant being of little significance. In both cases a kind of relentless automatism that converts human beings into comic puppets rules supreme.

One final observation by Bergson has relevance to Carroll's humor: *"Any incident is comic that calls our attention to the physical in a person, when it is the moral side that is concerned "* (93). The humor resides in one's perceiving the tension in a "soul tantalised by the needs of the body: on the one hand, the moral personality with its intelligently varied energy, and, on the other, the stupidly monotonous body, perpetually obstructing everything with its machine-like obstinacy" (93). Thus, he argues, we laugh at a public speaker who sneezes just at the most pathetic moment of his speech. Our attention is suddenly recalled from the soul to the body. Alice's frustrations in regulating her body size are cases in point. She longs to enter into "the loveliest garden you ever saw" but "she could not even get her head through the doorway." There are numerous passages in the *Alice* books, such as Alice's flood of tears and the Duchess's baby's uncontrollable sneezing, in which the human body baffles, betrays and embarrasses the soul.

One of the functions of humor, as Bergson sees it, is to make us human and natural during an age of mechanization. One of Carroll's early poems, "Rules and Regulations," establishes the fact that at the outset of his career he both prized and mocked rigidity. In his fascination with mechanical gadgets he possessed in microcosm a well-ordered, smoothly running universe. In the compulsive tidiness of both his personal life and his writings he achieved an order not inherent in nature. The cool geometry of Looking-Glass Land, however, offers only a temporary oasis in a mutable, biological, and mortal wasteland. Carroll recognized that the machinery of conventions and customs, mathematics and logic, helped to define by contrast and momentarily sustain and comfort the frightened, imperfect, and comic adventurer.

## Chapter Four
# The *Alice* Illustrations

*Alice's Adventures in Wonderland* and *Through the Looking-Glass* were published during a period when illustrated books were in vogue. Many of the great Victorian novelists, including Dickens, Thackeray, and Trollope, had drawings of their notable characters and scenes scattered throughout their novels. Illustrated children's books proliferated during the nineteenth century, a development enriched by such artists as Kate Greenaway, Walter Crane, Randolph Caldecott, Edward Lear, and John Tenniel. Victorian book reviewers, especially those attending to children's books, were inclined to give more critical attention to the illustrations than to the text. A writer in the *Times,* for example, after commenting at some length upon the extraordinary grace of John Tenniel's rendering of the White Rabbit, merely notes in passing that "the letterpress . . . by Mr. Lewis Carroll . . . may best be described as an excellent piece of nonsense."[1] While Lewis Carroll's fame soon overshadowed that of his illustrator, Tenniel's drawings continue to dominate and shape our memories of the *Alice* stories. Unlike the narratives that they accompany, the illustrations do not require a linear unfolding but are instantly available in memory. At the mere mention of such names as the Hatter, the Duchess, or Humpty Dumpty, one immediately conjures up Tenniel's definitive pictures of them. Despite the popularity and worldwide recognition of Tenniel's illustrations, until recently there has been remarkably little critical attention given to the importance of the *Alice* books as an integrated work of visual and verbal art.

The first illustrator of the *Alice* books was Lewis Carroll himself. Lacking any formal training in art and aware of the nineteenth-century convention that required comic writing to be illustrated, Carroll needed someone to improve upon his own drawings. Years earlier, in his productions of *Mischmasch* and the *Rectory Umbrella,* he took pains to illustrate his nonsense stories. When he prepared his hand-lettered manuscript of *Alice's Adventures under Ground* he included thirty-eight of his own drawings to complement the text. Keenly aware of his shortcomings as an artist, when he considered commercial publication of

Carroll's drawing of Alice at the Queen's croquet-ground.
*Alice's Adventures under Ground* (1864).

his story he sought out the assistance of a professional artist. If it were not for Carroll's sense of his own inadequacy as an artist, Tenniel might be remembered today only as a quaint political cartoonist for *Punch*.

Although Carroll arranged for a facsimile edition of his handwritten, illustrated manuscript to be published in 1886, the two *Alice* books illustrated by Tenniel had by that time established him as a renowned author who could well withstand the scrutiny of his amateurish artistic efforts. There is no question, however, that *the* "text"—in the sense of the whole work—that Carroll wanted to put before the public was his revised and expanded story as illustrated by Tenniel. These drawings, carefully supervised by Carroll and influenced by his own illustrations, are not decorative asides, but represent an essential part of the entire original published text. Carroll, Tenniel, and Macmillan worked out every conceivable detail of the printing of the *Alice* books. They painstakingly designed the volumes so that the text and illustrations could be coordinated on the page. Usually references in the text stand next to their pictorial counterparts and the narrative moments of text and illustration are visually synchronized.[2] Carroll obviously conceived of the books as an collaborative effort that integrated his narrative with the illustrations and their layout.

In working out his drawings for the book, Tenniel had three immediate influences to accommodate: the thirty-eight drawings that Carroll had already created for *Alice's Adventures under Ground*, Carroll's personal supervision of the new drawings, and, of course, the text of the revised and enlarged Alice story itself. Not a great deal is known about the specific details of the working relationship between Carroll and Tenniel. It is known, however, that Carroll was very difficult to please. He wrote to Tenniel complaining that Alice had been given too much crinoline and that the White Knight must not have whiskers nor be made to look old. Despite such strict supervision Tenniel sometimes ignored Carroll's demands, as in the case of the White Knight, whom he depicts as an old man with whiskers. Apparently Carroll's relentless scrutiny eventually got on Tenniel's nerves. Years later Tenniel wrote to Harry Furniss, who was about to illustrate *Sylvie and Bruno*: "I'll give you a week, old chap; *you* will never put up with that fellow a day longer."[3]

Tenniel was not unduly restricted in his work by Carroll's illustrations. He adds other characters, new arrangements of old ones, new faces, bodies, clothes, animals, and expressions. Nevertheless, he appears to have followed Carroll's lead in illustrating many of the same moments in the narrative of *Alice's Adventures under Ground*. In a few instances, he even adopts strikingly similar poses for his figures, as in his drawings of Alice in the pool of tears, Bill the Lizard, and Alice at croquet.[4] Carroll's rather crude sketches of the White Rabbit and the Caterpillar, on the other hand, bear only a rough resemblance to Tenniel's richly detailed drawings of the same creatures. When Carroll added chapters 6 and 7 ("Pig and Pepper" and "A Mad Tea-Party") for his expanded version of the story, he did not provide Tenniel with sketches of the Duchess, Cheshire Cat, Hatter, March Hare, or Dormouse. Working under Carroll's careful supervision, Tenniel made pre-

"'Well, I should like to be a *little* larger, sir, if you wouldn't mind,' said Alice, 'three inches is such a wretched height to be.'

'It's a very good height indeed!' said the caterpillar loudly and angrily, rearing itself up as it spoke (it was exactly three inches high)."

Carroll's drawing from *Alice's Adventures under Ground* (1864).

liminary pencil sketches of these and other characters to accompany the new text. It is problematic whether Carroll or Tenniel was the inspiration behind these renderings, but the fact remains that it is Tenniel's illustrations and not the narrative that enable us to visualize Carroll's characters.

At the time that Carroll hired Tenniel to illustrate *Alice's Adventures* Tenniel had established himself as one of the leading political cartoonists for *Punch*. A recent study has demonstrated the remarkable similarities between certain of his *Punch* cartoons and his illustrations in *Through the Looking-Glass*. Tweedledum, for example, is shaped and dressed like Master John Bull in Tenniel's political cartoons; the Cheshire Cat resembles his depiction of Abraham Lincoln as a raccoon treed by John Bull; and Humpty Dumpty and the Frog-Footman have their precursors in his drawing of a personified gooseberry and frog, a cartoon that satirized filler items in the press.[5] This discovery indicates that Tenniel had acquired a repertoire of designs, figures, and expressions during his tenure at *Punch* and that he brought some of these forms to bear upon Carroll's text. His background made him especially suited to his new task because as a political cartoonist he had developed a keen eye for the comic grotesque and knew how to capture the essence of an entire critical event in a single drawing.

Tenniel, who did not like to draw from life, based other of his illustrations upon such sources as paintings, drawings, photographs, or simply his own memories of people and places. His depiction of Alice, for example, appears to be a composite based upon his customary representations of middle-class girls and Carroll's drawing of Alice in *Alice's Adventures under Ground*. Alice Liddell, who wore bangs and had dark hair, clearly is not the model. Tenniel takes two traits from Carroll's drawing: Alice's long hair and her "impassive, almost pouty expression." Despite critics' association of Carroll with the White Knight, Tenniel's illustration looks nothing like Carroll. Instead, it appears that he may have drawn the White Knight after a caricature of Horace Mayhew, a *Punch* colleague, drawn by George du Maurier for a dinner invitation card for the magazine. Tenniel's memorable portrait of the Duchess in *Wonderland* seems to be based in part upon a painting of a grotesque old woman entitled *Portrait of the Duchess of Carinthia and Tyrol*, attributed to the sixteenth-century Flemish artist Quinten Massys. It is also likely that his illustration was influenced by F. W. Fairholt's engraving, *Misericord: Woman in Medieval Headdress.*[6]

Tenniel had the freedom to draw upon these varied sources of inspiration for his figures because Carroll's text is remarkably void of physical descriptions of his characters.[7] Were it not for the twenty-three drawings of Alice that embody Tenniel's conception of the heroine, for example, all we would know of her appearance from the narrative is that she had long, straight hair, shiny shoes, a skirt, small hands, and bright eyes. Given such paltry, general details, she would be a non-descript everygirl rather than the prim, moody, and mysterious Victorian child of the illustrations.

The White Rabbit, with six drawings, is second only to Alice as the visual star. Carroll describes him with more detail than he allotted his heroine. He informs us that the Rabbit has pink eyes, wears a waistcoat, and carries a watch, a pair of kid gloves, and a large fan. But the image we have of this colorful creature is largely Tenniel's. In the first illustration he is wearing the waistcoat with the watch that Carroll mentions, but he is also sporting a checkered jacket, a Gladstone collar, and a cravat, and is carrying under his arm a folded umbrella. In chapter 11, he holds a scroll in his left hand and a trumpet up to his mouth, two details recorded in the narrative, but only the illustration makes clear that he has completely changed his costume. He now wears a tunic covered with hearts and topped with a large round ruff, the sort worn by Sir Walter Raleigh and Queen Elizabeth, and there are large bows on his sleeves. In chapter 12 he appears for the last time in the illustration depicting the cards flying up at Alice. Partially hidden behind Alice's skirt, he appears for the first time in the nude—or more accurately, in the fur. Carroll does not mention this detail in the story, but Tenniel's drawing captures the essential transformation of dream into reality not only by showing the playing-card people reverting to "nothing but a pack of cards" but by undressing and dehumanizing the animals, especially the highly civilized White Rabbit.

Tenniel here goes beyond merely rendering the characters to reinforcing pictorially a major theme of the book, the play between dream and waking. It is the White Rabbit who leads Alice from her sister's sleepy book ("it had no pictures or conversations in it") and from an ordinary afternoon to the mad dream world of Wonderland. The reader first sees the White Rabbit standing fully dressed at the head of chapter 1 and last sees him as an ordinary rabbit in the book's final illustration. These two drawings thus frame the story and support its narrative structure as the reader, like Alice, emerges from a dream vision that reveals the fundamental instability of one's perceptions. The sudden appearance of the animals out of their clothes in the final drawing captures Alice's rejection of the mad sanity of Wonderland for the dull world of reality.

The Hatter, Hare, and Dormouse appear in the illustrations five, two, and three times, respectively. Carroll's description of the Hatter only indicates that he had a hat and a watch. Tenniel again fills in all of the memorable details: the top hat ("in this style 10/6"), the polka-dotted bowtie, Gladstone collar, and checkered vest and trousers. It has been said that he looks like Benjamin Disraeli and William Gladstone, but Tenniel's own drawings of those two men little resemble that of the Hatter. The Hatter more closely resembles *Punch*'s leading political satirist, Douglas Jerrold, a small, intense man with a prominent nose and small chin.

The March Hare and the Dormouse are not described at all and once again we depend upon Tenniel to visualize them for us. While the Dormouse looks very much like an overfed, sleepy squirrel, the Hare is given human characteristics. Except for his rabbit head, his body is that of a human. He is dressed in a jacket, striped trousers, and bowtie, and wears a random arrangement of weed stalks on his head, signifying his madness. As an embodiment of the phrase "mad as a March hare," the rabbit's physical appearance clashes with his civilized surroundings of china teacups, white tablecloth, and Alice's stuffed chair. Half human and half rabbit, he sits at the table in the first illustration as if he were civilized, but in the background of the drawing are the trees and woods to which his and the Dormouse's animal nature belong and to which they presumably will return upon Alice's waking from her dream.

Carroll captures the essential mystery of the Cheshire Cat in just two sentences. He introduces it in chapter 6 as "a large cat, which was lying on the hearth and grinning from ear to ear." Later, we hear Alice's response to the creature: "It looked good-natured, she thought; still it had *very* long claws and a great many teeth." Tenniel allotted four drawings to the Cheshire Cat. It is interesting to note that while he creates a wonderfully sinister grin and curious eyes for the cat, he does not show its claws, even though Alice called special attention to them. Tenniel usually does not mute the harshness of Carroll's text. By drawing the Cheshire Cat with its legs comfortably tucked under its body, Tenniel keeps the focus of his drawings more sharply upon the cat's perplexing expression. All cats have claws, but only this one grins. He does, however, add a detail to Carroll's portrait by making the cat a common striped one, in contrast to Alice's own Dinah (in *Through the Looking-Glass*), who is all black.

Like the Cheshire Cat, the Caterpillar is briefly but memorably described. As Alice stretches herself on tiptoe and peeps over the edge of the mushroom, her eyes "immediately met those of a large blue caterpillar, that was sitting on the top, with its arms folded, quietly smoking a long hookah, and taking not the smallest notice of her or anything else" (46). Tenniel's illustration of the Caterpillar in profile does not show its arms to be folded, though in Carroll's own drawing, which gives a frontal view, the "arms" are folded but the drawing is anatomically confusing. Tenniel's illustration captures the mystery and aloofness of the creature by shading its face in profile. Furthermore, he cleverly suggests both a nose and a chin by his depiction of the Caterpillar's forward feet.

The position of the illustration of the Caterpillar at the head of chapter 5 has a significant effect upon the reader's response. The themes of metamorphosis, growth, and sexuality are all prefigured in the drawing. The tube from the hookah, for example, forms a circle around the Caterpillar, suggesting the chrysalis mentioned by Alice. Furthermore, the Caterpillar towers over Alice, whose eyes merely reach the edge of the mushroom. This arrangement supports the Caterpillar's superiority and authority and emphasizes Alice's childlike size, out of which she will soon grow to threaten the Pigeon. It is noteworthy that this time only her neck grows to "an immense length" (74). The suggestion of the phallus here is pictorially foreshadowed in the drawings of the three mushrooms. Indeed, Alice's lower half itself resembles a mushroom. The subjects of sexuality and growth are thus appropriately related to the mysterious and shadowy Caterpillar even before the reader comes to the first sentence of the chapter.

Tenniel is always reading or interpreting the text for the reader-viewer, and nowhere is this more apparent than in his portrait of the Duchess, another character nearly invisible in the text but who puts in a dominating and unforgettable appearance in the illustrations. Tenniel makes Carroll's Duchess even more grotesque than that of Quinten Massys by enlarging her head and showing her in physical contact with her baby and Alice.

When we first meet the Duchess, in chapter 6, she is "sitting on a three-legged stool in the middle [of the kitchen] nursing a baby" (82). While the stool is not visible in the accompanying illustration, it presumably supports the Duchess. She is holding the baby but is not *nursing* it in the ordinary sense of the word—namely, "to suckle." It is true, of course, that in the nineteenth century the word *nurse* also meant "to fondle" and "to care for," and that is clearly the sense of the word that Tenniel has in mind in his drawing. How much more grotesque the scene would have been had he followed the more basic and accepted definition of the word.

In any event, our image of this monstrous female is derived in large part from Tenniel's illustration. She is wearing a dress with a floral print and an enormous, medieval-style hat, under which we see her black wavy hair and huge face with an equally huge pocketlike mouth. Her head is about four times as large as Alice's and she has powerful masculine features. These grotesque proportions are nowhere mentioned by Carroll, and, of course, since the "Pig and Pepper" chapter is an addition to the original manuscript, Carroll had not drawn any pictures of the Duchess. The only feature that Carroll does focus on in the text is her sharp little chin. He tell us that "the Duchess was *very* ugly" (120) and mentions the uncomfortably "sharp little chin" three times. Curiously, neither of the two illustrations with the Duchess shows her to have a chin that is either sharp or little. Rather, her jaw is very broad and fleshy. It seems, in this instance, that Carroll left the realization of the character to Tenniel and approved of what he created.

Even though she appears only twice in the illustrations, the Duchess is one of the most dominant visual figures in the book. The antithesis of conventional Victorian motherhood, she commands the central position of the drawing. Rather than looking to her crying baby, she stares coldly and threateningly out at the reader. Her leering masculinity undermines her maternal pose and makes her a ponderous, grotesque, and seemingly immovable figure. Her ambiguous sexual nature is further developed in chapter 9, where she appears with her hand around Alice's arm. Wearing a sinister grin and with her eyelids coyly half-opened, she appears to be seducing the young girl.

When the Duchess finally flings her baby at Alice and says, "Here! You may nurse him a bit, if you like!," Tenniel again interprets the word *nurse* in a general way and depicts Alice simply holding the pig-child. Nevertheless, she is holding it in the position of a mother suckling her baby, which subtly reinforces a grotesque maternal relationship. This drawing provides an interesting parallel with the one in which the Duchess is holding the baby. The Duchess holds up the baby's head with her right hand, and the other picture reverses this by having Alice support the pig-baby's head with her left hand. Neither the Duchess nor Alice look at their infants, but rather stare out at the reader. Alice's expression resembles that of Oliver Hardy, who would occasionally stop in the midst of a farcical situation that had befallen him and look out toward the theater audience as if to appeal for its support and sanity.

Based loosely upon Carroll's original drawings and upon the figures on the traditional playing cards, Tenniel's drawings of the King and Queen of Hearts enrich his models with great detail, texture, and expression of character and provide an important visual link with Carroll's text. The Queen of Hearts is basically an auditory creature, characterized by her recurrent shouts of "Off with her head!" Carroll tells us only that her face turned crimson, that she glared at Alice, and that she frowned "like a thunderstorm" (123). Tenniel fixes her face in a perpetual scowl, her brow casting dark shadows over her menacing eyes. The King of Hearts, on the other hand, maintains a more neutral expression characteristic of the face on the playing card. Carroll provides a few appropriate details by having the King put on his spectacles during the trial and wear his crown over his judicial wig: "the judge, by the way, was the King; and, as he wore his crown over the wig (look at the frontispiece if you want to see how he did it), he did not look at all comfortable and it was certainly not becoming" (144). Carroll's direct reference to the illustration on the frontispiece clearly acknowledges the important interdependence of illustration and text.

Tenniel added many details to this drawing that are not accounted for in the narrative but that provide visual clues for interpretation. The Knave, for example, with his eyes closed and his lips pursed, wears a smugly defiant expression. Tenniel also gives him a red nose (suggested by the hatching). One explanation for this oddity is that it supplies a visual link between the Knave and the tarts, for the Duchess's cook testifies that tarts are made mostly of red pepper. "It is in keeping with the rest of the Knave's disorderly trial that no one notices this incriminating evidence, as plain as the nose on his face."[8] Tenniel further enriched his drawing by including a satire of the legal profession. He depicts one of the barristers as a bird of prey and another as a parrot, suggesting thereby the rapacious and mindless nature of the profession.

In his drawings of the sobbing Mock Turtle with the ocean always in the background Tenniel recalls his earlier illustrations of Alice swimming in her own pool of tears. These drawings reinforce the theme that in Wonderland tears are deceptive and dangerous. With tears flowing from his eyes, the Mock Turtle sings a romantic, celebratory song about the soup that he will become. In *Through the Looking-Glass* the Walrus weeps uncontrollably while eating the oysters he presumes to lament. Carroll only partially describes the Mock Turtle, informing us that this creature has "large eyes full of tears" (126) and "drew the back of one flapper across his eyes" (131). The bizarre nature of the Turtle, however, is envisioned by Tenniel, who shows it to have the head, hind hooves, and tail of a calf, but the body and forelegs of a turtle. The illustration extends Carroll's playful notion that an abstract name has an object corresponding to it. It has been suggested that Tenniel's drawing may have been influenced by the fact that mock turtle soup is customarily made of veal.[9]

The Mock Turtle's associate, the Gryphon, has a ready-made image from Greek mythology, and Carroll makes little attempt to describe it. He simply states: "If you don't know what a Gryphon is, look at the picture" (124). When one looks at Carroll's own drawing, however, the Gryphon resembles a skinny rat with a bird's beak and talons more than it does the traditional figure from mythology, and the Mock Turtle appears as a rather scrawny turtle.

Why did Carroll look to a verbal-visual integration of his work to define his major characters and scenes? Several reasons may be inferred. Since the book was originally written for a child, there is the obvious reason that children simply enjoy looking at pictures. Alice, in fact, complains that the book her sister is reading to her has no pictures, and her boredom quickly sends her off to sleep and to Wonderland. Illustrations help to win a child's interest in a book; publishers demanded drawings to enhance the sales appeal of their volumes. Furthermore, there was a strong tradition of illustrated books in the nineteenth century, especially those designed for children, including such notable works as Grimms' *Fairy Tales* (1823), illustrated by George Cruikshank; Edward Lear's *Book of Nonsense* (1846), illustrated by the author; William Makepeace Thackeray's *The Rose and the Ring; or the History of Prince Giglio* (1855), illustrated by the author; and *The House that Jack Built* and *The History of Cock Robin* (1865–66), illustrated by Walter Crane.

Another important aspect of the illustrations is that they undermine any ambiguity about the characters and make our imaginative embellishment of them almost impossible. Tenniel's stark line drawings fix in our minds once and for all the physical presence of each character. By their precision and detail, the illustrations lead to our detachment from the characters in the narrative. We "know" them in one glance and, with the exception of the Cheshire Cat, they hold little depth or mystery. Most of the creatures are organized fictions with no referent in our world. Their abstract, impersonal nature is perfectly suited to their roles in the text—where, with mathematical precision, they articulate the logic of Wonderland.

The most important reason for Carroll's requirement of pictures, finally, is that the *Alice* books, unlike the typical Victorian novel, do not derive their power from creating the illusion of reality and believable characters who interact with one another in ways that we understand. Carroll's work is far more abstract and focuses upon language itself. Insofar as the text is concerned, the Hatter, the Caterpillar, the Cheshire Cat, and many of the other characters define themselves through their dialogues as witty masters of the language who seem eager to engage in verbal jousts with their curious visitor. They are intellectual creatures who play with language in a very sophisticated manner. By separating their language (the text) from their bodies (the illustrations), Carroll reinforces the essence of nonsense, namely, that it is a game and its playthings are words. Instead of human characters with complex emotions, the illustrations render the characters as fixed objects. Detachment is the name of the game, and consequently there is no room for such customary emotions as fear, grief, laughter, or affection.

When Carroll was a young boy he enjoyed putting on puppet shows to entertain his family. The *Alice* books are, in a sense, an extension of that same sort of production. Puppets, with their rigid expressions and postures, are fixed objects like the characters in illustrations. Both the puppets and the creatures in Wonderland, however, speak the language of the master wit, Lewis Carroll.

The wedding of Tenniel's illustrations to Carroll's *Alice* stories has produced two unique books that thrive on a vigorous and fundamental mutuality of image and word. In their collaborations Carroll and Tenniel scrupulously worked out the relationship of their productions, including the smallest details of the drawings and where precisely they were to be placed in the text. One would think, therefore, that the pictures and text could no more be separated than could the music of Arthur Sullivan from the lyrics of William Gilbert. Nevertheless, throughout the twentieth century publishers have brought out numerous editions of the *Alice* books with Tenniel's illustrations placed at random. More significantly, however, numerous editions have been published with illustrations by other artists. The critical assumption seems to be that the text is sacred but the pictures are merely decorative embellishments of that text and are therefore replaceable.

If, as I have argued, Tenniel's drawings are a vital, inextricable part of his and Carroll's mutual endeavor, that they planned the book and took great pains to publish it as a unified verbal-visual work of art,

then some interesting aesthetic questions arise when Carroll's narratives
are illustrated by other artists. What are the textual consequences when
new illustrations are introduced or old ones are reconceived? Can the
stories of the *Alice* books be read in the same way with new
illustrations?

Numerous artists have been so fascinated with the original stories
that they have reshaped the works according to their own artistic visions. They have chosen to fracture the original works and then rebuild
them with their own imagery. The carefully worked out relationships
between text and drawing that Carroll achieved with Tenniel are ignored in favor of a new interpretation of the texts. Indeed, it seems
that the most accurate way of describing these later editions is to call
them versions or interpretations of the originals.

The flood of illustrated editions of *Alice's Adventures in Wonderland*
began shortly after Carroll's death. The number of new illustrated editions increased even more dramatically after 1907, when the British
copyright to the book expired. By now *Alice's Adventures* has been illustrated by more artists than any other children's book. Among the
more memorable illustrations of this work are those by Thomas May-
bank, Arthur Rackham, Charles Robinson, Willy Pogany, Ralph
Steadman, and Salvador Dali. Among the notable illustrators of
*Through the Looking-Glass,* which has not elicited nearly the number of
newly illustrated editions as its predecessor, are Franklin Hughes, Ed-
gar Thurstan, Philip Gough, Mervyn Peake, Peter Blake, and Ralph
Steadman. [10]

Given that Carroll provides in his text only the scantiest physical
descriptions of his characters (since he knew that Tenniel, under his
supervision, would shape them), subsequent artists have an unusual
degree of freedom in devising their versions of Carroll's characters.
Writers like Charles Dickens and Arthur Conan Doyle, on the other
hand, provide such vivid descriptions of their characters that the artists' imaginations are constrained and their illustrations seem decorative and almost superfluous. We can conjure up the image of Mr.
Pickwick, even if we never saw the delightful illustrations of Hablot
Knight Browne. Similarly, Sherlock Holmes is recognizable without
the fine drawings of Sidney Edward Paget.

Arthur Rackham's illustrations of *Alice's Adventures* (1907)[11] provide
an interesting interpretation of the work through their addition of
color and detail. Unlike Tenniel's stark line drawings, Rackham's wa-

tercolors add a lush, sensual, and haunting dream quality to Alice's adventures. His emphasis upon the natural background with its gnarled trees, dark foliage, and mysterious shadows conveys a romantic spirit clearly not in the original work.

Willy Pogany, on the other hand, whose art deco edition[12] of the story appeared in 1929, converted Alice into an American bobbysoxer with a pageboy hairstyle. He depicts some of the playing cards as West Point cadets, others as members of the painters' union, and still others as a chorus line from the Ziegfield Follies. Pogany's Americanization of Alice was the first radical departure from the original text. His drawings elicit a network of new cultural associations derived from the era of *The Great Gatsby*. They displace the Victorian decorum and restraint found in the original illustrations with a sense of self-expression, social awareness, and rebellion.

Salvador Dali's lithographs for a limited edition of *Alice's Adventures*[13] in 1969 transform the work into a surrealistic series of adventures. Alice, with a skipping rope, appears in all of the drawings. Dali uses one of his famous melting watches to serve as the table top for the Hatter's tea party. As strange as these pictures may seem to the reader accustomed to Tenniel's illustrations, they dramatically render the atmosphere of a dream appropriate to the story, even if the dreamscape is Dali's and not that of Carroll and Tenniel.

Ralph Steadman, who has illustrated both *Alice's Adventures* (1967) and *Through the Looking-Glass* (1972),[14] is the most recent artist to offer a major reinterpretation of Carroll's works. His bold black and white drawings overwhelm the text. His illustration of Alice and the Sheep in the boat, for example, fills two whole pages. The mutuality between pictures and text that Carroll worked out so carefully with Tenniel is here sacrificed to showcase Steadman's overpowering artistic imagination. His Alice bears an uncanny resemblance to Meryl Streep (who, incidentally, played Alice in Joseph Papp's 1981 television production of *Alice at the Palace*). Steadman takes the accepted view that the White Knight is Carroll himself. His portrait of him clearly resembles the well-known photographs of Carroll.

An important distinction to be noted between critical interpretations of Carroll's stories and artistic interpretations of his characters is that the critics leave Carroll's text intact, whereas the artists replace Tenniel's illustrations with their own. There appears to be a remarkable arrogance in such an undertaking. Still, all illustrations are a form of reading and interpretation, and it is a tribute to the openness, complexity, and fertility of Carroll's work that so many renowned artists have tried their hands at reshaping it.

Carroll seemingly wanted to fix a text that cannot be fixed, a contradiction typical in his life. Despite his great efforts at defining the images of his characters once and for all, they have been and will continue to be reinterpreted by hundreds of artists. Besides the numerous illustrated editions of the *Alice* books there have been several British and American film and television versions of the stories. These works not only provide new images of the characters but they make significant changes in the text, frequently conflating parts of the two stories. It seems probable that today more people are familiar with Walt Disney's film version of *Alice* stories than they are with Carroll's originals. This popular film has apparently taken its toll upon the taste and judgment of its audience. In a course I taught on Carroll and Lear, I received a paper from a student who vigorously argued that the Disney version of *Alice* was clearly superior to Carroll's two *Alice* books.

Having created Alice and her wonderful associates, Carroll and Tenniel are now history. Alice has been appropriated by the critics and the artists. These foster parents have a tremendous responsibility for this Victorian dream child. As she continues to undergo new transformations in size and shape, we can only hope that the artistic genes and genius that first gave her birth are manifest in her thousand new faces.

# Chapter Five
# The *Sylvie and Bruno* Books

In 1867 Carroll wrote a short children's story entitled "Bruno's Revenge" for *Aunt Judy's Magazine.* This fairy tale was the germ for the novel *Sylvie and Bruno,* which Carroll worked on intermittently for over fifteen years: "It was in 1874, I believe, that the idea first occurred to me of making it the nucleus of a longer story. As the years went on, I jotted down, at odd moments, all sorts of odd ideas, and fragments of dialogue, that occurred to me—who knows how?—With a transitory suddenness that left me no choice but either to record them then and there, or to abandon them to oblivion." He goes on to declare in the preface that it would be courting disaster to revert to the style of the *Alice* books: "Hence it is that in 'Sylvie and Bruno,' I have striven—with I know not what success—to strike out yet another new path: be it bad or good, it is the best I can do."[1]

Carroll's interest in spiritualism was a crucial factor in his writing *Sylvie and Bruno.* He joined the Society for Psychical Research a year after its founding in 1882 and retained his membership until the year before his death. He owned numerous books about spiritualism and the occult, including A. Calmet's *The Phantom World* (1850), Edward Clodd's *Myths and Dreams* (1885), Daniel Dunglas Home's *Lights and Shadows of Spiritualism* (1887), Frank Seafield's *The Literature and Curiosity of Dreams* (1865), A. T. Thompson's *The Occult Sciences* (1846), C. H. Townshend's *Facts in Mesmerism* (1844), D. H. Tuke's *Sleep Walking and Hypnotism* (1844), and Alfred Wallace's *Miracles and Modern Spiritualism* (1875).[2] Carroll's interest in the spirit world goes back, of course, well before the 1880s; but in his earlier writings, such as *Phantasmagoria* (1869), he treated the subject more flippantly.

In *Sylvie and Bruno* Carroll combines the notions of spiritualists with his Christian belief in the supernatural and with his view of innocent children as emblems of angelic purity. He outlines the hypothesis upon which the story is based in the preface to *Sylvie and Bruno Concluded* (1893): "It is an attempt to show what might *possibly* happen, supposing that Fairies really existed; and that they were sometimes able to assume human form: and supposing, also, that human beings might sometimes become conscious of what goes on in the Fairyworld—by actual transference of their immaterial essence, such as we meet with in Esoteric Buddhism."[3] As he grew older Carroll began to adopt a form of Christian Platonism. In one of his letters he states, "I find that as life slips away (I am over fifty now), and the life on the other side of the great river becomes more and more the reality, of which *this* is only a shadow, that the petty distinctions of the many creeds of Christendom tend to slip away as well—leaving only the great truths which all Christians believe alike."[4]

Believing the actual world to be only a shadow of a greater spiritual reality, Carroll in his novel attempts to demonstrate how one's ordinary life is shaped and controlled by invisible forces of innocence and love. He explains that there are three psychical states exhibited by the various characters in his story. First, there is "the ordinary state," which precludes an awareness of Fairies. Second is the "eerie state," in which, while one is conscious of actual surroundings, one is also conscious of the presence of Fairies. And third, there is "a form of trance," in which, while unconscious of actual surroundings and apparently asleep, one's immaterial essence migrates to other scenes, in the actual world or in Fairyland, and is conscious of the presence of Fairies.[5] The anonymous narrator of the two *Bruno* stories experiences all three states at one time or another.

## Structure

Carroll organized his novel in such a way as to demonstrate the vital interaction between two seemingly disparate realms, the actual world and fairyland. In depicting the former, he adopts the form of the romance novel, with its conventional love story ending with marriage and happiness ever after. In portraying the latter, he draws upon the conventions of the folktale, with its rich array of fairies, secret gardens, and magical transformations. He develops his two plots simultaneously and brings them into focus through the Narrator, a London lawyer who suffers from heart trouble that induces states of semiconsciousness (or "eeriness," as Carroll would call it) and trances in which he visits the spirit world called Outland.

The plot that deals with the human characters is a simple one. A brilliant young doctor named Arthur Forester falls in love with Lady Muriel Orme, the daughter of an affectionate old earl. Believing she is in love with her handsome young cousin, Captain Eric Lindon, Arthur does not declare his feelings for her. Although Eric and Lady Muriel become engaged, Lady Muriel's religious scruples make the prospect of their marriage uncertain since Eric is not a believing Christian. Abandoning his hopes of ever marrying Lady Muriel, Arthur prepares to leave England for India where he has been offered a medical appointment. His selflessness and nobility are further affirmed by his hope that Lady's Muriel's religious character will help to convert Eric to Christianity. The book ends with a poetical invocation: "From the East comes new strength, new ambition, new Hope, new Life, new Love! Look Eastward! Aye, look Eastward!"[6]

In *Sylvie and Bruno Concluded* Carroll manages to bring Lady Muriel and Arthur together. Recognizing the depth of Lady Muriel's religious faith, Eric releases her from any moral obligation to marry him. With the help of the invisible sprites, Sylvie and Bruno, and the Narrator, Arthur and Lady Muriel are brought together and married. Shortly after their marriage Arthur goes off to help bring under control a plague that is ravishing a nearby town. Lady Muriel reads in the newspapers that her husband has died heroically while trying to save those afflicted with the disease. Her strong faith in him is rewarded later when it is learned that Arthur has survived the plague. Ironically, he is rescued by Eric, who comes to understand that there is a God who answers prayers. Eric, it turns out, has been an unwitting instrument of God's providence and love.

The second plot involves the invisible world. A realm named Outland is ruled by a Warden who withdraws from his governmental duties in order to go upon a journey disguised as a beggar. In his absence his brother Sibimet and Sibimet's wife conspire with the Chancellor to usurp the Warden's power. These characters, including Uggug, Sibimet's ugly son, are all cruel and selfish, taking sadistic delight in punishing the poor and exercising their novel powers. The Warden's two children, Sylvie and Bruno, are sweet-tempered, innocent spirits, who delight in play and in lavishing affection upon each other. The Warden's idealized, loving family has its evil counterpart in Sibimet's selfish and materialistic family. The former is a kind of holy trinity: a father, son, and angelic spirit. The latter is comprised of a father, mother, and unwholesome son. In *Sylvie and Bruno Concluded* the Warden returns, overthrows the conspirators, and proclaims the Empire of Love.

It becomes clear that there are several correspondences between the two worlds and the two plots. Lady Muriel has a face like Sylvie's and she shares with her spirit counterpart an open, honest, and loving character. Eric relinquishes his skeptical attitude toward religion and becomes a Christian; Sibimet undergoes a similar conversion as he begs forgiveness from his brother and declares him an honorable man. The Warden's return restores the rule of love to his kingdom even as Arthur's resurrection brings about the fulfillment of Lady Muriel's love. The bi-focal vision of the Narrator enables us to see these and other parallels between the two worlds. Carroll's implication here is that dream and reality coexist and are inseparable. In *Sylvie and Bruno* we never leave Wonderland, so to speak. Carroll's view of the world in this novel resembles Carlyle's idea of natural supernaturalism—namely, that all nature is the revelation of God and must therefore be deemed sacred.

## Critical Response

Edmund Wilson comments that "the opening railway journey, in which the Narrator is dozing and mixes with the images of his dream his awareness of the lady sitting opposite him, is of an almost Joycean complexity and quite inappropriate for reading to children."[7] Florence Becker Lennon suggests that the unity of the book is achieved by the complex unity of the author: "*Sylvie and Bruno* casts more light on the author than do his masterpieces. To the reader it presents a labyrinth of neurosis, whereas to him [Carroll] it may have represented a healthy exercise in which he reknitted his disintegrating elements. Whatever the reason, he had great affection for the book."[8]

The two worlds of *Sylvie and Bruno* clearly reflect Carroll's own duality: the strict separation he maintained between his identity as Lewis Carroll, the writer of nonsense books, and Charles Dodgson, the serious professor of mathematics; between his obsession with childhood innocence and play and his powerful sense of responsibility for his family; and between his sweet, nostalgic memories of life at the Croft Rectory and his regimented duties at Oxford. Lennon observes that "the two volumes and their prefaces are an omnium-gatherum of Carroll's and Dodgson's major interests. . . . Arthur pontificates on politics, religion, art, love, science, immortality, and ruined castles; the Professor . . . instructs his learners in the use of black light and various types of glass, a megaloscope, a minifying glass, and the old-fashioned looking-glass with backward arrangement of everything from time to logic."[9] She perceives the two volumes as a "protracted figure of which the themes are the Duchess and the White Knight,"[10] the tedious little tracts and pamphlets listed under Duchess, and the charming, whimsical fancies and left-handed inventions, under White Knight. As Lennon points out, "the book could easily fly into fragments again,"[11] but the presence of the Narrator, who easily and gently moves from the eerie state to the ordinary state, holds the work together.

In his essay "The *Sylvie and Bruno* Books as Victorian Novel," Edmund Miller argues that Carroll's novel is essentially modeled after the early Victorian romance with its emphasis upon the miracles wrought by the power of love. Replete with moral earnestness and sentimentality, *Sylvie and Bruno* organizes and unifies the energies of the fairy world to shape the events of the real world and proclaim the gospel of love. Miller believes that the structure of the romance binds the worlds of nonsense and reality together:

That *Sylvie and Bruno* attempts to show the playful underside of a rather prim moral and religious view of reality, that it illustrates what we might call a leavening of reality with nonsense, has probably been understood by everyone who has read it. But the complementary point seems to have been equally important to Carroll, and perhaps too many readers come to the book from the *Alice*'s with fixed expectations. Do we want to hear that nonsense sometimes has to give place to reality, to a Carrollian reality of moral platitudes and sentimentality? And Carroll's moral view of reality does seem to be the source of our trouble. Side by side with his nonsense, Carroll presents an ostensibly real world whose values are sentimental and where events fall out according to the artifices of romance. The plot that animates and coordinates the two worlds is certainly a romance.[12]

Although Lennon and Miller may be correct in arguing that the Narrator and the romance plot fuse the two worlds together, it is not a comfortable fusion. One is put in mind of Walt Disney's rather disconcerting motion picture *The Song of the South,* in which he attempted to blend cartoon characters with actual people. The fantasy figures and the real people each have a distinctive kind of reality that resists their melding. In a work like Alexander Pope's "The Rape of the Lock," on the other hand, the marriage of fantasy and reality is made acceptable by the narrator's witty, knowing, and satiric presence. But Carroll reserves his wit and intelligence for the nonsense world and expresses an uncritical sentimentality and moral earnestness in the supposedly real world of his novel.

There are other critics besides Miller who are reluctant to see a genius like Carroll fail, and there has been a recent trend to resurrect the *Sylvie and Bruno* books to declare them as unsung masterpieces. Jean Gattegno, for example, argues that Carroll was up to something new in his novel. He states that in the *Alice* books dreams depended upon desire but in the *Sylvie and Bruno* books "desire becomes intellectual or hides behind an urge for knowledge, and the dream becomes science and invites theorizing."[13] What interests Gattegno is not the plots but their juxtaposition: they relate to distinct universes, reality and dreams. "So, at first glance," he says, "one could believe they are opposed, but, in fact, they are not. The Preface to *Sylvie and Bruno Concluded,* along with the introductory poem in *Sylvie and Bruno,* underlines the fact that the disjunction is a mere hypothesis: 'Is all our Life, then, a dream?'" The solution, he continues, "in Carroll's eyes, is not to unite 'dream' and 'reality' but to bring the two worlds into contact, in a vision of mystical quality . . . as Sylvie—who still remains Sylvie—becomes an 'angel.'"[14] Lady Muriel has the same features as Sylvie, the spirit who occasionally steps into the real world. Lady Muriel (life) and Sylvie (dream) remain distinct but their characters overlay one another even as a dream overlays reality.

Gattegno concludes that the central thrust in the novel is to reshape multiplicity into unity. Mein Herr explains to Lady Muriel the paradox of Fortunatus's purse. The purse is created by combining two handkerchiefs by knots so as to join the four edges of an outer surface to the four edges of a circular opening. A version of Moebius's ring, the purse has but one surface and one side. Mein Herr thus explains that what is outside the purse is also inside the purse. Duality is therefore an illusion, and the implication of the paradoxical purse reverberates throughout the novel and recapitulates a central theme: the principle of sameness within difference.

Jan B. Gordon's analysis of the novel combines a linguistic and a biographical approach to the work. He notes that Carroll's moral test of literature, as stated in *Sylvie and Bruno,* is that one should not dare to live in any scene in which he dare not die. Gordon goes on to demonstrate the important role that disease and death play in the book. The Narrator, for example, is an octogenarian afflicted with an "illness of the heart," on a visit to Arthur Forester to seek a cure. The threat of death as a moral test of life hangs over him. As Gordon points out, "These books are about the difficulties of restoration—to health and to childhood, respectively—and as such they are much more akin to the literature of illness, like *The Magic Mountain,* than they are to Carroll's other achievements."[15]

Gordon's thesis argues that throughout the novel "salvation appears to lie in the denial of textuality." Instead of being absorbed with books and writing poems that never end, "the garden of eerie creates its own autonomous, yet ever-changing language."[16] The Narrator, given his age and declining health, is thus most interested in discovering how to live in the "pre-linguistic universe"[17] as long as possible. Ordinary discourse seems self-referential, having no origin except in previous discourse. The fear of the inevitable exhaustion of all language is found not only in the novel but in Carroll's statements that he wants to avoid the influence of his two *Alice* books and thereby write something entirely original. "The entire burden of the second volume [*Sylvie and Bruno Concluded*] is that of converting the autocratic tyranny of the text . . . into a world based upon *acts.*"[18] The first volume establishes a binary universe in which one must make clear choices, usually between right and wrong. Sylvie, for example, must choose which locket she desires: the one inscribed "All love Sylvie" or the one which reads "Sylvie will love all." The duality of this volume is further enhanced through the many correspondences between characters: Muriel and Sylvie, Mein Herr and the Professor, and Arthur and the Narrator. The parable of Fortunatus's purse, however, indicates that a new principle is replacing the binary one: the principle of sameness within difference. The messages on the lockets offered to Sylvie can now be fused. There is no need to choose between them. Similarly, Outland can become Elfland, Mein Herr can become the Professor, and vice versa.

Gordon points out that Carroll is attempting to deal with two extremes in language. On the one hand there is a world without metaphor, tyrannically ruled by the text. On the other hand, there is a world of metaphor in which all objects are potentially other objects and all discourse becomes self-reflexive. "Between these two extremes," Gordon writes, "Carroll locates the hope for stability in the principle of 'sameness within difference,' the notion that language is part of a binary set of relationships and proportions."[19] In chapter 16 of *Sylvie and Bruno Concluded* Carroll argues for the possibility of a transcendent language:

Now, may not our life a million years hence, have the same relation, to our life now, that the man's life has to the child's? And, just as one might try, all in vain, to express to that child, in the language of bricks and ninepins, the meaning of "politics," so perhaps all those descriptions of Heaven, with its music, and its feats, and its streets of gold, may be only attempts to describe in *our* words, things for which we *really* have no words at all. (*SBC* 643)

Gordon's analysis of Carroll's linguistic themes is thoroughly fascinating but finally leads to this rather abrupt dead end. As Lady Muriel observes, only a lunatic could write truly original works because his thinking would not have been shaped by the literary traditions of his culture. Furthermore, the lunatic would not have to experience Carroll's anxiety about writing the same book over again. Carroll really has no solution to his problem. How different, after all, is Alice's confusion over whether cats eat bats or bats eat cats from the inversion on Sylvie's amulet, "All will love Sylvie" and "Sylvie will love all"? It is only by extrapolating from the idea of love that one might argue that *because* Sylvie will love all that she will be loved by all or vice versa. The linguistic principle of inversion, however, seems the same in both cases. Language and its traditions are a closed box and no literary Houdinis have yet found a way out. In the passage quoted above, Carroll abandons logic and language for faith in a world for which no words exist, a Heaven that lies beyond the reach of metaphor.

Ironically, Carroll develops his novel, as Edmund Miller has shown, through the borrowed structure of the Victorian romance. Arthur Forester "dies" and is "reborn." The plague passes and even the Narrator, having regressed to a symbolic childhood, has achieved psychic renewal. Eric is converted to Christianity. Order is restored to the land and the kingdom of love is firmly established. Carroll thus fashions out of old literary patterns a new novel (a "sameness within difference") that would have us believe that the power of love transcends this prison-house of words and brings with it a rebirth and wholeness of spirit.

## Outlandish Nonsense

In the preface to the novel Carroll states that he has attempted "to strike out yet another new path" (*SB* 381) and to avoid repeating the pattern of the *Alice* books. Nevertheless there are numerous connections between *Sylvie and Bruno* and the *Alice* books—and it is important to note the connections before discussing why the book "remains one of the most interesting failures in English literature."[20] The Professor, for example, has a pair of boots for horizontal weather—they are small umbrellas worn about his knees in the event that it should rain horizontally. They are clearly reminiscent of the anklets on the White Knight's horse that ward off shark bites. The Gardener waters flowers with an empty can because it is lighter to hold, an absurdity comparable to the White Knight's box for clothing and sandwiches which hangs upside down to keep the rain from getting in. The Professor's Outlandish watch is related to the timepiece of the Hatter; the Wonderland concept that a person who befriends Time could turn the hands of a clock and skip from breakfast to dinner develops into the Outlandish watch.

In more general terms, the peculiar humor of nonsense that characterized the *Alice* books reasserts itself in the passages dealing with the Gardener (who is always singing some nonsense verse and provides most of the poetry in the work), the Professor, and the Other Professor. Furthermore, the basic contrasts between dreaming and waking states are carried over from the *Alice* books and emphasized to the point where the relationship between dream and reality becomes the subject. Once in Wonderland, Alice is totally enveloped in a series of absurd experiences, and we give our attention to her sundry encounters with Wonderland creatures rather than to the fact that she is dreaming. But in *Sylvie and Bruno* we are made to concentrate upon constantly shifting realities, from the actual world, to the fairy world, back to the actual world, and the relationships between both. The psychological process of perception is as important a part of the subject of the novel as are the two story lines. In this sense the Narrator not only unifies the two worlds—the actual and the spiritual—but as the central, unifying perceiver, is the intimate subject of his own story.

Finally, the ending of *Sylvie and Bruno* resembles those of the *Alice* books. In all three works a crescendo builds to a finale of contemptuous violence. Toward the end of *Alice's Adventures in Wonderland* Alice grows more assertive and finally, having reached her full size, announces, "You're nothing but a pack of cards!" Wonderland is subsequently undermined—the cards fly up in the air, and Tenniel depicts for the first time the various animals *without* their human characteristics. In *Sylvie and Bruno Concluded,* the Warden returns to Outland to forgive his cheating brother who usurped the throne, and Prince Bruno grows more aggressive in his contradicting the lying Sub-Warden. The scene darkens and a hurricane shakes the palace to its foundation, bursting open the windows. Through this violence the Sub-Warden is converted to honesty and he announces: "When my brother went away, you lost the best Warden you ever had. And I've been doing my best, wretched hypocrite that I am, to cheat you into making me an Emperor" (688). In both worlds the conclusions are marked not only by violence but by transformations.

In *Alice's Adventures in Wonderland*, for instance, characters become mere cards or animals losing their human traits as Alice wakes from her dream and returns to reality. Her strange experiences underground are clearly set forth as a dream framed by the actual world described in the first and last chapters. The transformations at the end of *Sylvie and Bruno*, however, are significantly different. Sibimet becomes an honest man, the old Beggar (the Warden in disguise) becomes the King of Elfland, the "dead" Arthur is resurrected, Uggug becomes a porcupine, and Sylvie becomes an angel. These transformations emphasize the coexistence of dream and reality, spirit and flesh. Thus the "dead" come back to life, a repulsive boy becomes an animal, and Sylvie, the fairy double of Lady Muriel, becomes an angel. The rule of love and justice thus prevails in both the visible and the invisible realms and the boundary between dream and reality remains happily uncertain.

Despite the similarities between the *Alice* books and *Sylvie and Bruno*, Carroll extends his original genius in his portrayal of such characters as Mein Herr and the Gardener. Unlike the conventional, straight characters, whose interests and activities seem only remotely connected to Carroll's own life, his eccentric characters embody his playful and visceral impulses and vibrate with an energy that engages both the reader's mind and his feelings.

Mein Herr, whose resemblance to the Professor suggests in the swirl of eeriness and actuality that they are one and the same, carries German ingenuity and inventiveness to a new high. He explains that in his country "we have gone on selecting *cotton-wool,* till we have got some lighter than air! You've no idea what a useful material it is! We call it "Imponderal!'" (*SBC* 607). The material is used chiefly for packing articles to go by parcel post. Asked how the postal clerk knows how much to charge for such packages, Mein Herr replies, "That's the beauty of the new system! They pay *us:* we don't pay *them*! I've often got as much as five shillings for sending a parcel!" (607).

Another project his nation developed is map making. They began with a scale of several inches to the mile and continued to decrease the ratio until they achieved a mile to the mile. The Narrator asks if they used such a map often and Mein Herr explains, "It has never been spread out, yet: the farmers objected: they said it would cover the whole country, and shut out the sunlight! So we now use the country itself, as its own map, and I assure you it does nearly as well" (609). This is an especially interesting passage in light of the recent criticism of this novel. Here the representation of an object becomes identified with the object itself. The map (the text or metaphor for the object) overlays the land (the real-world object). It is an interesting correspondence but, of course, still only a correspondence. To extend the dimensions of a metaphor (a map) to a literal representation of the real-world object is to destroy the essence of metaphor. However, to remain within the confines of representations and metaphors is to lose contact with the thing itself. Thus Carroll touches upon the dilemma of the artist who is doomed to work within a web of words, to repeat the conventions and traditions of his craft. Furthermore, this passage may also imply a criticism of the simple idea of Victorian realism that the word is identical with the thing designated.

Carroll includes in *Sylvie and Bruno Concluded* an amusing satire of the competition among English colleges for outstanding students. He begins this section in the manner of Jonathan Swift and concludes it through his unique mode of nonsense. Mein Herr describes the scene at the railway station:

Eight of nine heads of Colleges had assembled at the gates (no one was allowed inside), and the Station-master had drawn a line on the pavement, and insisted on them all standing behind it. The gates were flung open! The young man darted through them, and fled like lightning down the street, while the Heads of the Colleges actually *yelled* with excitement on catching sight of him! The Proctor gave the word, in the old statutory form, "*Semel! Bis! Ter! Currite!*", and the hunt began! (615–16).

The principal of one of the colleges is shaped like a sphere, which gives him an aerodynamic advantage over his competitors. His shape leads him to investigate the theory of Accelerated Velocity. Mein Herr explains to the Narrator how this principal arrived at a remarkable discovery: "the moving body, ever tending to *fall*, needs *constant support*, if it is to move in a true horizontal line. 'What, then' he asked himself, 'will give *constant support to a moving body*?' And his answer was 'Human legs!' *That* was the discovery that immortalized his name!" (616). Carroll seems to relish the wonderful naïveté of his scientists and inventors. Like the principal who discovers the importance of human legs,

like Mein Herr and the White Knight, they possess a childlike innocence of the world. They work out their problems in physics and math
in the peculiar towers of their own minds and imaginations. Like children, they are filled with curiosity and mental energy, exercising their
minds with the same abandon as a child at play.

The episode with the Outlandish Watch provides another pleasant
interlude of nonsense amid the sensible dullness of the novel. The
Professor explains how the device works: "It *goes,* of course, at the
usual rate. Only the time has to go *with* it. Hence, if I move the
hands, I change the time. To move them *forwards,* in *advance* of the
true time, is impossible: but I can move them as much as a month
*backwards*—that is the limit. And then you have the events all over
again—with any alterations experience may suggest" (*SB* 503). Upon
moving the hands of the clock backwards the narrator is treated to
witnessing a "ghostly banquet": "An empty fork is raised to the
lips: there it receives a neatly-cut piece of mutton, and swiftly conveys it to the plate, where it instantly attaches itself to the mutton
already there. Soon one of the plates, furnished with a complete slice
of mutton and two potatoes, was handed up to the presiding gentleman, who quietly replaced the slice on the joint, and the potatoes
in the dish" (518). Carroll anticipates here the fun of viewing a
motion picture run backwards, an event he would have applauded.
Carroll, it will be recalled, also played with the idea of "living
backwards" in *Through the Looking-Glass.* There, however, the reversal
of time was not a mere spectator sport but a curiously conscious process. The White Queen screamed, her finger bleeding, as she coolly
anticipated pricking her finger on a brooch when she would fasten her
shawl.

One of the most memorable nonsense characters in *Sylvie and Bruno*
is the Gardener. He is the keeper of the door out of the garden in which
Sylvie and Bruno occasionally find themselves. He is a vigorous, merry
creature who stands on one leg while watering the flowers with the
empty watering can and singing of fantastic things. A perfect singer
of nonsense, the Gardener paradoxically admits, "I never means nothing" (418), and his songs bear him out:

> He thought he saw a Rattlesnake
> That questioned him in Greek:
> He looked again, and found it was
> The Middle of Next Week.

> "The one thing I regret," he said,
> "Is that it cannot speak!"
>
> (415)

Most of his songs are set in the same meter but through their sing-song innocence he asserts a disconcerting message: the world is neither stable nor consistent and our perceptions shift like a series of mirages. Nevertheless, we (perhaps foolishly) draw grand conclusions (namely, that life is bitter) from the incoherent swirl of visions and experiences. The following song reinforces this sense of perceptual dislocation:

> He thought he saw an Elephant,
> That practised on a fife:
> He looked again, and found it was
> A letter from his wife.
> "At length I realise" he said,
> "The bitterness of Life!"
>
> (408)

Amusing in themselves, the songs also reinforce the theme of dream and reality that permeates the entire story. Things are not what they seem at first and second looks oftentimes reveal startling new sights. Throughout the novel the Narrator's vision fades in and out of reality as images of Outland and Fairyland overlay those of the more conventional Elveston: Sylvie becomes Lady Muriel and Mein Herr becomes the Professor.

Phyllis Greenacre sees a relationship between the Gardener, Father William, and the White Knight: "all are older men, parodied, foolish inferior characters, but merry and glamorously enchanting in their unexpectedly acrobatic behavior and lilting rhythms."[21] She finds "the acrobatic, swaying, jigging, snorting rhythm" to be "a typical dream representation of sexual excitement" and that "these figures all appear as memories which are represented in dreams":

The gardener's song always comes at the point of a shift from one state to another [between dreaming and consciousness]. The repetitiveness of this excited figure and his constant association with a secret garden, the concern about whether the memory is good in the onlooker and the reciprocal questions whether the silly old fellow's brain has been injured—whether his behavior is merrily exciting or a comfort in a state of distress—would lead to the conclusion that there was some actual but repressed memory of the author's which was insistently recurring in hidden forms: that probably in his childhood Charles had been stirred at the sight of an older man, perhaps a gardener, in a state of sexual excitement.[22]

Greenacre's psychoanalytical reading offers a credible and perceptive explanation as to why the straight part of Carroll's writings is so dull and conventional and the nonsense part so alive and unusual. Despite his extreme self-discipline, his dependence on orderliness, his suppression of strong emotions, and his concern for accuracy and detail, a spirit of a "primitive type of 'feeling-thought'" asserts itself in his best writing and "it awakens in the reader a feeling of fantastic familiarity with an extravaganza of outlandish nonsense."[23]

It is exactly this fusion of thought and feeling that brings about the dynamic energy of the *Alice* books, where puzzles, riddles, and chess moves combine with powerful emotions (sexual anxiety, fear of death and annihilation, the obsession with order). The Tweedle brothers' defense of Bishop Berkeley's idea that all material things, including people, are only items in the mind of a dreaming God simultaneously presents Alice with an interesting philosophic notion and a powerful visceral message that if the Red King awakens she will go out like a candle. Similarly, in *Sylvie and Bruno* the Gardener's presence signals a shift in the narrative (between dream and reality)—a shift reinforced by the dislocations within his songs—while his obsessive body movements and regular poetic meters convey a pleasing, compulsive, and guilty sexual rhythm.

## An Outlandish Failure

Given the similarities between the nonsense in *Sylvie and Bruno* and that in the *Alice* books, why, then, is the former unsuccessful as a work of literature? The first volume sold 13,000 copies by the time of Carroll's death; the second volume was not so popular. What little success the story had in Carroll's own day was probably due to the reputation of the *Alice* books. The reviewers did not like it, and Carroll commented on their displeasure in a letter he wrote to his publisher in 1884: "If the reviewers are right the book does not deserve to sell: if they are wrong, it will gradually get known by people recommending it to their friends."[24] In 1904 Carroll's brother Edwin attempted, with small success, to revive interest in the work by publishing an abridgement that featured only the fairy sections. In our own day the work is relatively inaccessible, hardly read, and only recently examined by Carroll critics and scholars. In 1937 Edmund Wilson wrote *"Sylvie and Bruno,* which is never reprinted, ought to be made available."[25] Hardly a clarion call for *Sylvie and Bruno's* resurrection, Wilson's essay does recognize the psychological complexity that makes the book interesting to the modern reader. He also notes its chief faults: "In the 'straight' parts of *Sylvie and Bruno,* Lewis Carroll was mawkishly Victorian to the point of unintentional parody."[26] In the prefaces to *Sylvie and Bruno* and its sequel one first discerns the sermonizing that characterizes the novel. After providing a few details about the composition of the book, Carroll digresses to make moral reflections of all kinds— the need for a children's Bible, the danger of a sudden death for a person unprepared to meet his Maker, and the insincerity of elaborate church rituals. As Hudson notes, "these prefaces warn us of what is coming. The artist has not been snuffed out, but he has been overlaid by the moralist."[27] By attempting to fuse the fantasy to the conventionally uplifting didacticism of a period novel Carroll destroyed the book as a whole. The point already made with regard to Carroll's poetry applies here as well—namely, that when Carroll abandons nonsense in order to write "straight," he falls prey to outrageous sentimentality and tedious moralizing. Having so ably handled moralizing in the *Alice* books (through the Duchess, the parodies, and Alice's own moral code) he now evades the constraints of his comic perspective and writes:

"Sylvie will love all—all will love Sylvie." Bruno murmured, raising himself on tiptoe to kiss the "little red star." "And, when you look *at* it, it's gentle and blue like the sky?"

"God's own sky," Sylvie said, dreamily.

"God's own sky," the little fellow repeated, as they stood, lovingly clinging together, and looking out into the night. "But oh, Sylvie, what makes the sky such a *darling* blue?"

Sylvie's sweet lips shaped themselves to reply, but her voice sounded faint and very far away. The vision was fast slipping from my eager gaze: but it seems to me, in that last bewildering moment, that not Sylvie but an angel was looking out through those trustful brown eyes, and that not Sylvie's but an angel's voice was whispering

"IT IS LOVE." (*SBC* 698)

Derek Hudson summarizes a response to the work that has prevailed for many years: *"Sylvie and Bruno* bears the same relation to Lewis Carroll's earlier works, *mutatis mutandis,* as *Finnegans Wake* to the more intelligible earlier productions of James Joyce. It is worth giving time to it, though not too much, as the honourable experiment of a remarkable mind."[27] Although some recent critics have given considerable time to analyzing the novel, providing Carroll scholars with thought-provoking and illuminating insights, it is doubtful that the *Sylvie and Bruno* books will ever enjoy a popularity outside of academe.

The books lack well-rounded, interesting characters, the staple of any good novel. Perhaps this difficulty arises, in part, from genre expectations. The reader anticipates finding believable characters in the novel, and Carroll is setting up these expectations by using a genre he cannot command. The shifting states of mind of the Narrator have a powerful interest but the worlds that he visits during these dreaming moments are not in themselves of great interest. His sorties into the prelinguistic worlds of Sylvie and Bruno, idealized children walking together in an embrace of love, are rather abstract and dull. The recent analyses of such scenes may demonstrate their structural significance but they certainly cannot make them any more compelling. Reading a careful analysis of this story is akin to having someone explain why a joke that no one laughed at is actually funny.

Characters like Arthur Forester, Lady Muriel, and Eric are simply cardboard figures drawn to intersect with the much more lively fairy tale characters. Given Carroll's desire to write an original story, his "real life" characters betray him at every turn with their stereotypical behavior formulated in previous Victorian romances. Arthur is the conventional earnest, long-suffering lover who, out of respect for his lady's feelings, willingly waits in the shadows. Eric, his competitor, is the typical dashing young military man from the romance. Lady Muriel herself is a standard romantic heroine, possessing the scruples and sensibilities of Victorian morality. When these characters are not being stereotypical they act like puppets manipulated by their academic creator. Carroll frequently has Lady Muriel engage in conversations dealing with such bizarre topics as the minimizing of ideas in books and the creation of original literature by lunatics. When he allows Arthur several pages of speech it turns out to be a long, tedious lecture to the Narrator about material wealth and charity.

If the characters and plot cannot engage the modern reader it is unlikely that many people will be willing to plunge beneath the surface with recent critics to examine the more sophisticated subtext. In his preface Carroll states that his novel was written "not for money, and not for fame, but in the hope of supplying, for the children whom I love, some thoughts that may suit those hours of innocent merriment which are the very life of Childhood" (*SB* 381). It seems clear that he has not succeeded in reaching either his intended child audience or the general public. Recalling the mental gymnastics of the Professor, the Other Professor, and Mein Herr, however, we should not be surprised that the *Sylvie and Bruno* books are at least gaining an appreciative audience among academic critics.

## Chapter Six
# Man of Diverse Interests

## Photographer

Lewis Carroll was one of the most visually oriented writers of his time. In contrast with an author such as Charles Dickens, however, Carroll did not develop striking physical descriptions of scene and character in his writings; in fact, his prose and poetry are fairly abstract and spartan. His visual response to the world is largely isolated from his writing and relegated to his sketches, photography, and supervision of other artists' illustrations for his books. If one has a mental picture of the Hatter or the White Rabbit, the odds are that it is derived from Tenniel's illustrations and not from Carroll's prose descriptions.

From childhood, when he illustrated his own magazines, through the period of *Alice's Adventures under Ground,* to the last years of his life, Carroll enjoyed sketching. He adopted the Victorian habit of carrying sketchbooks with him on vacation and filled them with drawings of young girls he met by the seaside. He was constantly frustrated, however, by his inability to draw. In a letter to Gertrude Thomson, from whom he took lessons, Carroll wrote, "I *love* the effort to draw, but I utterly fail to please even my own eye—tho' now and then I seem to get somewhere *near* a right line or two, when I have a live child to draw from. But I have no time left now for such things. In the next life, I do *hope* we shall not only *see* lovely forms, such as this world does not contain, but also be able to draw them."[1] Later letters to Miss Thomson show him still sketching young girls from life, to within three months before his death. Despite his lifelong interest in drawing, Carroll's work, when compared to that of Tenniel, Harry Furniss, and Henry Holiday, appears primitive and naive.

It was commonplace for authors to have their books illustrated during the Victorian period, but it is curious to reflect that few books are so clearly remembered for their pictures as are the two *Alice* stories. Once cannot explain this phenomenon simply by attributing the success to Tenniel—for how many people can recall other illustrations by that artist? The explanation, perhaps, lies in the perfect marriage of art and nonsense. There is a more natural affinity between the two than there is between art and some other forms of literature, such as the psychological novel. In reading a work such as *Middlemarch,* one might be displeased with a drawing of Dorothea Brooke, for her psychological complexity and ambiguity would be threatened by a fixed physical representation of her. It is precisely because nonsense eschews ambiguity, as Sewell has observed, that the illustrations are so effective: "The providing of pictures is a regular part of the Nonsense game. They sterilize the mind's powers of invention and combination of images while seeming to nourish it, and by precision and detail they contribute towards detachment and definition of the elements of the Nonsense universe."[2] The characters in Wonderland, for example, do not have a psychological reality; they are, for the most part, mindless. Their existence is comprised solely of their nonsense statements (which do not seem to arise from any intelligible core of being) and their physical appearance as delineated in the precise illustrations.

The visual aspect of Carroll's work that strengthens his nonsense derives from his obsession with looking. Phyllis Greenacre comments: "The spirit of both *Alice* books is that of an unplanned sight-seeing trip through a marvelously strange country. The title, *Alice's Adventures in Wonderland* in the one instance, and the entrance through the *Looking-Glass* into an extraordinary country in the other, reemphasize the voyeuristic theme."[3] In *The Hunting of the Snark,* the Baker is punished by annihilation in the act of seeing the Boojum. Greenacre explains the Boojum as "some representation of the primal scene, in which the sexual images of the parents are fused into a frightening or awe-inspiring single figure" and sees the last "fit" as "an acting out of the primal scene with the Baker first standing 'erect and sublime' and then plunging into the chasm between the crags."[4] Unlike his abstract mathematical interests, Carroll's visual curiosity leads him toward the sometimes guilty pleasures of the physical world.

One of the most satisfying outlets for Carroll's psychological interest in looking came in photography. What began as a hobby in 1856 became a passionate devotion for nearly twenty-four years. During that period Carroll became one of the most skillful portrait photographers of his day. He did his own developing and printing at a time when this was an exceedingly complicated and exacting job. Photography had only become available to the public a few years before Carroll took it up. He was now able to approach his favorite subject, the beautiful girl child, in a new and exciting way. Like the Butcher in the *Snark* who "thought of his childhood, left far far behind— / That blissful and innocent state," Carroll throughout his life looked back on his childhood with nostalgia. Now, through photography, he could freeze images of youthful innocence through countless photographs of young girls.

Although he frequently sought out eminent men and women to photograph—such as Dante Gabriel Rossetti, Ellen Terry, and Alfred Tennyson—he achieved greater artistic success in his pictures of children.[5] He was simply more relaxed in the company of children and could work with them more effectively as subjects. He owned a large variety of costumes, many of which were from the Drury Lane pantomimes, and he dressed up the little girls as Chinese women, Cinderellas, parlor maids, beggar maids, and Little Red Riding Hoods. The majority of his girl sitters were the daughters of clergymen, of Oxford professors, and of well-know writers and artists. There was a snobbish streak in Carroll that made it impossible for him to photograph real beggar maids. In a letter to Beatrice Hatch he wrote that "below a certain line, it is hardly wise to let a girl have a 'gentleman' friend." Attracted by a twelve-year-old girl he saw talking to Hatch, Carroll hesitates to ask for an introduction: "I fear I must be content with her *name* only: the social gulf between us is probably too wide for it to be wise to make *friends*. Some of my little *actress*-friends are of a *rather* lower status than myself."[6]

Carroll considered children's simple nightdresses most attractive and had a number of little girls pose in them. He was especially fond of having his young models pose in white flannel because the texture and color of the material made it more photogenic and enhanced the naturalness of the child. Gernsheim condemns the costume pictures for their lamentable concession to Victorian taste but as a photographer of unadorned children he feels that Carroll "achieves an excellence which in its way can find no peer."[7]

In a letter to Mrs. James Chataway, Carroll goes a step beyond nightdresses in requesting permission to photograph her daughter Gertrude in the nude: "with some I know (Londoners chiefly) I would not venture to propose even taking off their shoes: but with a child like your Gertrude, as simple-minded as Eve in the garden of Eden, *I* should see no objection (provided she liked it herself) to photographing her in Eve's original dress."[8] But he carefully discriminated between naked boys and naked girls. In a letter to Gertrude Thomson he writes: "I confess I do *not* admire naked boys in pictures. They always seem to me to need *clothes*: whereas one hardly sees why the lovely forms of girls should *ever* be covered up!"⁹ Carroll took great pains, however, to avoid ever offending the propriety of either parents or children. He wrote, "If I had the loveliest child in the world, to draw or photograph, and found she had a modest shrinking (however slight, and however easily overcome) from being taken nude, I should feel it was a solemn duty owed to God to drop the request altogether."¹⁰ Many of his models obviously did not shrink from his careful requests, for Carroll eventually took a number of photographs of nude girls.

For many years it was believed that none of Carroll's photographs of nude children had survived. Before he died he destroyed most of the negatives and prints of his nude studies and requested that his executors destroy those that remained after his death. He had sent copies of some of these pictures, however, to his various sitters and their families. While most of these have probably been lost or destroyed, a few survived. In 1978 Morton Cohen published four of these nude studies that he discovered among Dr. A. S. W. Rosenbach's collection of Carroll materials.

Cohen makes out a good case for the innocence of these photographs. He argues that there were two traditions running through the Victorian period: the evangelical and the Romantic. The former stressed original sin and the need to protect the child from the evil of the world. The Romantic tradition, on the other hand, viewed the child as the epitome of innocence and purity. Followers of the views of Blake, Wordsworth, and Coleridge thus "believed that the child, and especially the female child, was a divine creation sent from heaven in a state of grace. The child's exterior, naturally soft, beautiful, and unblemished, was an outward manifestation of inner goodness."¹¹ Cohen places Carroll clearly on the side of the Romantics. Furthermore, he points out that Victorian parents who shared Carroll's attitude allowed their children to romp about in warm weather without any clothes on, especially at the seaside. I should add to Cohen's discussion that the great photographer of Whitby, Frank Meadow Sutcliffe, took several pictures of nude children. His most famous picture, "The Water Rats," taken in 1886, shows a group of nude boys playing around a boat in Whitby harbor. King Edward VII, then the prince of Wales, saw the picture in an exhibition and ordered an enlargement to be hung in Marlborough House. The local clergy, however, excommunicated Sutcliffe for showing such an indecent print that they were convinced would corrupt the morals of young women. The puritanical severity of the evangelical

churchmen blinded them to the Romantic innocence embodied in
these pictures.

The four photographs that Cohen reproduces were all taken in Carroll's studio. The original black and white pictures do not seem to have
survived. What we have are pictures that apparently were colored by
an artist that Carroll hired. Besides tinting the photographs, the artist
added background scenes—oceans, rocks, lakes, and trees. Unlike Sutcliffe's more natural photographs, these are of the typically posed variety. The unknown artist surrounds the children with rather crude
imagined scenes that give the pictures a bizarre quality. Plate 4, for
example, shows two nude girls, one sitting on and one leaning against
a rocky promontory jutting out into the sea. In the background is a
shipwreck. The dreamy, distracted, almost bored expression of the girls
seems to have no relationship whatsoever to the dramatic shipwreck
behind them.

The photograph of Evelyn Hatch (plate 3), however, stands out
among the four as the most erotic. She is posed lying on her back, her
arms up behind her head, and her hips turned toward the viewer. Lying
in what appears to be an open field, with her soulful eyes directed
towards the observer, she strikes the pose and has the color of a Rubens
figure. The pictorial allusion to a sensual artistic tradition makes this
picture much less innocent than the others. Unlike Sutcliffe's photograph of boys being boys, Carroll's picture captures a girl being a
woman.

Carroll's interest in photography is inextricably related to his interest in young girls. He apparently derived a great deal of satisfaction
from the elaborate and socially acceptable ritual of photographing his
youthful subjects. He was constantly on the lookout for new little girls
to photograph. In his diary he records, for example, that a Mrs. Colo-
nel Franklin's "little girl was one I observed at the school-feast and had
enquired her name, with a view to getting Mrs. Cameron to photograph her for me."[12] Later, he wrote to his sister, Louisa: "I was
lounging about on the beach, and came on the same little unknown
child—such a little gypsy beauty, rich brown complexion and black
eyes."[13] Finally, several days later, he managed to photograph the girl
himself. A diary entry for March 1863 reveals a list of 107 names of
girls "photographed or to be photographed."[14] In 1877 he saw a girl
named Connie Gilchrist playing a part in the children's pantomine
*Goody Two Shoes* and noted in his diary that she was "one of the most

beautiful children, in face and figure, that I have ever seen. I must get an opportunity of photographing her."[15] About three months later he got to meet her and wrote "I was decidedly pleased with Connie, who has a refined and modest manner, with just a touch of shyness, and who is about the most gloriously beautiful child (both face and figure) that I ever saw. One would like to do 100 photographs of her."[16] I could cite scores of similar entries throughout the quarter of a century that Carroll tirelessly pursued his photography. It is noteworthy that many of these entries reveal that his first response to seeing a young girl is a desire to photograph her—not talk to her, take her somewhere, play with her, hold her, or any of a number of other possible responses. It was careful and intense observation of the mysterious Franklin girl that led Carroll to want to photograph her—his mental picture of her was apparently never satisfactory until he got her image aligned through the camera lens and later fixed on the film.

If photography for Carroll became a surrogate ritual for seduction and possession, then its intricacies had to be mastered as in any complex art form. "The main charm of photography for his artist soul," writes Lennon, "was its difficulty."[17] When photography became simplified by the invention of the convenient dry plate process, he abandoned the art. Over the years Carroll's photography, like his manner of living, became strictly patterned. From finding new sitters to pasting the finished photograph in his album, Carroll transformed a hobby into an elaborate ritual—and the idea of replacing the complex wet plate process for a new and easy method must have threatened the entire ritual.

Many of Carroll's photographs were taken in Oxford, at the Deanery, Christ Church, in his rooms, and at a hired studio. When, in 1868, he moved into a suite of rooms in Tom Quad he had erected on the flat college roof a photographic glass house. It was to this magical room that numerous girls climbed in order to be transformed into Turks, parlor maids, and fisherboys. One of his sitters later recalled the experience:

Perhaps the most vivid memories of the Oxford children are connected with the great experience of being photographed. How well they can remember climbing up the dark oak staircase leading out of Tom Quad to the studio of the top floor of his rooms! The smell of certain chemicals will still bring back a vision of the mysterious dark cupboard where he developed his plates, of the dressing-room where strange costumes had to be donned, and of the rather awe-inspiring ceremony of being posed, with fastidious care, as Turk, China-man, fisher-boy, or in a group with several others to form a picture.[18]

Having secured a desirable sitter (oftentimes obtained only after much correspondence, meeting friends of friends who had an attractive daughter, wrangling invitations, etc.) and having set up the elaborate equipment of the glass house, Carroll could proceed with the final stages of the photographic ritual. He had created in his rooms a para-dise for children, the atmosphere of which would help bring them to just the right mood to be photographed. There was an array of dolls and toys, a distorting mirror, a clockwork bear, a flying bat that he had made, a collection of music boxes, and an organette that played perforated sheet music. When she grew tired of these amusements Car-roll would sit a child on his knee and tell her fascinating stories, illus-trating them with humorous drawings on scraps of paper. When she seemed thoroughly elated by the procedures, he would pose her for a photograph before the appropriate mood had passed. Sometimes he would allow the children to go into the darkroom and watch him de-velop the large glass plates.

Without casting a sinister light upon Carroll's relationship with his sitters, one may nevertheless note the compelling parallel between his photographic adventures and the sexual adventures of a typical bachelor (which Carroll obviously was not). Both keep an eye out for attractive girls, strategically work out meetings, establish a proper atmosphere of entertainment and relaxation that serves as a kind of fore-play, and then proceed to the crucial moment of possession. Even Carroll's list of 107 names of girls "photographed or to be photographed" fits into this pattern of seduction and possession. In a letter to Gertrude Thom-son a year before he died Carroll playfully writes of his potential models as "victims": "Your description of the sands, and the naked children playing there, is very tempting, and I might *possibly* make an expedi-tion there, some day . . . , on the chance of getting some picturesque victims to sketch." He goes on to ask Gertrude to photograph a nude girl for him: "And if you chance to make friends with any exceptionally *nice* little nudity . . . who is willing to be victimized for my benefit, I will send you a book to give her."[19] Considering the likelihood that he never loved any woman in an adult fashion, it is not surprising that he should adopt the conventional procedures of the bachelor on the hunt for dealing with little girls who, after all, in Carroll's own words, comprised three-fourths of his life.

Whatever the driving forces behind Carroll's photography may have been, his work was well known and admired by his contemporary photographic artists. Only two years after he purchased his first camera, in 1858, four of his pictures were shown in the fifth annual exhibition of the Photographic Society of London. In 1860 his reputation had grown to the point where the *Illustrated Times* asked him to write a review of that year's Photographic Society exhibition. As Cohen observes, Carroll's artistry consists in large part "in the way he manages, on the one hand, to break away from those who saw photography as a means of rivalling or imitating the art of painting, and, on the other hand, to keep his photographic art out of the fuzzy, unfocused realm of impressionism. He worked between these extremes, striving for and achieving a fidelity to human nature, a relaxed realism that distinguished his work."[20]

## Wizard of Math and Logic

Lewis Carroll was a competent but not an extraordinary mathematician. As a lecturer in Christ Church and as a tutor, he was concerned with elementary aspects of mathematics—arithmetic, algebra, trigonometry, plane and solid geometry, and less sophisticated portions of calculus and differential equations. Despite his devotion to math, however, his interest "was never coupled to a deep knowledge or a large natural talent." "Formal logic," Warren Weaver contends, "is the one subject to which Dodgson can be said to have made any real contribution."[21] W. W. Bartley, however, argues convincingly that Carroll's work in mathematical logic set him apart from his more traditional associates at Oxford and earned him a place in the history of logic. He contends that Carroll's *Symbolic Logic* (1896) "was the only logical work of any importance whatever to be produced at Oxford."[22] While most of his colleagues at Oxford were working out of the Aristotelian tradition, Carroll, according to Bartley, was closer in his approach to logical theory and practice to his contemporaries at Cambridge, such as John Venn, John Neville Keynes, and W. E. Johnson. Adopting the principles of the influential English mathematician and logician George Boole, Carroll attempted to popularize algebraic logic. As Bartley points out, it was the first and last such attempt, for after

1910, with the publication of Bertrand Russell's *Principia Mathematica,* studies in logic and mathematics were forever altered.[23]

Carroll appeared to view logic as a complex game, an attitude expressed in the title of his first book on the subject, *The Game of Logic.* As with his writing, his mathematics, when it stays on the orthodox side of Wonderland, is uninspired—but when he allows his bizarre imagination to take charge both his writing and mathematics come alive. As W. W. Bartley notes, "[*Symbolic Logic, Part 1*] was quite interesting but not innovative in a major way. . . . By contrast, Carroll's examples and exercises manifested genius. Here he has no rivals."[24] John Fisher makes a similar point, stating that Carroll possessed "a magician's instinct for tracking down the impossible," and that he "was able to supply something more than the straightforward academic approach to his studies in mathematics and logic."[25] His interest in baffling and mystifying others could be realized through the infinite means of these two fields of study. Ideas for games, puzzles, and riddles occupied his mind at all hours, and he recorded them in his books and essays throughout his life. Like mathematics itself, these games and puzzles provided Carroll with a psychic defense against an untidy, flawed, and disordered reality.

Games are games and most of them are not worth discussing here, for they have an anonymous sort of quality. There are, however, several examples that have the distinctive literary flavor of his nonsense books. *Dynamics of a parti-cle,* a small pamphlet of political satire published in 1865, contains some interesting mathematical puns. They are strikingly similar to those in the Mock Turtle's account of his education, when he studied Uglification, Distraction, and Derision. The first three definitions from this pamphlet give a flavor of Carroll's wit:

1. PLAIN SUPERFICIALITY is the character of a speech, in which any two points being taken, the speaker is found to lie wholly with regard to those two points.
2. PLAIN ANGER is the inclination of two voters to one another, who meet together, but whose views are not in the same direction.
3. When a Proctor, meeting another Proctor, makes the votes on one side equal to those on the other, the feeling entertained by each side is called RIGHT ANGER.[26]

*The Offer of the Clarendon Trustees,* published in 1868, proposes a number of additions at Oxford that would accommodate students in their mathematical calculations:

B. A piece of open ground for keeping Roots and practising their extraction: it would be advisable to keep Square Roots by themselves, as their corners are apt to damage others. . . .

E. A narrow strip of ground, railed off and carefully leveled, for investigating the properties of Asymptotes, and testing practically whether parallel Lines meet or not: for this purpose it should reach, to use the expressive language of Euclid, "ever so far."

This last process, of "continually producing the Lines," may require centuries or more: but such a period, though long in the life of an individual, is nothing in the life of the University.[27]

*Euclid and His Modern Rivals* further illustrates Carroll's fusion of mathematics with literary whimsy, a union clearly relevant to *Through the Looking-Glass*. Carroll's purpose in writing this book was to demonstrate that with only very slight changes Euclid is the best geometry book on the market. The form of his argument, however, is that of a five-act comedy. The opening scene presents the Mathematical Lecturer in the guise of Minos, talking to himself as he grades examination papers:

So, my friend! That's the way you prove I. 19 is it? Assuming I. 20? Cool, refreshingly cool! But stop a bit! Perhaps he doesn't "declare to win" on Euclid. Let's see. Ah, just so! "Legendre," of course! Well, I suppose I must give him full marks for it: what's the question worth?—Wait a bit, though! Where's his paper of yesterday? I've a very decided impression he was all for "Euclid" then: and I know the paper had I. 20, on it . . . Ah, here it is! "I think we know the sweet Roman hand." Here's the proposition, as large as life, and proved by I. 19. "Now, infidel, I have thee on the hip!" You shall have such a sweet thing to do in *viva-voce*, my very dear friend! You shall have the two propositions together and take them in any order you like. It's my profound conviction that you don't know how to prove either of them without the other. They'll have to introduce each other, like Messrs. Pyke and Pluck. But what a fearful confusion the whole subject is getting into![28]

The human or literary element that generates the "fearful confusion" is the life-giving force of this book, for it is constantly at war with the rigidity of a pure mathematical system. This is essentially the same battle that was waged by the supple, fallible Alice in a world of unyielding rules of logic and games.

In Scene ii, Minos sets out to review modern geometries without the aid of Euclid's mathematical discoveries:

*Min.:*   It will be weary work to do it all alone. And yet, I suppose you cannot, even with *your* supernatural powers, fetch me the authors themselves?

*Euc.:*   I dare not. The living human race is so strangely prejudiced. There is nothing men object to so emphatically as being transferred by ghosts from place to place. I cannot say they are consistent in this matter: they are forever "raising" or "laying" us poor ghosts—we cannot even haunt a garret without having the parish at our heels, bent on making us change our quarters: whereas if *I* were to venture to move one single boy—say to lift him by the hair of his head over only two or three houses, and to set him down safe and sound in a neighbour's garden—why, I give you my word, it would be the talk of the town for the next month!²⁹

Ghosts and the supernatural in a book on geometry! Euclid could as easily appear in *Phantasmagoria* or *Sylvie and Bruno.* His proposed elevation of the boy is comparable to Alice's lifting the White King to the table.

In act 2 the reader is introduced to Herr Niemand [nobody] in a manner clearly suggestive of the Cheshire Cat's entrance, grin first: "Minos sleeping: To him enter, first a cloud of tobaccco-smoke, secondly the bowl, and thirdly the stem of a gigantic meerschaum; fourthly the phantasm of Herr Niemand, carrying a pile of phantom-books, the works of Euclid's Modern Rivals, phantastically bound."³⁰

Before going on to a difficult discussion of a system of codifying the various methods of treating parallel lines, Carroll treats his reader to a madcap satire of the Association for the Improvement of Geometrical Teaching:

Enter a phantasmic procession, grouped about a banner, on which is emblazoned in letters of gold the title "Association for the Improvement of Things in General." Foremost in the line marches Nero, carrying his unfinished "Scheme for the Amelioration of Rome": while among the crowd which follows him may be noticed—Guy Fawkes, President of the "Association for raising the position of Members of Parliament"—The Marchioness de Brinvilliers, Foundress of the "Association for the Amendment of the Digestive Faculty"—and The Rev. F. Gustrell (the being who cut down Shakespeare's mulberry tree) leader of the "Association for the Refinement of Literary Taste." Afterwards enter on the other side, Sir Isaac Newton's little dog, "Diamond," carrying in his mouth a half-burnt roll of manuscript. He pointedly avoids the procession and the banner, and marches past alone, serene in the consciousness that he, single-pawed, conceived and carried out his great "Scheme for the Advancement of Mathematical Research," without the aid of any association whatever.[31]

The playfulness exhibited in Carroll's mathematical writings is even more forcefully apparent in his two small works on logic, *The Game of Logic* and *Symbolic Logic, Part 1.* R. B. Braithwaite has observed that "Carroll regarded formal and symbolic logic not as a systematic knowledge about valid thought nor yet as an art for teaching a person to think correctly, but as a game."[32] Carroll's procedure in *The Game of Logic* is to present not a series of facts, but a game for the reader to enter into. He proposes certain "universes" that contain all members of a certain class. Thus, there might be a "universe of Cakes," a "Universe of Hornets," or a "Universe of Dragons." With regard to the latter, Carroll declares: "Remember, I don't guarantee the Premises to be *facts*. In the first place, I never even saw a Dragon: and, in the second place, it isn't of the slightest consequence to us, as *Logicians,* whether our Premises are true or false: all *we* have to make out is whether they *lead logically to the Conclusion,* so that, if *they* were true, *it* would be true also."[33] Following the game logic of this passage we can more clearly understand the happy coexistence of such *Looking-Glass* creatures as the Rocking-horse fly, the Snap-dragon fly, and the Bread-and-butter-fly.

In *Symbolic Logic,* Carroll takes his argument a step further: "I maintain that any writer of a book is fully authorised in attaching any meaning he likes to any word or phrase he intends to use."[34] As he already noted, the accepted facts of logic vary according to logician. There is a clear relationship between the artificial and arbitrary system of logic advocated by Carroll in his books on logic and the closed system of play in such works as *The Hunting of the Snark.* The famous "Rule of Three," for example, is entirely consistent with Carroll's observations about premises and the adoption of one's own rule. The Bellman practiced what Carroll preached.

Carroll the mathematician and logician, then, is inseparable from Carroll the nonsense writer: the principles of order, logic, and gamesmanship hold the same for both. Nearly all of Carroll's jokes are jokes either in pure or applied logic. Some of the humor derives from the fact that a word or a phrase used in one particular context cannot be used in some other context "and the attractiveness of Carroll lies in the fact that his use of a phrase in an apparently correct but really non-sensical way appears as plausible to him as to the child."[35] Throughout his nonsense writings Carroll creates numerous personae to articulate his puns, paradoxes, and logical twists of thought. Listening to Humpty's statement, "When *I* use a word, it means just what I choose it to mean—neither more nor less," we realize that we are actually in the presence of a very self-conscious logician. Humpty Dumpty's definition of glory as "a nice knock-down argument" is notably defended in *Symbolic Logic,* a defense that serves as an important reminder that Lewis Carroll and Charles Dodgson are one and the same person.

## Miscellaneous Essays

Carroll wrote a number of essays on miscellaneous topics throughout his life. The limited range of his interests is reflected in the titles of some of these pieces: "Eight or Nine Wise Words about Letter Writing," "Three Years in a Curatorship," "Resident Women-Students," and "The New Belfry of Christ Church, Oxford." In the haven of Tom Quad, immersed in a world of mathematics, logic, nonsense, and children, Carroll spent little time worrying or writing about the great social and economic problems of his day.

Occasionally, however, something outside of academe would trigger a strong response from him as when, in 1875, a letter appeared in the *Spectator* on the subject of vivisection. A week later Carroll published a long letter in the *Pall Mall Gazette.* "Vivisection as a Sign of the Times" uses the subject of vivisection as a springboard to attack the new secular education made possible by the Education Act of 1870: "How far may vivisection be regarded as a sign of the times, and a fair specimen of that higher civilization which a purely secular State education is to give us?" He flatly rejects the logic that suggests that a nation's moral conduct will be improved through scientific education. Carroll himself had taken up the study of anatomy in 1872 after helplessly watching a man in convulsions. That sight may have led him to ask, "Can the man who has once realized by minute study what the nerves are, what the brain is, and what waves of agony one can convey to the other, go forth and wantonly inflict pain on any sentient being?" He comes to the conclusion that secular education without religious or moral training not only diminishes one's moral growth but actually encourages selfishness: "The world has seen and tired of the worship of Nature, of Reason, of Humanity; for this nineteenth century has been reserved the development of the most refined religion of all—the worship of Self." Selfishness is the keynote of all secular education and vivisection is "a glaring, a wholly unmistakable case in point." The nineteenth century will thus foster the unprincipled man of science who, "looking forth over a world which will then own no other sway than his, shall exult in the thought that he has made of this fair green earth, if not a heaven for man, at least a hell for animals."[36]

Four months after he published the preceding letter he wrote an article entitled "Some Popular Fallacies about Vivisection" for the *Fortnightly Review*. After considering man's right only to inflict a painless death upon an animal, Carroll proceeds to distinguish between killing for food and killing for knowledge. He contends that the effect of vivisection is more damaging to the scientist than to the animal: "The hapless animal suffers, dies, 'and there is an end': but the man whose sympathies have been deadened, and whose selfishness has been fostered, by the contemplation of pain deliberately inflicted, may be the parent of others equally brutalized, and so bequeath a curse to future ages." In this connection one may recall that the Baker, Carroll's most notorious hunter, was destroyed by the hunt. Carroll's thirteenth fallacy, however, is the most horrifying (and prophetic of the ghoulish experiments performed in the Nazi concentration camps): "*That the practice of vivisection will never be extended so as to include human subjects.*" He sees the day coming "when anatomy can claim as legitimate subject for experiment, first, our condemned criminals—next, perhaps, the inmates of our refuges for incurables—then the hopeless lunatic, the pauper hospital-patient, and generally 'him that hath no helper.'"[37]

Viewing a sound education in the liberal arts as the basis for a sane and humane society, Carroll's "Natural Science at Oxford," published in the *Pall Mall Gazette,* attacks the new emphasis upon science in the university curriculum. Almost crotchety in his conservatism, he complains that Latin and Greek may both vanish from the curriculum and that logic, philosophy, and history may follow. He fears the day when Oxford falls into the hands of those whose only education has been in science. This view is part of the more general issues of the time, especially the concern over the lack of morality in a scientific education. He also laments the decay of English language evident in much scientific writing. Having corrected some pages of the *Anthropological Review* for the press, he exclaims that he has never read "even in the 'local news' of a country paper, such slipshod, such deplorable English." As a general principle he argues that the exclusive study of any *one* subject does not really quite educate a person: "therefore it is that I seek to rouse an interest, beyond the limits of Oxford, in preserving classics as an essential feature of a University education."[38] This essay, taken with the two on vivisection, sets forth an argument similar to John Henry Newman's in *The Idea of a University.* Newman had argued that "to give undue prominence to one [branch of knowledge] is to be unjust to another,"[39] and, of course, had demanded the inclusion of religion and morality in his idea of the liberal arts.

Carroll's essay "Feeding the Mind" arose out of an illness he experienced in July 1883. He diagnosed his malady as "a sort of ague, with cystitis" and noted that he suffered "two miserable feverish nights, in a state between waking and sleeping, and worrying over the same idea (something about Common Room ledgers) over and over again."[40] During this period he spent many hours lying on his sofa reading novels. This experience led him to see that the mind must be trained and nourished no less than the body—for never before did he abandon himself so completely to the reading of fiction.

"Feeding the Mind" was originally planned as a lecture that Carroll delivered for W. H. Draper, vicar of Alfreton, in September 1884. Although Carroll suffered another attack of feverish ague while he was at Alfreton, he nevertheless dutifully delivered his promised lecture. The Reverend Draper noted Carroll's "nervous, highly strung manner as he stood before the little room full of simple people"[41] to speak on the importance of feeding the mind. A delightful talk, characteristic of Carroll's whimsy, it was not published until 1907.

The metaphor of food, which unifies the essay, was probably suggested to Carroll by Francis Bacon's essay "On Studies," in which Bacon argued that some books are to be tasted, others to be chewed, and still others to be swallowed and digested. Carroll imagines a dialogue that might ensue were one able to take his mind to be examined by a physician:

"Why, what have you been doing with this mind lately? How have you fed it? It looks pale, and the pulse is very slow."

"Well, doctor, it has not had much regular food lately. I gave it a lot of sugar-plums yesterday."

"Sugar-plums! What kind?"

"Well, they were a parcel of conundrums, sir."

"Ah, I thought so. Now just mind this: if you go on playing tricks like that, you'll spoil all its teeth, and get laid up with mental indigestion. You must have nothing but the plainest reading for the next few days. Take care now! No novels on any account."[42]

One is clearly reminded in this passage of Carroll's illness and his subsequent indulgence in novel reading. It was not atypical of a Victorian gentleman, especially one reared in a religious household, to consider the reading of novels as a frivolous, if not sinful, activity. There is no indication that Carroll considered novels to be serious works of art. His own reading was usually carefully balanced: novels were a mere spice to a diet of mathematical, logical, technical, and theological writings. He goes on to say that the effects of reading "the unwholesome novel" are "low spirits, unwillingness to work, weariness of existence—in fact . . . mental nightmare."[43] He makes novel reading sound as detrimental as lotus eating.

This Calvinistic turn of mind is further demonstrated by his belief that the mind should be nimble and athletic (not unlike the disciplined bodies of the young boys in Arnold's Rugby School). He ponders the idea of mental gluttony: "I wonder if there is such a thing in nature as a FAT MIND? I really think I have met with one or two: minds which could not keep up with the slowest trot in conversation; could not jump over a logical fence, to save their lives; always got stuck fast in a narrow argument; and, in short, were fit for nothing but to waddle helplessly through the world."[44] Carroll's body, like his mind, was trim and nimble throughout his life, and he obviously views fat minds, like fat people, as self-indulgent and comical.

Finally, one can see from this essay Carroll's compulsive orderliness as he ridicules the thoroughly well-read man who cannot organize his learning well enough to respond to simple questions: "all this for want of making up his knowledge into proper bundles and ticketing them."[45] One is pleased to remember that the Baker, in *The Hunting of the Snark,* "had forty-two boxes, all carefully packed, / With his name painted clearly on each: / But, since he omitted to mention the fact, / They were all left behind on the beach." And so, it seems, even a well-fed, orderly mind like the Baker's is only an asset insofar as it does not exhibit the classical professorial malady, absentmindedness.

## Chapter Seven
# Surviving the Critics

*Alice's Adventures in Wonderland* is one of the world's most translated books, and Carroll is one of the world's most quoted authors. The characters he created have lived in the imaginations of his audience to an extent unattained by any other English writer save Shakespeare, Dickens, and Conan Doyle. This vast popularity of his works has made the role of the critic a difficult one. There has been and still is a feeling that any serious evaluation of Alice and her friends is inherently ridiculous and results in an unintentional parody of criticism and scholarship. This attitude is clearly expressed in John Fisher's edition of Carroll's puzzles, *The Magic of Lewis Carroll* (1973):

This volume has been an attempt to bring forward some of the magic and fun of Lewis Carroll smothered by the spate of serious criticism and analysis of the author that has gushed forth in recent years. Academics, often earnestly seizing upon the *Alice* books as a coat-hanger for their own fantasies, have variously interpreted Carroll's representation of Alice Liddell as pastoral swain and phallic symbol, as Jungian anima and the first acid-head in children's literature; have laid bare the books themselves as allegories of philosophical systems and Darwinian evolution, of the Oxford Movement and Victorian toilet training.[1]

It is precisely this antiintellectual attitude that led Edmund Wilson, in 1932, to write: "If the Lewis Carroll centenary has produced anything of special interest, I have failed to see it. C. L. Dodgson was a most interesting man and deserves better of his admirers, who revel in his delightfulness and cuteness but do not give him any serious attention."[2] Since 1932 Carroll has received volumes of serious critical attention, some of it brilliant, some of it bad. It is certainly debatable to argue that "the spate of serious criticism" has "smothered" the fun of Carroll's writings. Fun is an intellectual as well as an imaginative exercise, as exemplified by the very puzzles and riddles Mr. Fisher has collected. The psychoanalytical perspective of Phyllis Greenacre, the linguistic analysis of Elizabeth Sewell, and the biographical discussions of Morton Cohen are all intellectually stimulating. If, as Plato has said, the unexamined life is not worth living, then perhaps the unexamined *Alice* is not worth rereading. Not all of the critical approaches are compatible, but most of them provide insights and explanations that enrich one's reading of the works themselves. Carroll's books have come of critical age and the public no longer requires the paternalistic defense of Carroll admirers who view Freud and Jung, allegorists and formalists, biographers and psychoanalysts as dangerous enemies of enjoyment. Samuel Johnson and G. Wilson Knight have not diminished the comic stature of Falstaff any more than William Empson and Phyllis Greenacre have tarnished the joys of Wonderland.

The danger in Carrollian criticism, as in all interpretation, is the possessive spirit of the critic who presumes to offer a definitive reading or interpretation. The early allegorical interpretations of *The Hunting of the Snark,* for example, use the text of the poem as a jumping-off point from which to construct parallel narratives, presumably encoded in the original. The notion that there is a hidden key to the poem appears to close rather than open the work to analysis. Even the eclectic critic, therefore, must reject such rigid and closed readings as aesthetically damaging and intellectually untenable. One must boldly assert that the Snark is not the atomic bomb, that the Boojum is not a symbol of a business slump, and that the whole poem is not an antivivisectionist tract. The recent existential, linguistic, and psychoanalytical readings of the *Snark,* however, do manage to offer insights into the work without closing off other interpretations. With these less presumptive critical approaches, one may pick the most appealing blossoms from among the burrs and brambles of Carroll's growing critical garden.

The psychoanalytical readings of the *Alice* books do not purport to exhaust their "meaning" but to explain why some things appear there as they do. To view the sea of tears in which Alice swims as the amniotic fluid bathing the fetus is not to preclude seeing it as Lethe. Alice can be the anima, the genteel Victorian child, the swain, and the eternal ingenue all at once. Although some of the Freudian critics imply a psychological allegory (girl = phallus, rabbit hole = vagina), they are primarily concerned with the *Alice* books as revelations of the author's subconscious mind, and are thereby a different breed from the critics who impose a rigid conscious allegory upon the works. Anyone who is amused with Humpty Dumpty's ability to interpret "all the poems that ever were invented—and a good many that haven't been invented just yet" ought to welcome and relish "the spate of serious criticism" that has "gushed forth." The flood of criticism is a clear sign that Alice is alive and well. Here is what Carroll himself, writing about *The Hunting of the Snark,* has to say on the subject. "Still, you know, words mean more than we mean to express when we use them; so a whole book ought to mean a great deal more than the writer means. So whatever good meanings are in the book, I'm glad to accept as the meaning of the book."[3] This is a remarkably modern insight that anticipates the concept of the intentional fallacy set forth by the twentieth-century critic W. K. Wimsatt.

## Alice's Survival

Alice is no more the property of the critics than she is of Lewis Carroll. She has been adopted and adapted by all people in practically every country of the world. Alice and the other characters of Wonderland and Looking-Glass Land have appeared on biscuit tins, playing cards, and greeting cards; have been shaped into glass and silver figurines; and have shown up in puppet shows and professional stage plays and on film and television.

Carroll himself encouraged the popularization of the *Alice* stories by granting permission for several stage performances based upon *Alice's Adventures in Wonderland* as well as for an operetta by Savile Clarke in 1886. He also worked closely with his publisher in seeing his stories translated into other languages. Afraid of exploitation of his success, he wrote to Macmillan asking that the two *Alice* books be copied out in dramatic form and be duly registered as two dramas. Over the years, however, he discovered that he had little legal control over adaptations as *Alice* quickly became available to an ever increasing audience. In 1898 the *Pall Mall Gazette* took a survey of the popularity of children's books, and *Alice's Adventures in Wonderland* led them all. In our own day the *Alice* stories are available in countless children's versions, not to mention the many paperback editions of the complete tales. They have been translated into numerous languages, from Swedish to Swahili, making Alice a universal emblem of childhood.

In 1933 Paramount produced a version of *Wonderland* with W. C. Fields as Humpty Dumpty, Cary Grant as the Mock Turtle, and Gary Cooper as the White Knight. In 1951 Walt Disney's animated version made its disappointing appearance, with the voices of Ed Wynn as the Hatter, Sterling Holloway as the Cheshire Cat, Jerry Colonna as the

March Hare, and Kathryn Beaumont as Alice. In both the redrawing and retelling of the original, Disney produced a sentimental adaptation that appeals primarily to children. Jonathan Miller's 1972 live-action production features *Punch* editor Malcolm Muggeridge as the Gryphon, Sir Michael Redgrave as the Caterpillar, and Peter Sellers as the March Hare. Surpassing these earlier versions is the 1988 film *Alice* by the Czech animator Jan Svankmajer. Alice, played by a little girl named Kristyna Kohoutova, moves in a claustrophic world of puppet figures and animated objects rebelling against her attempts to order her small world.

Among the notable dramatic adaptations of *Wonderland* are those by Eva le Gallienne and Florida Friebus at the Civic Repertory Theatre in 1932, by Clemence Dane in 1943 at the Scala Theatre in London, and Andre Gregory's *Alice* in 1970, in New York. Edward Albee's *Tiny Alice* (1964) is also indebted to Carroll. There have also been several musical renditions, including an Afro-American soul musical in New York, and, of course, Deems Taylor's *Through the Looking-Glass*. Employing the style and setting of the old music hall, Joseph Papp produced a stunningly creative musical for television in 1981. Starring Meryl Streep as Alice, who is supported by a small repertory group who take on the roles of the various other characters, *Alice at the Palace* incorporated various musical styles—ranging from country-western and mock-flamenco to soul music and rock.

The *Alice* books have provided the world with an inexhaustible fairy tale. There are simply too many aspects of Alice for them ever to be finally dramatized, illustrated, or explicated. In his art Carroll has achieved a purity that, in the words of Edmund Wilson, "is almost unique in a period so cluttered and cumbered, in which even the preachers of doom to the reign of materialism bore the stamp and stain of the industrial system in the hard insistence of their sentences and in the turbidity of their belchings of rhetoric. They have shrunk now, but *Alice* still stands."[4]

## The Legacy of Play

Although Carroll is primarily remembered for the enormous success and unique artistry of the *Alice* books, his other works have also proven to be of lasting value. *The Hunting of the Snark, Euclid and His Modern Rivals, Rhyme? and Reason?, A Tangled Tale, The Game of Logic, Sylvie and Bruno, Sylvie and Bruno Concluded, Symbolic Logic,* and *Three Sunsets and Other Poems* display an extraordinary intelligence and creativity. Each of these volumes, like the *Alice* books, affirms a similar thesis: the inestimable value of play, an activity that releases man from mechanical routine and enhances his human spirit. In a letter to one of his child friends Carroll wrote: "Do you ever play at games? Or is your idea of life 'breakfast, lessons, dinner, lessons, tea, lessons, bed, lessons, breakfast, lessons,' and so on? It is a very neat plan of life, and almost as interesting as being a sewing-machine or a coffee-grinder."[5] Games, like laughter, remind us of our humanity in so far as they free us of mechanical routine. Logic, to Carroll, is essentially a game. Euclid is a comic character in a drama (*Euclid and His Modern Rivals*) as well as a propounder of axioms. The Snark hunters are involved in an elaborate hunt that entails the observance of the rules and regulations of a game. The object of that game is to capture a Snark. The players are told the five unmistakable signs of a Snark and the precise method of seeking it out (with thimbles, care, forks, and hope). The freedom and spontaneity of the players are carefully controlled and limited by the arbitrary set of rules.

The view of life as a game is essentially a comic (not frivolous) one, and such a view, with its focus upon objectivity and upon spontaneity within rigidly defined limits, arouses and engages our human instincts. When Carroll brought together his intellect and playfulness "he made structures so complex and entire that, for whatever reason we come to them, and whatever we take from them, we can be held within them simply by the pleasure of watching Dodgson playing, this time, with the stuff of his very life, and at the very top of his game."[6]

Behind all of the writings is his sense of life as an enormous puzzle, one to be worked at to the end, and one never completely to be solved. Writing to his brother Skeffington, who invited him to preach a sermon in Worcester (in 1893), Carroll said: "I am glad to take opportunities of saying 'words for God,' which one *hopes* may prove of some use to somebody. I always feel that a sermon is worth the preaching, if it has given *some* help to even *one* soul in the puzzle of Life."[7] Judith Bloomingdale's view of Carroll reinforces this idea: "As Jung has also stated, the man possessed by the *anima* sees all of life as a game or puzzle. This perception seems to be the missing link between the two personalities of Charles Dodgson and Lewis Carroll."[8] It is little wonder, then, that such men as Ludwig Wittgenstein and James Joyce were drawn to Carroll's writings, for in them they discovered a sophisticated play with language and an attempt to create a self-contained world of words, an attempt that would distil the essence of civilized play and human understanding. If the puzzle of life could not be solved, at least one could create his own universe, complex but regulated, puzzling but rational. Joyce has thus appropriately addressed Carroll in *Finnegans Wake* as "Dodgfather, Dodgson and Coo,"[9] Dodgson as Father, Son, and Holy Spirit.

His nonsense makes him "a central figure, as important for England, and in the same way, as Mallarme is for France."[10] Such authors as T. S. Eliot, James Joyce, Franz Kafka, and Wallace Stevens are all practitioners of nonsense. They owe a debt of gratitude to Carroll for his daring confrontation with the absurd and his creative and comic triumph over its devastating implications. Carroll was a modernist in his sense of the absurd, in his surrealist drawings and conceptions, and in his realization of the paradoxical force of language—a force that liberates the human spirit but that ultimately fails to transcend the confines of the imagination in its attempt to engage an outer reality.

Carroll's unique vision of the world has now been assumed into our own dream life, our imaginations, and our popular culture. Unlike the above named authors, Carroll's writings appeal to a wide audience. Sophisticated novelists, poets, playwrights, and critics, along with the general reader and the millions of people who have seen versions of his work on film, at the theater, and on television all share in the fascination and entertainment provided by his vision of an alien, disorienting, and absurd world made comfortable by the grace of wit and laughter.

# Notes and References

*Chapter One*

1. Preface to *The Selected Letters of Lewis Carroll,* ed. Morton N. Cohen (New York: Pantheon Books, 1982), x.
2. *The Letters of Lewis Carroll,* ed. Morton N. Cohen, 2 vols. (New York: Oxford University Press, 1979), 184.
3. Quoted in Stuart Dodgson Collingwood, *The Life and Letters of Lewis Carroll* (London: T. Fisher Unwin, 1898), 8.
4. Phyllis Greenacre, *Swift and Carroll: A Psychoanalytic Study of Two Lives* (New York: International Universities Press, 1955), 217.
5. Florence B. Lennon, *Victoria through the Looking-Glass: The Life of Lewis Carroll* (London: Cassell, 1947), 14.
6. *The Annotated Alice: "Alice's Adventures in Wonderland" and "Through the Looking-Glass,"* ed. Martin Gardner (New York: Clarkson N. Potter, 1960), 308.
7. Lennon, *Victoria through the Looking-Glass,* 22.
8. *Letters,* 2:1154.
9. Quoted in Derek Hudson, *Lewis Carroll: An Illustrated Biography* (New York: New American Library, 1977), 38.
10. *The Diaries of Lewis Carroll,* ed. Roger Lancelyn Green, 2 vols. (London: Cassell, 1953), 1:9–10.
11. Ibid., 10.
12. *The Rectory Umbrella and Mischmasch,* with a foreword by Florence Milner (New York: Dover, 1971), 8; hereafter cited in the text.
13. Ibid., vi.
14. *Diaries,* 1:12.
15. Quoted in Hudson, *Lewis Carroll,* 52.
16. Ibid., 55.
17. Ibid., 59.
18. *Letters,* 1:17.
19. Ibid., 26.
20. Hudson, *Lewis Carroll,* 71.
21. *Diaries,* 1:50.
22. Ibid., 70.
23. Ibid., 77–78.
24. Ibid., 78.
25. Ibid., 79.
26. Ibid., 86.
27. Helmut Gernsheim, *Lewis Carroll, Photographer* (New York: Chan-

ticleer Press, 1949), 28. The Gernsheim Collection of Lewis Carroll's photograph albums resides at the Humanities Research Center at the University of Texas.

28. *Diaries,* 1:125.
29. *Letters,* 1:151, fn 1.
30. Ibid., 152–53.
31. Hudson, *Lewis Carroll,* 101.
32. *Diaries,* 1:83.
33. Ibid., 111.
34. *Letters,* 1:44.
35. Ibid., 116.
36. *Diaries,* 1:181–82.
37. Ibid., 182.
38. Ibid., 230–31.
39. *Letters,* 1:520n.
40. Quoted in Hudson, *Lewis Carroll,* 124.
41. Ibid.
42. Jeffrey Stern, "Lewis Carroll the Pre-Raphaelite 'Fainting in Coils,'" in *Lewis Carroll Observed,* ed. Edward Guiliano (New York: Clarkson N. Potter, 1982), 167–68.
43. Ibid., 171.
44. Ibid., 178.
45. *Letters,* 2:902.
46. *Letters,* 1:86.
47. "Journal of a Tour in Russia in 1867," *The Works of Lewis Carroll,* ed. Roger Lancelyn Green (Feltham: Spring Books, 1965), 968; hereafter cited in the text.
48. Hudson, *Lewis Carroll,* 142.
49. Lennon, *Victoria through the Looking-Glass,* 152.
50. *Diaries,* 2:263.
51. Quoted in Collingwood, *The Life and Letters of Lewis Carroll,* 131.
52. Anne Clark, *Lewis Carroll* (London: J. M. Dent, 1979), 161.
53. *Letters,* 1:94.
54. *Diaries,* 2:272.
55. Quoted in Hudson, *Lewis Carroll,* 180.
56. *Letters,* 1:373.
57. *Letters,* 2:807–8.
58. *Diaries,* 2:501.
59. Ibid., 400.
60. Ibid., 411.
61. Hudson, *Lewis Carroll,* 200.
62. *Letters,* 2:719.
63. Hudson, *Lewis Carroll,* 203.

64. Ibid., 204.
65. *Diaries*, 2:445.
66. "*Alice* on the Stage," *Works of Lewis Carroll*, ed. Roger Lancelyn Green, 237.
67. *Diaries*, 2:469.
68. *Athenaeum* (4 January 1890), 11–12.
69. *Letters*, 1:337.
70. *Letters*, 2:821–22.
71. *Diaries*, 2:501.
72. *Letters*, 2:1100.
73. Ibid., 1155.
74. Ibid., 1155–56.
75. Quoted in Cohen, *Selected Letters*, 283.

*Chapter Two*

1. Donald Rackin, "Blessed Rage: Lewis Carroll and the Modern Quest for Order," in *Lewis Carroll: A Celebration* (New York: Clarkson N. Potter, 1982), 15.
2. Ibid., 16.
3. *The Humorous Verse of Lewis Carroll* (New York: Dover, 1960), 404. All of the poems in section 1 are from this book; page numbers will be cited in the text.
4. John Skinner, "Lewis Carroll's Adventures in Wonderland," in *Aspects of Alice,* ed. Robert Phillips (New York: Vanguard, 1971), 299.
5. Derek Hudson, *Lewis Carroll: An Illustrated Biography* (New York: New American Library), 159.
6. Alexander L. Taylor, *The White Knight* (London: Oliver and Boyd, 1952), 31.
7. Collingwood, *The Life and Letters of Lewis Carroll*, 355.
8. See Morton Cohen, "The Actress and the Don: Ellen Terry and Lewis Carroll," in *Lewis Carroll: A Celebration*, 1–14.
9. Elizabeth Sewell, *The Field of Nonsense* (London: Chatto and Windus, 1952).
10. Ibid., 20.
11. Ibid., 112.
12. Ibid., 113.
13. W. H. Auden, "Today's 'Wonder-World' Needs Alice," in *Aspects of Alice,* 6.
14. *The Humorous Verse of Lewis Carroll*, 10–11.
15. Sewell, *The Field of Nonsense*, 96.
16. *The Humorous Verse of Lewis Carroll*, 7–8.
17. Greenacre, *Swift and Carroll*, 214.

18. *The Rectory Umbrella and Mischmasch,* 96–103.

19. Gardner, *The Annotated Alice,* 159.

20. Ibid., 159.

21. Ibid., 158.

22. *The Rectory Umbrella and Mischmasch,* 136–39.

23. Ibid., 143–47.

24. *The Humorous Verse of Lewis Carroll,* 44–46.

25. Gardner, *The Annotated Alice,* 311.

26. "Phantasmagoria," *The Humorous Verse of Lewis Carroll,* 115–157. Subsequent references to this poem will be indicated by page number in the text.

27. *Letters,* 1:413.

28. Ibid., 7.

29. Ibid., 471–72.

30. All of the poems quoted below are from Gardner, *The Annotated Alice*; subsequent page references will be cited in the text.

31. John Ciardi, "A Burble through the Tulgey Wood," in *Aspects of Alice,* 258.

32. Sewell, *The Field of Nonsense,* 100–101.

33. Donald Rackin, "Alice's Journey to the End of Night," *PMLA* 81 (October 1966):324.

34. Gardner, *The Annotated Alice,* 140.

35. Gardner, *The Annotated Alice,* 192.

36. Sewell, *The Field of Nonsense,* 118.

37. Ibid., 119–20.

38. Ibid., 122.

39. Michael Holquist, "What is a Boojum? Nonsense and Modernism," in *Alice in Wonderland,* ed. Donald J. Gray, Norton Critical Edition (New York: Norton, 1971), 412.

40. Taylor, *The White Knight,* 80.

41. Ibid., 80–81.

42. Gardner, *The Annotated Alice,* 197.

43. Ibid., 235.

44. Ibid., 237.

45. Sewell, *The Field of Nonsense,* 113.

46. Gardner, *The Annotated Alice,* 333.

47. "*Alice* on the Stage," *Works of Lewis Carroll,* 235–36.

48. *Athenaeum* (8 April 1876), 495.

49. "*Alice* on the Stage," *Works of Lewis Carroll,* 236.

50. The above readings of the poem are cited in *The Annotated Snark,* ed. Martin Gardner (New York: Simon and Schuster, 1962), 19–20.

51. Auden, "Today's 'Wonder-World' Needs Alice," in *Aspects of Alice,* 3–12.

52. In *Alice in Wonderland* (Norton Critical Edition), 404–5.

53. Ibid., 412–16.

54. Ibid., 417.

55. Gardner, *The Annotated Snark,* 56; page numbers for subsequent quotations will be cited in the text.

56. Greenacre, *Swift and Carroll,* 244:45.

57. Gardner, *The Annotated Snark,* 23.

58. Edward Guiliano, "A Time for Humor: Lewis Carroll, Laughter and Despair, and *The Hunting of the Snark,*" in *Lewis Carroll: A Celebration,* 130.


*Chapter Three*

1. Hudson, *Lewis Carroll: An Illustrated Biography,* 128.

2. Taylor, *The White Knight.*

3. William Empson, "*Alice in Wonderland*: The Child as Swain," in *Some Versions of Pastoral* (New York: New Directions, 1960), 241–82.

4. Donald Rackin, "Alice's Journey to the End of Night," 313–26.

5. These quotations are cited in *Diaries,* 1:236–37.

6. *Athenaeum* (16 December 1865), 844.

7. Elsie Leach, "*Alice in Wonderland* in Perspective," in *Aspects of Alice,* 89–90.

8. Quoted in Gardner's introduction to *The Annotated Snark,* 11.

9. Jan B. Gordon, "The *Alice* Books and the Metaphors of Victorian Childhood," in *Aspects of Alice,* 94.

10. Gardner, *The Annotated Alice,* 26; page numbers for subsequent quotations will be cited in the text.

11. Empson, *Some Versions of Pastoral,* 256–57.

12. Lennon, *Victoria through the Looking-Glass,* 123.

13. Gardner, *The Annotated Alice,* 30.

14. Gordon, "The *Alice* Books and the Metaphors of Victorian Childhood," in *Aspects of Alice,* 102.

15. James R. Kincaid, "Alice's Invasion of Wonderland," *PMLA* 88 ( January 1973): 96.

16. Nina Auerbach, "Alice in Wonderland: A Curious Child," *Victorian Studies* 17 (September 1973): 46–47.

17. Empson, *Some Versions of Pastoral,* 255.

18. Rackin, "Alice's Journey to the End of Night," 316.

19. Empson, *Some Versions of Pastoral,* 260.

20. Gardner, *The Annotated Alice,* 48.

21. Empson, *Some Versions of Pastoral,* 259.

22. Ibid., 258.

23. Rackin, "Alice's Journey to the End of Night," 320.

24. Elizabeth Sewell, *The Field of Nonsense,* 113.

25. Roger W. Holmes, "The Philosopher's *Alice in Wonderland,*" in *Aspects of Alice,* 161.

26. Rackin, "Alice's Journey to the End of Night," 321.

27. Leach, *"Alice in Wonderland* in Perspective," in *Aspects of Alice,* 91–92.

28. Ibid., 92. Carroll was obviously fascinated by *Goody Two Shoes,* for in 1873 and 1877 he attended several theatrical productions in which children acted out the story in pantomime.

29. Empson, *Some Versions of Pastoral,* 263–64.

30. Rackin, "Alice's Journey to the End of Night," 324.

31. Shane Leslie, "Lewis Carroll and the Oxford Movement," in *Aspects of Alice,* 216.

32. Leach, *"Alice in Wonderland* in Perspective," 92.

33. Rackin, "Blessed Rage: Lewis Carroll and the Modern Quest for Order," in *Lewis Carroll: A Celebration,* 18.

34. Quoted in Collingwood, *The Life and Letters of Lewis Carroll,* 142.

35. Gordon, "The *Alice* Books and the Metaphors of Victorian Childhood," in *Aspects of Alice,* 111.

36. Holmes, "The Philosopher's *Alice in Wonderland,*" in *Aspects of Alice,* 169.

37. Ibid., 170.

38. Patricia Spacks, "Logic and Language in *Through the Looking-Glass,*" in *Aspects of Alice,* 269.

39. Taylor, *The White Knight,* 101.

40. Gardner, *The Annotated Alice,* 172.

41. Taylor, *The White Knight,* 98.

42. Gardner elaborates upon some of these techniques in *The Annotated Alice,* 180–83.

43. Empson, *Some Versions of Pastoral,* 271.

44. See Empson, *Some Versions of Pastoral,* for a fuller treatment of the theme of the nineteenth-century child's relationship to nature.

45. Gardner, *The Annotated Alice,* 239.

46. Empson, *Some Versions of Pastoral,* 277.

47. *Lewis Carroll's Symbolic Logic,* ed. William Warren Bartley (New York: Clarkson N. Potter, 1977), 232.

48. J. B. Priestley, "A Note on Humpty Dumpty," in *Aspects of Alice,* 264.

49. Judith Bloomingdale, "Alice as *Anima*: The Image of Woman in Carroll's Classic," in *Aspects of Alice,* 388.

50. Empson, *Some Versions of Pastoral,* 253.

51. Rackin, "Love and Death in Carroll's *Alices,*" in *Soaring with the Dodo: Essays on Lewis Carroll's Life and Art,* eds. Edward Guiliano and James R. Kincaid (New York: The Lewis Carroll Society of North America, 1982), 27.

52. Ibid., 41.

53. Ibid., 43.

54. Gardner, *The Annotated Alice,* 296.

55. *Letters,* 1:441.

56. Lionel Morton, "Memory in the *Alice* Books," *Nineteenth-Century Fiction* 33 (December 1978): 299.

57. Ibid., 304.

58. Tenniel's letter to Carroll is reprinted in facsimile in *The Wasp in a Wig: A "Suppressed" Episode of "Through the Looking-Glass and What Alice Found There,"* ed. Martin Gardner (New York: The Lewis Carroll Society of North America, 1977), xii–xiv.

59. Ibid., 3.

60. Ibid., 5.

61. Ibid., 13. Subsequent quotations from "The Wasp in a Wig" are taken from the edition above and will be cited in the text.

62. Robert Dupree, "The White Knight's Whiskers and the Wasp's Wig in *Through the Looking-Glass,"* in *Lewis Carroll: A Celebration,* 120.

63. Henri Bergson, "Laughter," in *Comedy,* introduced by Wylie Sypher (New York: Doubleday, 1956), 63; page numbers for subsequent quotations will be cited in the text.

*Chapter Four*

1. (London) *Times* (26 December 1865), 5.

2. See Michael Hancher, *The Tenniel Illustrations to the "Alice" Books* (Columbus: Ohio State University Press, 1985), 120–32.

3. Quoted in *Early Children's Books and Their Illustrators,* ed. Gerald Gottlieb (Boston: David Godine, 1975), 233.

4. Hancher, *The Tenniel Illustrations,* 27–34.

5. Hancher, *The Tenniel Illustrations,* 3–26.

6. Hancher, *The Tenniel Illustrations,* 103, 69–74, 41–47.

7. For a fuller discussion of the relationship between Carroll's text and Tenniel's illustrations, see my essay, "If you don't know what a Gryphon is: Text and Illustration in *Alice's Adventures in Wonderland,"* in *Lewis Carroll: A Celebration,* 62–74.

8. Hancher, *The Tenniel Illustrations,* 35.

9. This idea is suggested by Martin Gardner in *The Annotated Alice,* 124.

10. See *The Illustrators of "Alice in Wonderland" and "Through the Looking-Glass,"* ed. Graham Ovenden (New York: St. Martin's Press, 1972).

11. *Alice's Adventures in Wonderland* (London: Heinemann, 1907).

12. *Alice's Adventures in Wonderland* (New York: Dutton, 1929).

13. *Alice's Adventures in Wonderland* (New York: Random House / Maecenas, 1969).

14. *Alice's Adventures in Wonderland* (London: Dobson, 1967); *Through the Looking-Glass* (London: MacGibbon & Kee, 1972).

*Chapter Five*

    1. Preface to *Sylvie and Bruno,* in *The Works of Lewis Carroll,* ed. Roger Lancelyn Green, 379, 381.
    2. See *Lewis Carroll's Library,* ed. Jeffrey Stern (Silver Spring, Md.: The Lewis Carroll Society of North America, 1981).
    3. Preface to *Sylvie and Bruno Concluded,* in *Works of Lewis Carroll,* 539.
    4. Quoted in Collingwood, *The Life and Letters of Lewis Carroll,* 340.
    5. Preface to *Sylvie and Bruno Concluded,* 539.
    6. *Sylvie and Bruno,* in *Works of Lewis Carroll,* 533; quotations from both *Sylvie and Bruno* and *Sylvie and Bruno Concluded* are from the above edition, and subsequent page references will be cited in the text.
    7. Edmund Wilson, "C. L. Dodgson: The Poet Logician," in *Aspects of Alice,* 202.
    8. Lennon, *Victoria through the Looking-Glass,* 220.
    9. Ibid., 219.
    10. Ibid., 227.
    11. Ibid., 220.
    12. Edmund Miller, "The *Sylvie and Bruno* Books as Victorian Novel," in *Lewis Carroll Observed,* 136.
    13. Jean Gattegno, "*Sylvie and Bruno,* or the Inside Outside," in *Lewis Carroll: A Celebration,* 169.
    14. Ibid., 171.
    15. Jan. B. Gordon, "Lewis Carroll, the *Sylvie and Bruno* Books, and the Nineties," in *Lewis Carroll: A Celebration,* 181–82.
    16. Ibid., 184.
    17. Ibid., 185.
    18. Ibid., 187.
    19. Ibid., 191.
    20. Hudson, *Lewis Carroll: An Illustrated Biography,* 230.
    21. Greenacre, *Swift and Carroll,* 227.
    22. Ibid., 230
    23. Ibid., 211.
    24. *Lewis Carroll and the House of Macmillan,* eds. Morton N. Cohen and Anita Gandolfo (Cambridge: Cambridge University Press, 1987), 306.
    25. Wilson, "C. L. Dodgson: The Poet Logician," in *Aspects of Alice,* 203.
    26. Ibid., 202.
    27. Hudson, *Lewis Carroll,* 289.


*Chapter Six*

    1. Quoted in Collingwood, *The Life and Letters of Lewis Carroll,* 197.
    2. Sewell, *The Field of Nonsense,* 112.

3. Greenacre, *Swift and Carroll,* 212.

4. Ibid., 240.

5. Gernsheim, *Lewis Carroll, Photographer,* 16.

6. *Letters,* 2:1007.

7. Gernsheim, *Lewis Carroll, Photographer,* 21.

8. *Letters,* 1:253.

9. *Letters,* 2:947.

10. Quoted in Lennon, *Victoria through the Looking-Glass,* 317.

11. Morton Cohen, *Lewis Carroll, Photographer of Children: Four Nude Studies* (New York: Clarkson N. Potter, 1979), 6.

12. *Diaries,* 1:221.

13. *Letters,* 1:67.

14. Noted by Gernsheim, *Lewis Carroll, Photographer,* but this entry is omitted by Green in his edition of the *Diaries.*

15. *Diaries,* 2:359.

16. Ibid., 362.

17. Lennon, *Victoria through the Looking-Glass,* 165.

18. Evelyn Hatch, *A Selection from the Letters of Lewis Carroll to His Child Friends* (London: Macmillan, 1933), 3.

19. *Letters,* 2:1134–35.

20. Cohen, *Lewis Carroll, Photographer of Children,* 3–4.

21. Warren Weaver, "The Mathematical Manuscripts of Lewis Carroll," in *Alice In Wonderland,* ed. Donald J. Gray, Norton Critical Edition (New York: Norton, 1971), 291.

22. *Lewis Carroll's Symbolic Logic,* ed. William Warren Bartley (New York: Clarkson N. Potter, 1977), 30.

23. Ibid., 28–29.

24. Ibid., 29.

25. *The Magic of Lewis Carroll,* ed. John Fisher (New York: Simon and Schuster, 1973), 8.

26. *Works of Lewis Carroll,* ed. Roger Lancelyn Green, 908.

27. Ibid., 901–2.

28. *Euclid and His Modern Rivals* (New York: Dover, 1973), 1–2.

29. Ibid., 17.

30. Ibid., 54.

31. Ibid., 182–83.

32. R. W. Braithwaite, "Lewis Carroll as Logician," in *Alice in Wonderland* (Norton Critical Edition), 298.

33. *Mathematical Recreations of Lewis Carroll: "Symbolic Logic" and "The Game of Logic"* (New York: Dover, 1958), 25.

34. *Lewis Carroll's Symbolic Logic,* 232.

35. R. W. Braithwaite, "Lewis Carroll as Logician," 301–2.

36. *Works of Lewis Carroll,* 1089, 1090, 1092.

37. Ibid., 1099.

38. Ibid., 964.

39. John Henry Newman, *The Idea of a University* (New York: Longman's, Green, 1947), 88.

40. *Diaries,* 2:418.

41. Quoted in Hudson, *Lewis Carroll,* 284.

42. *Works of Lewis Carroll,* 1071.

43. Ibid., 1072.

44. Ibid., 1072.

45. Ibid., 1074.

*Chapter Seven*

1. *The Magic of Lewis Carroll,* 274.

2. Wilson, "C. L. Dodgson: The Poet Logician," in *Aspects of Alice,* 198.

3. Quoted in Gardner, *The Annotated Snark,* 17.

4. Wilson, "C. L. Dodgson: The Poet Logician," in *Aspects of Alice,* 202.

5. *Letters,* 1:333.

6. Donald J. Gray, introduction to *Alice in Wonderland* (New York: Norton, 1971), x–xi.

7. *Letters,* 2:946.

8. Judith Bloomingdale, "Alice as *Anima*: The Image of Woman in Carroll's Classic," in *Aspects of Alice,* 383.

9. James Joyce, *Finnegans Wake* (New York: Viking Press, 1939), 482.

10. Elizabeth Sewell, "Lewis Carroll and T. S. Eliot as Nonsense Poets," in *Aspects of Alice,* 119.

# Selected Bibliography

## PRIMARY WORKS

### Books

*Alice's Adventures in Wonderland*. London: Macmillan, 1866.

*Alice's Adventures under Ground, Being a Facsimile of the Original Ms. Book Afterwards Developed into "Alice's Adventures in Wonderland."* London and New York: Macmillan, 1886.

*Curiosa Mathematica, Part 1. A New Theory of Parallels*. London: Macmillan, 1888.

*Curiosa Mathematica, Part 2. Pillow Problems*. London: Macmillan, 1893.

*Euclid and His Modern Rivals*. London: Macmillan, 1879.

*The Game of Logic*. London: Macmillan, 1887.

*The Hunting of the Snark*. London: Macmillan, 1876.

*The Nursery Alice*. London: Macmillan, 1889.

*Phantasmagoria and Other Poems*. London: Macmillan, 1869.

*The Rectory Umbrella and Mischmasch*. Foreword by Florence Milner. New York: Dover, 1971.

*Rhyme? And Reason?* London: Macmillan, 1883.

*Sylvie and Bruno*. London and New York: Macmillan, 1889.

*Sylvie and Bruno Concluded*. London and New York: Macmillan, 1893.

*Symbolic Logic, Part 1*. London and New York: Macmillan, 1896.

*A Tangled Tale*. London: Macmillan, 1885.

*Three Sunsets and Other Poems*. London: Macmillan, 1898.

*Through the Looking-Glass, and What Alice Found There*. London: Macmillan, 1872.

### Diaries, Journals, and Letters

*The Diaries of Lewis Carroll*. Edited by Roger Lancelyn Green. 2 vols. London: Cassell, 1953.

*The Letters of Lewis Carroll*. Edited by Morton N. Cohen. 2 vols. New York: Oxford University Press, 1979.

*Lewis Carroll and the House of Macmillan*. Edited by Morton N. Cohen and Anita Gandolfo. New York: Cambridge University Press, 1987. Carroll's letters to his publisher.

*Lewis Carroll and the Kitchens.* Edited by Morton N. Cohen. New York: The
Lewis Carroll Society of North America, 1980. Twenty-five letters, nine-
teen photographs.

*The Russian Journal and Other Selections from the Works of Lewis Carroll.* Edited
by John Francis McDermott. New York: Dutton, 1935.

*The Selected Letters of Lewis Carroll.* Edited by Morton N. Cohen. New York:
Pantheon, 1982.

*A Selection from the Letters of Lewis Carroll to His Child Friends.* Edited by Evelyn
Hatch. London: Macmillan, 1933.

*Editions and Collections*

*Alice's Adventures in Wonderland: A Critical Handbook.* Edited by Donald
Rackin. Belmont, Calif.: Wadsworth Publishing, 1961. Reproduces the
Rosenbach facsimile of *Alice's Adventures under Ground* and the text of
*Alice's Adventures in Wonderland,* based upon a number of editions super-
vised by Carroll.

*Alice in Wonderland.* Edited by Donald J. Gray. Norton Critical Edition. New
York: Norton, 1971.

*The Annotated Alice: "Alice's Adventures in Wonderland" and "Through the Looking-
Glass."* Edited by Martin Gardner. New York: Clarkson N. Potter, 1960.

*The Annotated Snark.* Edited by Martin Gardner. New York: Simon and Schuster, 1962.

*The Collected Verse of Lewis Carroll.* London: Macmillan, 1932. Reprinted as
*The Humorous Verse of Lewis Carroll.* New York: Dover, 1960.

*The Lewis Carroll Picture Book. A Selection from the Unpublished Writings and
Drawings of Lewis Carroll.* Edited by Stuart Dodgson Collingwood. Lon-
don: T. Fisher Unwin, 1899. Reprinted in facsimile as *The Unknown
Lewis Carroll.* New York: Dover, 1961.

*Lewis Carroll's "The Hunting of the Snark."* Edited by James Tanis and John
Dooley. Los Altos, Calif.: William Kaufman, 1981. Centennial edition.

*Lewis Carroll's Symbolic Logic.* Edited by William Warren Bartley, III. New
York: Clarkson N. Potter, 1977.

*The Magic of Lewis Carroll.* Edited by John Fisher. New York: Simon and
Schuster, 1973. Carroll's games and puzzles.

*Mathematical Recreations of Lewis Carroll.* 2 vols. New York: Dover, 1958.
Volume 1 reprints *Symbolic Logic* and *The Game of Logic;* volume 2 reprints
*Pillow Problems* and *A Tangled Tale.*

*The Wasp in a Wig: A "Suppressed" Episode of "Through the Looking-Glass and
What Alice Found There."* Edited by Martin Gardner. New York: The
Lewis Carroll Society of North America, 1977.

*The Works of Lewis Carroll.* Edited by Roger Lancelyn Green. Feltham: Spring
Books, 1965.

## SECONDARY WORKS

*Collections of Criticism*

(Some of the essays from these collections are listed individually as well.)

Gray, Donald J., ed. *Alice in Wonderland.* New York: Norton Critical Edition, 1971. Contains nine critical essays.

Guiliano, Edward, ed. *Lewis Carroll: A Celebration.* New York: Clarkson N. Potter, 1982. Fifteen essays on the occasion of the 150th anniversary of Carroll's birth.

———, ed. *Lewis Carroll Observed.* New York: Clarkson N. Potter, 1976. A collection of unpublished photographs, drawings, and poetry by Carroll, and fifteen essays about his work.

Guiliano, Edward, and James R. Kincaid, eds. *Soaring with the Dodo.* New York: The Lewis Carroll Society of North America, 1982. Ten essays on Carroll's life and art.

Phillips, Robert, ed. *Aspects of Alice: Lewis Carroll's Dreamchild as Seen Through the Critics' Looking-Glasses.* New York: Vanguard, 1971. The largest single collection of critical essays; includes a useful bibliography of items from 1865 through 1971.

Rackin, Donald, ed. *Alice's Adventures in Wonderland: A Critical Handbook.* Belmont, Calif.: Wadsworth Publishing, 1961. Contains eleven critical articles.

*Books and Parts of Books*

Auden, W. H. "Today's 'Wonder-World' Needs Alice." Reprinted in *Aspects of Alice,* 3–12. Alice is an adequate symbol for what every human being should try to be like.

Auerbach, Nina. "Falling Alice, Fallen Women, and Victorian Dream Children." In *Soaring with the Dodo,* 46–64. Sees Carroll's Victorian triumph in his amalgamation of the fallen woman with the unfallen child.

Bergson, Henri. "Laughter." In *Comedy,* introduction by Wylie Sypher, 61–190. New York: Doubleday, 1956. Analyzes the basic principles of humor.

Blake, Kathleen. *Play, Games and Sport: The Literary Works of Lewis Carroll.* Ithaca, N. Y.: Cornell University Press, 1974. Examines Carroll's philosophy of play.

Bloomingdale, Judith. "Alice as *Anima*: The Image of Woman in Carroll's Classic." In *Aspects of Alice,* 378–90. A Jungian study of Alice as Carroll's anima.

**Ciardi, John.** "A Burble Through the Tulgey Wood." Reprinted in *Aspects of Alice,* 253–61. Discusses three of the poems in the *Alice* books.

**Clark, Ann.** *Lewis Carroll.* London: J. M. Dent, 1979. A thorough, well-researched biography; sympathetic but lacking in analysis.

**Cohen, Morton N.** "The Actress and the Don: Ellen Terry and Lewis Carroll." In *Lewis Carroll: A Celebration,* 1–14. Argues that Carroll's relationship with the actress was one of affection, not romantic love.

————. *Lewis Carroll, Photographer of Children: Four Nude Studies.* New York: Clarkson N. Potter, 1979. The eagerly awaited first reproduction of Carroll's nude photos.

**Collingwood, Stuart Dodgson.** *The Life and Letters of Lewis Carroll.* London: T. Fisher Unwin, 1898. The standard family biography, by Carroll's nephew.

**Dupree, Robert.** "The White Knight's Whiskers and the Wasp's Wig in *Through the Looking-Glass.*" In *Lewis Carroll: A Celebration,* 112–22. Examines the hair motif in the story and argues that the Wasp in a Wig episode fits into the pattern.

**Empson, William.** *Some Versions of Pastoral,* 241–82. New York: New Directions, 1960. A Freudian reading of Alice as "swain."

**Gattegno, Jean.** *Lewis Carroll: Fragments of a Looking-Glass.* Translated by Rosemary Sheed. New York: Crowell, 1976. A potpourri of analytical snippets that probe Carroll's psychology. Stimulating, though highly speculative, readings.

————. "*Sylvie and Bruno,* or the Inside and the Outside." In *Lewis Carroll: A Celebration,* 167–75. Argues that Carroll brings together the two worlds of dream and reality in a mystical vision revealing that multiplicity is unity.

**Gernsheim, Helmut.** *Lewis Carroll, Photographer.* New York: Chanticleer Press, 1949. A comprehensive study of Carroll's photographic art, with sixty-four photographic plates.

**Gordon, Jan B.** "The *Alice* Books and the Metaphors of Victorian Childhood." In *Aspects of Alice,* 93–113. Argues that the *Alice* books are decadent adult literature.

————. "Lewis Carroll, the *Sylvie and Bruno* Books, and the Nineties: The Tyranny of Textuality." In *Lewis Carroll: A Celebration,* 176–94. Sees the three main themes of the novels as the relationships of the child to the man, the literal language of necessary texts to metaphoric language, and earth to heaven.

**Greenacre, Phyllis.** *Swift and Carroll: A Psychoanalytic Study of Two Lives.* New York: International Universities Press, 1955. The most intelligent and provocative psychoanalytic study of Carroll to date.

————. "A Time for Humor: Lewis Carroll, Laughter and Despair, and *The Hunting of the Snark.*" In *Lewis Carroll: A Celebration,* 123–31. Reads the *Snark* as the expression of Carroll's despair over the threat of nonexistence.

**Hancher, Michael.** *The Tenniel Illustrations to the "Alice Books."* Columbus:

Ohio State University Press, 1985. Traces the artistic roots of Tenniel's illustrations of the *Alice* books to his work for *Punch,* the paintings of various artists, photographs, and Carroll's own drawings.

Holmes, Roger W. "The Philosopher's *Alice in Wonderland.*" Reprinted in *Aspects of Alice,* 159–74. Discusses the reality of names, identity, and time.

Holquist, Michael. "What is a Boojum? Nonsense and Modernism." Reprinted in *Alice in Wonderland* [Norton Critical Edition], 402–18. Argues that *The Hunting of the Snark* can only be understood as a closed system of language.

Hudson, Derek. *Lewis Carroll: An Illustrated Biography.* New York: New American Library, 1978. The best biography to date, despite its defensive attitude towards psychological interpretations of Carroll's life and work.

Kelly, Richard. " 'If you don't know what a Gryphon is': Text and Illustration in *Alice's Adventures in Wonderland.*" In *Lewis Carroll: A Celebration,* 62–74. Examines the intimate relationship between Tenniel's drawings and Carroll's story.

Leach, Elsie. "*Alice in Wonderland* in Perspective." Reprinted in *Aspects of Alice,* 88–92. A study of *Alice in Wonderland* against the background of Victorian children's literature.

Lennon, Florence Becker. *Victoria through the Looking-Glass: The Life of Lewis Carroll.* London: Cassell, 1947. A somewhat disorganized study that contains much information found in no other biography and offers some excellent literary criticism and psychological insights.

Leslie, Shane. "Lewis Carroll and the Oxford Movement." Reprinted in *Aspects of Alice,* 211–19. Examines the *Alice* books as allegories of the Oxford Movement.

Miller, Edmund. "The *Sylvie and Bruno* Books as Victorian Novel." In *Lewis Carroll Observed,* 132–44. Sees the romance structure of Carroll's work as typical of Victorian novels.

Otten, Terry. "After Innocence: Alice in the Garden." In *Lewis Carroll: A Celebration,* 50–61. Views Alice's innocence as her ability to journey into Wonderland and her fallen nature as her inability to remain there.

Ovenden, Graham, ed. *The Illustrators of "Alice in Wonderland" and "Through the Looking-Glass."* New York: St. Martin's, 1972. Provides a good sampling of the drawings of various artists but a scanty and inadequate examination of their work.

Pitcher, George. "Wittgenstein, Nonsense, and Lewis Carroll." Reprinted in *Alice in Wonderland* [Norton Critical Edition], 387–402. Demonstrates that Wittgenstein and Carroll were both professionally concerned with nonsense.

Priestley, J. B. "A Note on Humpty Dumpty." Reprinted in *Aspects of Alice,* 262–66. Argues convincingly that Humpty Dumpty is a satire of the solemn literary pedant.

Pudney, John *Lewis Carroll and His World.* London: Thames and Hudson,

1976. A brief biography enriched with many illustrations and photographs.

**Rackin, Donald.** "Blessed Rage: Lewis Carroll and the Modern Quest for Order." In *Lewis Carroll: A Celebration,* 15–25. Views Carroll's writings as a search for a new coherent vision of the human condition.

————. "Laughing and Grief: What's So Funny About *Alice in Wonderland?*" In *Lewis Carroll Observed,* 1–18. Sees the comedy of the work arising from the tension between the reader as adult and the adult reader as child.

————. "Love and Death in Carroll's *Alices.*" In *Soaring with the Dodo,* 26–45. Argues that the *Alice* books are great and good because they rest upon the warm, fusing morality and sentiment cherished by Victorians and not because they entertain modern critics with their games and wit.

**Sewell, Elizabeth.** *The Field of Nonsense.* London: Chatto and Windus, 1952. A brilliant and influential study of the principles of nonsense, based upon logical and linguistic considerations.

————. "Lewis Carroll and T. S. Eliot as Nonsense Poets." Reprinted in *Aspects of Alice,* 119–26. Examines the principles of nonsense that are exhibited in the work of both Eliot and Carroll.

**Skinner, John.** "Lewis Carroll's Adventures in Wonderland." Reprinted in *Aspect of Alice,* 293–307. A psychoanalytic approach to Carroll's writings.

**Spacks, Patricia Meyer.** "Logic and Language in *Through the Looking-Glass.*" Reprinted in *Aspects of Alice,* 267–75. Argues that language is a theme that underlies virtually all of the episodes in *Through the Looking-Glass.*

**Stern, Jeffrey, ed.** *Lewis Carroll's Library.* Silver Spring, Md.: The Lewis Carroll Society of North America, 1981. Lists books in Carroll's personal library.

————. "Lewis Carroll the Surrealist." In *Lewis Carroll: A Celebration,* 132–53. Examines what is Carrollian about surrealism and what is surrealist about Carroll.

**Taylor, Alexander L.** *The White Knight.* London: Oliver and Boyd, 1952. Relates the *Alice* books to contemporary religious controversies.

*Tenniel's Alice: Drawings by Sir John Tenniel for "Alice's Adventures in Wonderland" and "Through the Looking-Glass."* Cambridge, Mass.: Harvard College Library and the Metropolitan Museum of Art, 1978. Reproduces many of Tenniel's pencil drawings and preliminary sketches.

**Weaver, Warren.** "The Mathematical Manuscripts of Lewis Carroll." Reprinted in *Alice in Wonderland* [Norton Critical Edition], 291–98. Contends that Carroll's mathematical writings are elementary but often enlivened through whimsy and nonsense.

**Williams, Sidney Herbert, and Falconer Madan, eds.** *The Lewis Carroll Handbook.* Revised by Roger Lancelyn Green; further revised by Denis Crutch. Kent, England: Dawson, 1979. A bilbiographic account of Carroll's writings and a history of their composition and development.

**Wilson, Edmund.** "C. L. Dodgson: The Poet Logician." Reprinted in *Aspects* *of Alice,* 198–206. A brilliant but brief commentary on Carroll and Carrollian criticism.

Wood, James Playsted. *The Snark Was a Boojum.* New York: Pantheon, 1966. A biography of Carroll distinguished mainly by David Levine's excellent drawings.

*Articles*

Anon. Review of *Alice's Adventures in Wonderland.* (London) *Times,* 26 December 1865, 5.

————. "Children's Books." *Athenaeum,* 16 December 1865, 844.

————. Review of *The Hunting of the Snark. Athenaeum,* 8 April 1876, 495.

————. Review of *Sylvie and Bruno. Athenaeum,* 4 January 1890, 11–12.

Auerbach, Nina. "Alice and Wonderland: A Curious Child." *Victorian Studies* 17 (September 1973):31–47. Emphasizes Alice's oral aggressiveness and sees her to be implicated in the "troubled human condition."

Hinz, John. "Alice Meets the Don." *South Atlantic Quarterly* 52 (1953):253–66. Relates the *Alice* books to *Don Quixote.*

Kincaid, James R. "Alice's Invasion of Wonderland." *PMLA* 88 ( January 1973):92–99. Sees Alice as bringing death, predation, and egoism into the comic harmony of Wonderland.

Madden, William A. "Framing the Alices." *PMLA* 101 (May 1986):362–73. Argues that the framing poems and prose of the *Alice* books and the text of the stories are mutually dependent; the lyrical poems modify the reader's sense of reality as preparatory to the dream world of the tales.

Morton, Lionel. "Memory in the *Alice* Books." *Nineteenth-Century Fiction* 33 (December 1978):285–308. Views Alice as a mediating figure between Carroll and the mother hidden in memory, comprising elements of both.

Rackin, Donald. "Alice's Journey to the End of Night." *PMLA* 81 (October 1966):313–26. An existential reading of *Alice's Adventures in Wonderland* in which Alice's experiences represent man's search for meaning in a meaningless world.

# Index

(The works of Carroll are listed under his name)